The F

C

Enlightenment

TANYA SAVAGE

Published by Goldcrest Books International Ltd
www.goldcrestbooks.com
publish@goldcrestbooks.com

ISBN: 978-1-913719-96-8

For Donna, who said 'write!'

Chapter 1

The year was 1273, according to the calendar of Eden. This was the year I discovered that the world around me consisted of lies.

By the time I had finished school, I already had a niggling suspicion something else lingered beneath the town of Eden. Not a physical monster. But a monstrous charade. However, my true awakening began only days after my nineteenth birthday, on a night with one of the worst thunderstorms I could recall.

As was my usual custom, when the stars shone like a thousand lanterns, I had ventured into the old citadel on the hill to be closer to the glittering orbs. The night-time curfew meant that I was the only human wandering the cobblestone streets and passages. But I had a fellow wanderer: my dog, Envy.

After dark I could enjoy the freedom of the old citadel without the horde. The citadel was mine, and mine alone. No one was around to brush past me in the narrow lanes. There were no loud conversations to shatter my earholes. No one standing on top of me in the food ration queue. I'm sorry to say, but at times I couldn't relate to my fellow humans. I was as terrified of humans as I was of spiders, depending on the size …

of the spider that is. Both could cause my heart rate to rise and my palms to sweat. One had too many eyes, and too many legs. The other had an excessive number of peculiarities, most of which I could never get my head around. A gathering of humans meant too much chitter-chatter. Too much confusion. People didn't always mean what they said. I had to read between the lines apparently. What lines, I wondered? Anyway, I found it all exhausting to deal with.

As a consequence, I preferred the old citadel at night when it was abandoned. I can understand how you would think this selfish of me. However, I sometimes felt like a complete anomaly to others. I couldn't understand why I struggled with everyday expectations. My apparent differences confused even me. All I wanted was to be understood. But alone with Envy, I didn't have that problem. We had a bond which didn't require cryptic conversation. And I spoke to her all the time. I couldn't explain to you why I had no problem talking to my dog.

Envy and I had set off for the citadel once darkness consumed the day. Eden became a place of peace after curfew.

The suburbs of Eden spread out down the slopes from the citadel and into the river valley, and the townsfolk referred to the suburbs as the town. Eden was my entire world. I had no idea what lay beyond the outer walls and dense forest. And I had no idea of the vastness to which I – and the other townsfolk – truly belonged.

The sky above the citadel promised an uneventful evening weather-wise. Illumination from the streets and townhouses below created an amber glow, while the large waxing moon radiated above. Some of the gas lamps had already gone out, but most remained burning in the old citadel as I crept along the winding cobbled streets. Despite the pleasant warmth which Eden experienced during the daytime, the evenings were yet to acknowledge the beginning of spring. Therefore, I had wrapped myself in an extra layer under my coat.

Envy trotted at my heels. As she always did.

My grandfather had said I should have named her Shadow, as wherever I stomped, Envy stomped too. She was a dusky grey-and-white, short-haired terrier type, with a broad chest and strong shoulders. My favourite thing about Envy was her beautiful inquisitive face. My second favourite thing about her was that the length of the white markings on her paws gave the impression she wore socks.

We sat on a bench in the square near one of the glowing gas lamps, opposite the water fountain. The fountain featured three damaged statues and faced my favourite abandoned building in the citadel. I didn't know it at the time, but the architecture of this building was in the style of classical antiquity. It had large Ionic columns and deep alcoves where statues had once stood. The building also had a small tower on the roof.

Behind my favourite building lay another striking building, whose more dominant towers pierced the night sky. They sat atop the humongous Temple of the First Ancestors.

The gentle trickle of water from the fountain proved a soothing backdrop to stargazing. Not a single cloud floated above to disrupt the glittering vastness. A cluster of golden light arched across the dark violet sky. I thought about how the planets glide with grace through their respective orbits. And how the asteroid belt rumbled through its trapped trajectory. Those broken and deformed rocks will never shine like the planets and stars.

I had my lantern and a book on the planets with me. It was entitled *Discourse on the Planets and Moons*. The book was one of my favourites and it used to be my father's. I lit my lantern for a closer inspection of the page on Jupiter and the gas giant's four celestial companions.

A shriek broke through the sky, as a shock of lightning struck the small tower atop my favourite abandoned building, shattering the calm. This was followed by a monstrous bellow.

Envy whined.

I realised the stars had disappeared. The pitch-black threatened to swallow the entire citadel.

Another shock of lightning struck the central tower on the Temple of the First Ancestors. It appeared to reverberate off the tower and shoot out in all directions across the old citadel and beyond, along with a deafening growl.

A flicker of light caught my eye. The tallest temple tower was aflame.

I wondered if that was what had happened to the two buildings which sat in the top right corner of the square. Both had been gutted by fire at some point in history. And both buildings had been left to decay. I considered it lucky the flames from the historical fire hadn't spread any further. For they would have destroyed my favourite abandoned building, which stood to the left of the damaged buildings and to the right of the Guildhall.

I advanced towards the Guildhall, with the intention of retreating down the side street and onto the gardens, which surrounded the Temple of the First Ancestors.

I already regretted my late-night venture when the sky morphed into a river. To my surprise the rain felt warm. It also carried a bitter acrid scent which burned my nostrils. And I thought the rain dispersed intermittent wafts of sulphur.

Blinded by the tumultuous downpour, I darted for shelter under the porch of the Guildhall. I considered staying there with Envy until the storm passed. However, the night sky had other ideas.

I believe Envy noticed them first. She grumbled and cowled, backing herself into a corner by the entrance door.

Spectres floated above us through the deluge.

I wondered if these were the ancestral spirits from the Forest of Ancients. Perhaps these ones didn't know that they should have passed on through to the other realm. I wondered what they were doing in the citadel. The ancestral spirits were supposed to be confined to the forest, while the townsfolk were confined to the town.

Tiny orbs of light appeared in addition to the spectres, and they all danced before me.

I thought I heard singing, like how my mother used to sing to me when I was a child. But I must have imagined the song. Sometimes my ears could deceive me. Even at home, I sometimes thought I could hear my mother singing from another room, only to find her sitting in silence. My mother hadn't sung in years.

I followed Envy's lead and I also sank into a corner. My body slumped like a wet rag against the cold stone. I lost sight of the sky, as the porch roof blocked the panoramic vista. I would have ripped open the door of the Guildhall if I could, but the door was made of a solid dark wood, and inevitably locked long before the evening curfew.

Some of the ghostly figures descended upon the square. Through the shower I could discern that the spectres moved as though almost human. But the movements of these almost human figures were more graceful and free. And despite my fear, for a brief moment I must have become quite mesmerised. Even Envy had ceased grumbling.

As I observed these gliding spirits, one grew larger than the others. Until I realised too late that it had not grown larger at all. It had slunk closer. And it hovered before the porch.

Large dark eyes stared in my direction as the clock atop the Guildhall began its elegant chime.

I deemed the ghost to be a young male. I don't know how I gathered this information from a floating white blob. I couldn't fathom what else he could be other than a spirit from the forest. I supposed the ancestral spirits were the reason we had a night-time curfew in Eden. Perhaps they could become lost and creep in on occasion. And then I realised, I'd never had the misfortune to witness the restless spirits in the citadel before. I hadn't even caught a glimpse of them beyond Eden, in the forest where they were supposed to reside. I had only ever heard about them. To see them up close was terrifying. I wondered if perhaps, when an ancestral spirit saw you, it might carry you off back to the Forest of Ancients, and there you would remain, in their realm forever.

I think I screamed. But alas not in tune with the gentle song from the clock which jingled across the square, despite a slight drowning of the sound by the torrent. The Guildhall clock provided the only music in Eden.

Somehow I recovered the use of my limbs and flung myself from the porch back out into the flood. I may or may not have persisted in screaming as I sped through the square, with Envy charging at my flank. We were surrounded on all sides by these unwelcome spirits who had forgotten their place.

The chimes ceased, and the clock paused, before the crescendo.

The bell in the clock tower struck once, then twice, and continued.

I knew then it was already midnight as I raced through the slippery streets. I slid a few times on the wet cobblestones. It didn't help that it was all downhill towards any three of the old bridges, which would eject you from the citadel wall and into the surrounding town. The bridge I required was the only bridge with large gatehouses at either end. I had always found this to be the most charming of the bridges over the river, and tonight it would be my saviour. But I had to get past the nightwatchman first.

I had no grip on the bottom of my shoes. The soles had worn down long ago and I couldn't afford new ones. No one could afford new anything, what with the war and everyone rationing. I had to make do with what I had and some handed-down clothes from my mother. It was the first time since the war had begun that I wished for tougher footwear. Plus, my over-the-knee skirt restricted my leg span.

I slipped on the final bend leading on to the first gatehouse. But I recovered my balance as Envy bolted on ahead.

'Oi,' said a male voice. 'What the—'

It was the nightwatchman. He had stumbled out of the gatehouse at the opposite end of the bridge.

The nightwatchmen were supposed to guard the citadel and look out for any townsfolk breaking curfew. If anyone was caught breaking curfew, they were sent to one of the lock-ups for a few nights. If they were caught repeatedly breaking curfew, they were sent to the prison. I had never been caught. I think because I chose to wander the streets only on perfectly clear evenings – which restricted my outings – and more importantly when it was late, by which time the nightwatchmen were already dozing.

This particular nightwatchman was useless. We had found him snoring in his chair about an hour ago as we had crept past his quarters. Now he was fully awake, and flailed around, trying to grab Envy.

'Hey, ya little bugger,' he said, as she squeezed past his legs.

The nightwatchman caught sight of me as I emerged into the lamplight on the bridge. He appeared to forget all about my companion, who now stood waiting for me just beyond his menacing frame.

'What are you doing up here?' he hollered. 'You're not supposed to be up here.'

I lunged forward as I decided the only way out was through.

I'm not a good judge of expressions, but I do believe the nightwatchman had a look of bewilderment as I hurtled onwards with some force. I either had to face him or the ancestral spirits currently floating around the citadel behind me and the prospect of being carried off to the Forest of Ancients. Life seems a little easier when you have limited choices. I didn't much fancy either. But at this point I just wanted to get home to safety. Besides, despite my worn-down soles, my shoes made a grating click-clack as I sprinted along the bridge. The noise caused me to grit my teeth. Or perhaps it was my determined focus which made my jaw lock. Anyhow, I wanted out of the old citadel.

The nightwatchman opened his arms wide as I loomed upon him.

'Sorry, sir,' I said, as I smacked into him.

'What in the blazes—' he said, as he went spinning off to one side.

I caught up with Envy and we exited the bridge down the slope.

'Do you know what time it is?' he yelled after us.

'Yes,' I said, wheeling round to face him. 'It's midnight. I heard the gongs. Didn't you?'

'Are you being funny?' he asked.

At least I think that's what he said. The rain continued to pour, and it muffled his voice.

'One of the towers on the Temple of the First Ancestors was on fire you know,' I said. 'Before the rain came.'

With that revelation, he staggered off across the bridge and disappeared into the darkness of the old citadel.

I would have breathed a sigh of relief since Envy and I were now clear of the bridge, but we still had some way to go.

As we passed the fire station, I wondered if the nightwatchman would alert the men to the fire. But since the flames appeared to have expired, I expected not. Some of the firemen had been recruited as soldiers when the war broke out but were still manning the station when not patrolling the citadel during the day. The rest of the firemen had been sent off to fight.

Envy and I surged on through the town.

All the gas lamps continued to burn here. And light glimmered in a few of the townhouses. There is nothing more inviting than an amber glow from behind a window. It gave me comfort. I thought of my own cosy home on the outskirts of Eden, although I expected my mother would have retired to bed. And my grandfather would have fallen asleep in his favourite armchair in front of the log burner.

The rain had begun to ease off as Envy and I approached the beehives, allotments, abandoned manor house, and thatched cottages at the edge of town. I assumed the sheep in the fields beyond the cottages had sought shelter under the trees.

My legs ached as we reached the top of our lane. I stumbled along the path by the row of greenhouses and willed my legs to keep going a little further. Envy didn't appear tired at all, but she had four legs to carry her to safety, and no need for footwear which had seen better days.

An owl hooted at me from a nearby tree as I flung open the little wooden gate outside our cottage. In my exhaustion I fell onto the front lawn. The grass felt a little damp, but not soaked. Unlike me.

Envy licked my face, as if to say: 'Come on, we're home now, just a few more steps to the front door.'

A guttural growl came from the dark Forest of Ancients beyond the outer town wall.

That got me standing again. I squinted at the treeline. I thought I could see a faint glimmer of illumination and a little movement, as though a chain of forest creatures armed with lanterns were taking a slow march through the trees. Aside from the ancestors haunting the forest, legend had it that after dark more evil spirits prowled. Not to mention the other horrendous creatures and abnormal humans who inhabited the woods. The townsfolk had to leave the woodland for them: those who dwelt in the forest realm. As a result, going beyond the outer wall was forbidden. I had often wondered how the birds could come and go as they pleased, without incident. The bees also frequented the forest. Numerous times I had witnessed them escape the small field behind our garden and disappear over the stone partition. Something had enticed them. Even the sheep grazed right up against the wall, unperturbed by the skulking spirits.

I had almost forgotten the terror which had caused me to run. It wasn't the storm and heavy shower. It had been the spectre with dark eyes.

I thrust open the front door and clapped eyes on my grandfather. He was sitting slumped in his favourite armchair and he snored with a gentle rhythm.

As I placed my key by the lamp on the table, I realised I no longer had my lantern. And even more annoyingly, I no longer had possession of my book. I must have left them behind during my fright and flight from the old citadel. I didn't recall putting them down anywhere. The lantern wasn't important. Although, I did consider I could be in trouble if my elders noted we were one short. But the book was precious, a gift handed down from my father. I didn't have another one like it. There was at least one newer edition of *Discourse on the Planets and Moons* available in the little bookshop in the citadel, but books were expensive. Because of this we had few books in the house. And now we had one less.

I lit the small fire in my bedroom and hung my wet clothes over a chair. Envy snuggled next to me on the bed as I towel dried my hair.

I vowed to retrieve my father's book. Which meant I would have to go back into the old citadel first thing the following morning. This filled me with dread. The citadel would swarm with the townsfolk. I recalled my grandfather had an appointment with the optician in the morning. I would go with him. I considered that a good enough excuse.

As I drifted off to sleep, I had no cause to believe that night would be my final night of ignorance. I suppose I had been content with my life. I knew no different. I was unaware that anything lay beyond our solar system other than the glittering stars. I was unaware of the limitations of my knowledge. My world was Eden. My place was in Eden. But as I was soon to discover, it was also out there.

Chapter 2

My stomach twisted into knots at the thought of going into the old citadel when it would heave with the townsfolk. But at least I knew I was going into the citadel, and I had time to prepare myself for the dreaded morning ahead. It would have been far worse if my mother or grandfather announced at the last minute that I had to go in for some reason. I wouldn't have had the time to process the information and accept it. I most likely would have vomited. As it was, I couldn't get my breakfast down that morning. I felt nauseous enough from the advanced knowledge. I allowed my grandfather to finish my second slice of toast and honey. We would have had eggs, but the hens hadn't laid any. I had commented that the storm must have frightened them in the night. Both my mother and grandfather said they hadn't heard a storm. My mother thought she had heard a little rain, but nothing substantial. Perhaps the shower hadn't amounted to much on the outskirts of Eden.

Since my recent visit to the doctor, I had been even more anxious whenever I went into the citadel during the day. She had said I appeared stressed, and she thought I had some kind of condition of the mind. She said she would look into it further for me, and we could discuss it at my next appointment. I suppose the doctor meant well. But knowing I had a *condition of the mind* made me feel as though I had a big sign atop my head which read: Look at me, aren't I odd. And it meant something lurked underneath my exterior. As I said before, I had always thought there was something wrong under the surface of Eden. But perhaps there was nothing wrong with my town. Perhaps there was only something wrong with me.

The reason I had gone to the doctor in the first place was because I had fainted twice in the space of a week. And I often felt sick. I could make myself sick from worrying about things. Then I would worry that I would feel sick from worrying, and the worrying about feeling sick brought on the sickness again. My grandfather had said the war had brought on my stress, and I was simply sensitive to change. Plus, the rationing would make anyone faint. Everyone in Eden suffered. But perhaps my sensitivity exacerbated the trauma.

My grandfather had once said that, despite the fact I often missed what he and others noticed, he thought it rather beautiful when I noticed things he missed. He was always surprised when I pointed things out to him, like how Envy had different barks for various scenarios: throw the ball, let me outside, let's go for a walk, isn't it time I had something to eat? I also noticed when the wireless had been turned up a notch. Or when the temperature dropped by one degree. And when the *pinch* of rosemary in the stew was more than a smidgin. My grandfather said I was just Andromeda. It didn't matter what other people thought. I had him, my mother, and Envy. They were the people who mattered. I loved my grandfather dearly. And knowing I would get to spend the morning with him calmed some of my nerves about having to go to the citadel during daylight hours, amidst the crush of the townsfolk.

A divine scent lingered in the air as I stepped out the front door. Our wisteria bloomed around the door and window frames. A few of our neighbours also had wisteria. Plus, we all had an array of flowers and plants in our gardens, which burst with an intoxicating aroma.

All the thatched cottages had small windows and doors, which we needed to duck to get through, as though some of the descendants of the First Ancestors had been small. The cottages gleamed in the sunshine, as the entire town and citadel were made from a glorious warm honey stone.

Sheep grazed in the fields surrounding the cottages. Behind the fields lay the outer wall. And beyond the outer wall, the Forest of Ancients spread up the hillside.

My grandfather and I, along with Envy, waited for the next omnibus at the end of our lane. Since we lived on the outskirts of Eden, we were the first pickup when the omnibus turned around to head back for the citadel.

The sunshine bounced off the varnished wood of the omnibus as it approached with a gentle clip-clop of horse hooves. The horses who pulled the omnibuses were known as Edenshire horses, and they were much larger and stronger than the horses who pulled the smaller carriages. Seeing the horses was one positive with regards to going into the citadel during the day. Eden had no omnibuses after curfew, for obvious reasons. Hence why all my night-time adventures were on foot. I was glad we took an omnibus that morning, as my legs still ached.

'Shall we sit up top?' I asked my grandfather.

'Why not, poppet. It's a pleasant day. And I'm feeling sprightly.'

Envy leapt up the narrow stairs at the back of the omnibus. My grandfather struggled a little with his stick, but I shoved him up the small flight of steps to the top deck.

The driver waited for us to sit. And my grandfather bowed and touched the front of his cap as a gesture of thanks.

The omnibus pulled away with a jolt, before finding a groove.

Delicate lavender swayed in one of the fields behind the cottages, creating waves of lilac amongst lush pastures.

We passed the abandoned manor house. The grounds were overgrown and the wrought-iron gates had rusted away from their stone posts. The gates lay lost amongst the weeds and wild flowers. When I was younger, I thought I saw a ghost at one of the windows. I had been counting all the windowpanes. It astonished me to think it was one house. I wondered if each window represented one room, or whether rooms could have more than one window. When I got to the fifteenth pane, I caught sight of a ghost behind the glass. I have never stopped to count the windowpanes since. I had supposed it was the ghost of a former resident and they hadn't wanted to leave.

We rolled on by another abandoned building. Creeping plants strangled the façade and some of the roof had fallen in. It looked like a large house with a tall tower which reached to a sharp point. The doors were unusual. They reminded me of the doors on the Temple of the First Ancestors; these too were pointed at the top in line with the arch above. The grounds were also overgrown. But unlike the manor house, these grounds contained broken stone slabs which poked through the undergrowth. We had other buildings like it across Eden. They too remained in equal decay. It was forbidden to enter any abandoned building in the town and citadel.

Women tended to the vegetables in the allotments. Each had their hair wrapped up under a scarf, and they wore trousers, which I assumed made their labour easier. Prior to women taking work in the fields and allotments, no females had ever worn trousers in Eden. The current fashion for women was an over-the-knee skirt, blouse or jumper, and heeled pumps. The pumps could be worn with either ankle socks for young women, or stockings for more mature ladies. I wondered if the women in the allotments ever wore anything else at the end of their day. Looking back on it, I expect they collapsed at home from exhaustion still wearing their trousers.

In a field on the other side of the road, bees buzzed with fury around a beekeeper, who was destroying all their hard work. I felt sorry for the insects. All that effort and then we come along and help ourselves to their food source. It didn't prevent me from enjoying honey though. Honey drizzled on toast, or even better crumpets, was a welcome sweet indulgence.

Leaving the fields and cottages behind, we began passing the modest houses. I called them modest houses because these homes lay between the humble cottages on the periphery and the grandeur of the townhouses on the main streets.

We approached a small gathering of women next to an omnibus stop. They boarded and sat downstairs.

The omnibuses were quite a compact mode of transport. I would say there would have been enough room for twelve people to sit inside the omnibus downstairs. Fourteen if either of the long seats were taken up by children, but everyone would be squashed in, with no standing room. In fact, you couldn't even stand inside if you wanted to. The confined space of the lower deck meant you had to crouch through the little door to get on the omnibus, and then slide along the seat.

I considered that the omnibus would soon get full and other passengers would join us on the top deck. And when they did, I wouldn't be able to have a private conversation with my grandfather.

'You didn't hear the storm last night then?' I asked.

'Can't say I did. Bad, was it?'

'The worst one I've ever seen. Lightning struck two of the towers in the citadel.'

'Oh, you were up there again were you,' my grandfather said. 'You'll be seen one night. Then you'll be in trouble. And then we'll all be in trouble.'

Envy grumbled in agreement with my grandfather. At least I think she did.

'The lightning struck the central tower on the Temple of the First Ancestors, and it caught fire,' I said.

'Did it? It would be a shame to lose a tower.'

'The downpour put the fire out though.'

'That's good,' my grandfather said. 'Wouldn't want such a beautiful building turning to ash and ruins. We should pay a visit to the temple while we're in the citadel.'

'I'd like that.'

A visit to the temple would also make the morning worthwhile, I thought, as I watched the modest houses go by.

'The storm wasn't the only thing that happened last night,' I said.

'No?'

'I thought I saw something unusual. It's just ...'

'I'm not getting any younger you know,' my grandfather said. 'If you've got something to tell me you'd better get to it before I die on this omnibus.'

'You're not going to die on an omnibus, Grandad.'

'How do you know? You never know when your time is up. Besides, the fresh air is cutting through me a little now.'

'Sorry,' I said. 'We'll sit downstairs on the return journey.'

'Agreed. Now what was it you saw?' my grandfather asked.

'Spirits. In the storm.'

'That's unusual alright. Were you a bit tired?'

'I don't think so. I was looking at the stars,' I said.

'Perhaps you nodded off and were half dreaming?'

'I was awake. It began pouring down.'

'You think the citadel has spirits?' my grandfather asked.

'I thought they might be forest spirits, but they'd got lost.'

'Balderdash,' he said. 'Forest spirits indeed.'

'But the forest is their resting place, isn't it? It's the realm of the dead,' I said. 'Plus, the evil spirits would do harm, wouldn't they?'

'We should always question the things we've been told. Why would evil spirits only appear after dark? A bit too specific if you ask me. And that's even if you believe in spirits.'

We turned onto one of the main streets, and the elegant

townhouses rose around us. Most of the townhouses had been converted into apartments. Although I was convinced some remained as five-storey homes.

The omnibus stopped again.

'We'll say no more for now,' my grandfather whispered.

I glanced over the side as an elderly couple clambered onboard and sat downstairs.

More women also boarded, this time with their children. Most of them came upstairs to join us. Envy received some fuss from the youngsters and a woman smiled at me, but I didn't know why. I wasn't sure if she thought she knew me. I attempted a smile back, but it must have been inadequate, as the woman turned away from me and I had the feeling she wouldn't look upon me again.

My grandfather and I didn't utter another word while the omnibus rolled along the main road. After the grand houses, the most significant building on the main road was the fire station. Its wide façade dominated the approach to the old gatehouse bridge.

The gatehouse bridge didn't actually have any gates on it. I supposed it must have had gates at some point, but these were long gone. If there had still been gates on the bridge, it would make my occasional night-time adventures a lot more challenging.

As we reached the bridge, we stopped to allow an oncoming omnibus to cross first. I took the opportunity to peer into the room on the lower floor of the gatehouse. I wanted to see if the nightwatchman lingered inside. He might recognise me and run out shouting. I would have died from embarrassment. But through the open door I caught sight of a different man. I should have realised the nightwatchman wouldn't be there. It's daytime. This man would be the *day*watchman. I cringed inside from my own stupidity.

With the other omnibus clear, we passed under the first gatehouse. Despite only two Edenshire horses pulling the omnibus, the acoustics on the bridge gave the impression twenty horses drew us along, as their clip-clopping intensified upon the old stones. I have always loved that clip-clop sound.

Disgruntled ducks quacked in the river below as the swans flapped their large wings to demonstrate they were the true bosses of the waterway.

I thought of the First Ancestors. They gave us life. They gave us the land. And the river teaming with fish. We had a home, fresh water, and a food source. Later, their forebears gave us the buildings.

The beauty of the old citadel always filled me with wonder. As we ascended through the winding streets, even my grandfather gazed with admiration at the handsome architecture. Some of the buildings appeared a little wonky. While some buildings complemented their neighbour, others were completely unique. This added to the charm in my opinion. All the tall and crooked buildings within the citadel walls had a variety of shops on the lower floors, some of which closed when the war began. I wondered if those shopkeepers would ever return. We still had several cafes and restaurants. Although the townsfolk couldn't always afford to go to these anymore, what with rationing for the war effort. It was a shame to see them so empty. Most of the townsfolk queued outside one of the bakeries for their daily allowance of one small loaf of bread per family. Depending on the size of the family, you could obtain another half loaf. The butcher shops had smaller queues due to the number of coupons required for meat, and because meat was not a daily allowance. Plus, meat was imported in from somewhere beyond Eden, and sometimes they wouldn't provide any. Whoever *they* were. No one knew why we imported food from outside. Outside meant hostile. Yet Eden exported wool to these hostile enemies. We received various other goods in return. I suppose it made sense to someone somewhere, but it always puzzled me as an arrangement. Especially as we were now at war with at least one of these towns.

If we had enough coupons over by the end of the week, my mother would purchase some flour and yeast and bake a large loaf. I felt grateful we lived at the edge of town. We had hens in our garden, and therefore free eggs, which we sometimes swapped for other food items if we had plenty. We had a small patch on one of the allotments near the cottages and grew our own vegetables. A poster had recommended we do this.

War posters decorated the citadel. They adorned the sides of buildings and community message boards. I wasn't too keen on some of the garish colours. Some posters told us to mend our own clothes, which we did. Another poster stated we needed to do our duty for Eden, which I think referred to growing your own food and mending clothes again. One informed us scrap metal could be used for tanks. Another encouraged women to work in the fields, which they did. My mother wasn't obligated to work in the fields. She was a seamstress. She made uniforms, amongst other items. And I helped.

The most garish of the posters had a giant V for victory. But we hadn't won. I wondered if we ever would.

As the omnibus arrived in the main square, the clock began to chime, as it did every quarter-hour.

Most of the buildings surrounding the square had more imposing façades than the crooked buildings. Their frontages were wider and more ornate, including the Guildhall, the hospital, one of the town's schools, and my favourite of the abandoned buildings in the citadel.

Some mothers dropped their young children off at the school. Once they had done that, they joined the largest queue in the citadel, outside the Guildhall. This was where everyone received their coupons and a new ration book when required. The ration books were stamped in the shops, as proof we had purchased the daily allowance of bread, milk, and cheese, for example. No one could cheat and go back for more later. The stamp never lied. Each family had only been allowed to register with one bakery and one grocer shop. You couldn't go to one you were not registered with.

Soldiers strolled about the square, while others loitered within the narrow passages between the shops and cafes. They wore a dark brownish green uniform and carried rifles. I couldn't tell you who they were expecting to shoot. I suppose the enemy could have charged over the outer wall and marched up to the citadel. But in the six years we had been at war, nothing had happened to our town. Apart from elderly men and young boys, the soldiers were the only males left in Eden. All men, and boys over the age of sixteen, had been sent off to fight in the war, including my father. It angered me. Why couldn't my father be one of the men who got to stay behind and be a soldier in the square? He could have loitered down a side passage while wearing a black hat and smart uniform with shiny buttons. Why was he sent off? We didn't even know where he was. Frontline, the authorities said. But where was the town of Frontline? Did we fight the townsfolk of Frontline? Or was Frontline just where the fighting was taking place?

My father said he would write to us. We received two letters, eight weeks apart, and then silence. The first letter arrived with a photograph of my father in his uniform. The second letter was folded around a group photograph of four men, including my father. My father sat next to one of the men, and the other two stood behind them. He had made friends in the war. It seemed both photographs were taken by a professional photographer in a studio. But both photographs left me with a sense of unease. I thought the men, including my father, all had a distant expression. I often caught my mother re-reading those letters, as though she attempted to locate something else in them. Perhaps a clue, or secret code, hidden amongst all his words. The last time I took the letters from a drawer in her bedroom, to examine them again myself, I noticed some of the ink had splodged from her tears. My father was gone and my mother mourned his absence by dying inside. I felt as though I had lost both my parents.

'I've got ten minutes to get to the opticians,' my grandfather said, interrupting my thoughts. 'Where shall I meet you when I'm done, poppet?'

'I'll meet you by the fountain. I'm going to stay in the square.'

'Good idea. Then we'll go to the temple. And maybe we'll get a little treat afterwards,' he said, tapping the side of his nose.

He patted Envy goodbye on the head and hobbled off to the opticians.

Now I could search for my father's book.

The long line of women outside the Guildhall grew larger with every passing minute.

The clock struck nine and I watched two little painted men, wearing red coats and black hats, pop out from below the clock face. They approach each other, took it in turns to bow several times, turned around and headed back inside. Most people in the citadel ignored the display, but I still thought it wonderful.

With the little mechanical men back behind the clock face, I sauntered past the queue and began snooping around the porch.

'Excuse me, miss, do you think you're more important than everybody else?'

It took me a few seconds to realise the woman closest to the door was addressing me.

'Sorry?' I said.

'Everyone else is in the queue. Queueing,' she continued.

I could feel heat rising within, as all eyes fell upon me. I must have blushed, as my cheeks burned.

'Sorry, I—'

The women in the queue began jibber-jabbering away all at

once, and I couldn't keep up with who said what. The air was a cacophony of words, which overwhelmed me. Not that it mattered. The upshot of it was they were all having a go at me. I couldn't look any of them in the eye.

A clanking noise came from behind the main door of the Guildhall, and one of the double doors swung open with a creak.

'No pushing in,' a woman said. 'You can wait to get your coupons like everyone else here.'

'I'm not push—'

'Is this young lady pushing in?' asked the white-haired man who had opened the door.

'Yes,' some of the women said in unison.

'No,' I protested. 'I'm looking for something.'

'Right at the front of the queue?' a woman asked.

'Yes, I dropped something here last— yesterday.'

'How convenient,' she said, rolling her eyes.

'It wasn't convenient actually,' I said, staring at the ground, my skin still burning with embarrassment. 'It was my favourite book.'

'Your dog is sniffing around the door now,' said the woman at the front of the queue. 'Is he going to collect your coupons for you?'

A few of the women sniggered.

'She's a girl dog,' I snapped. 'And I can't see my book, so I'm going now. Come on, Envy.'

I stomped off in anger, but at the same time I could have cried. I felt humiliated. There was no need for them to be rude. I regretted coming into the old citadel during the day. I should have known something would cause embarrassment. I wanted to change my attire and pick up a hat to cover my red hair, so none of the women would recognise me if we walked past each other later. But of course, that would have been ridiculous. Plus, I didn't possess enough coupons to purchase new clothes. Since the war, only two clothing shops remained open, and they sold no more than the most basic of necessities.

I hid with Envy behind a column on the large porch of my favourite abandoned building. The wide porch sat atop a flight of steps. I could spy on the women who had insulted me, and re-emerge when they disappeared. Also, I would be able to see my grandfather as he approached the fountain.

I hung back by the huge wooden door. Some faded lettering remained above the doorway, like a watermark upon the stone. I think I could just make out an E and an R. The other letters had vanished through time. Closed wooden shutters prevented prying eyes from peeking through the windows. A bronze plaque coated in a green fuzz nestled high up on the façade. From where I stood, the fuzz made the plaque illegible.

But from this position on the porch, I detected something dark lying under a bench close to the Guildhall.

I assumed this dark object might be my book. I must have dropped it under the bench. My lantern could be there too. But I couldn't go back over there. Not with those women ready to throttle me for having the audacity to go looking for an item next to a queue.

Not long after the clock gonged ten, my grandfather appeared in the distance. Envy and I bounded over to him as he reached the broken stone block which sat in the centre of the square. At the time, I had never questioned what the broken stone had once been. I had never questioned why it appeared that someone had taken a chisel to parts of the remaining stone in order to eradicate something. I had never questioned anything about anything.

Envy leapt all over my grandfather's legs in excited greeting. You would have thought she hadn't seen him for a week.

'Let's go to the temple now, Grandad,' I said.

'I could do with a sit down first, poppet.'

'Didn't you sit down at the opticians?'

'Yes, and I'd like to sit down again. I've just walked up a bit of the hill you know.'

'Okay, sorry,' I said.

My grandfather shuffled towards a bench. He landed in the seat with a thud.

Two women were sitting upon the bench with the dark object underneath. Even though I was closer now, I still couldn't discern if the item was my book. But I wasn't prepared to go snooping around the bench and receive another barrage of rudeness.

'How are your eyes?' I asked my grandfather as I sat next to him.

'Perfect vision.'

'Really?'

'Only when I'm wearing my glasses,' he said, with a cheeky grin.

'You don't need a new pair?'

'No, the ones I have are fine. Good job too, since I'd have to use up a lot of coupons towards a new pair.'

'We would have to sell something if you needed new glasses,' I said.

'It's a terrible crime when people have to sell their household goods in order to get by. Absolute disgrace. I don't even understand why we're rationing. I can't see why we have to almost starve just because someone somewhere wanted to start a fight. All our men off fighting and dying for what? We must be living at a time of utmost human suffering. I suppose peace is not a given. It's only a gift for so long. Our ancestors must've had to fight for what they believed in,' my grandfather said with a sigh.

I slumped down onto the bench when I noticed some of the women who had chastised me outside the Guildhall had formed a queue for the next omnibus out of the citadel. Each woman carried multiple food items wrapped in brown paper and string in their shopping basket.

'Can we go to the temple now, Grandad?' I asked, as I sprang up and attempted to lift him from the bench.

‘Careful. I’m fragile you know.’

‘Sorry. It’s just … I want to go before it gets too busy.’

‘It never gets busy. The townsfolk are more concerned with other things these days,’ he said. ‘They don’t appreciate the magnificence standing before them.’

The Temple of the First Ancestors stood within its own complex behind the Guildhall and two large abandoned buildings. The temple perched upon the highest point of the hill, overlooking the river below. The river ran in a horseshoe shape around the old citadel and flowed out into the dark forest beyond the outer town wall. Looking up at the temple from the town below gave the impression that it floated above the treelined cliff. The view from atop the wall and lookout towers surrounding the temple gardens was spectacular. You could see for miles, although the view was nothing but forested hillside which rose up from the snaking river valley.

We had been told strange people roamed parts of the forest. They obviously didn’t have a problem living alongside the ancestral spirits. These people didn’t look like us. These humans were deformed. Instead of human heads, they had dog heads. We were also told that actual dogs the size of humans lived in the forest, and these dogs could rip you apart in a heartbeat. A boy in school said he had seen one, and it had killed his older brother. No one believed he had seen a giant dog. The forest was forbidden for a start. He and his brother had no business going into the forest. It was to be left for the ancestral spirits. That’s what the outer town wall was for. Anyway, days later, another boy confirmed he had seen the deceased older brother in a café in the citadel. Apparently, the older brother looked remarkably well for a boy who had been torn to shreds. But that wasn’t to say we didn’t believe in the giant dogs, or the dog-headed humans, or the forest spirits. Everyone knew they existed. These were known facts passed down through the generations.

Aside from the night sky, I had always found the view of the forest beguiling. I couldn't understand how something so intriguing from a distance could crawl with monsters and evil.

The Temple of the First Ancestors was a striking old crumbling structure. I wondered how the First Ancestors could have even built it. It dominated the skyline and seemed to belong to another world. Its warm honey-coloured pillars soared skywards and the enormous main entrance door was constructed for a giant. The descendants of the First Ancestors confused me. Some must have been ginormous, judging by the size of the temple doors, but others had also been small, judging by the cottages.

The gardens around the temple were a haven for wildlife. Squirrels darted down trees and bounced across the lawn. Crows swooped and commenced their waddling walk along the grass. Pigeons flapped and scrambled together as they cooed and nodded incessantly. The squirrels didn't come too close, as the skittish pigeons and large crows appeared to disturb their delicate nature. The overconfident pigeons thoroughly annoyed the crows. The gardens erupted with flowers, but the lawn and flower beds were uneven, as though the soil had been disturbed many times throughout history. The gardens had the appearance of being turned over by giants as they rummaged in search of something. These had been the giants who lived inside the temple I presumed.

It was forbidden to stray from the pathways and walk on the lawn amongst the flowers. Years ago, my grandfather said this was because bodies lay within the earth. My grandmother refuted this. She had said he must have been having one of his funny turns if he'd thought such a beautiful place would be surrounded by the dead. My grandfather never mentioned it again, but I wondered if he still believed in his statement.

We entered the cavernous temple with Envy in tow. There was no sign stating you couldn't bring a dog in. Besides, birds nested in the roof arches, and their droppings ran down some of the giant pillars. They had easy access to the temple as the windows had no glass. It appeared pointless as to why the huge wooden doors remained, since anyone could climb in through the lower windows. And just like my grandfather had predicted, the temple was void of other townsfolk. Everyone truly had forgotten the magnificence and tranquillity of the temple.

'Something about this place makes my heart feel light,' my grandfather said as we strolled along, going deeper into the body of the temple.

'In what way?'

'It's a sanctuary for the soul,' he said. 'A place of peace in a mad world.'

'The world is mad?'

'If the world isn't truth, then it's mad.'

'We don't know the world. We only know our town,' I said.

'Exactly. And what do we really know about Eden? And what do we know about this war? Nothing.'

I thought again of my father. Sent away to a distant part of the land. Perhaps the town of Frontline had dog-headed humans.

Dead leaves danced across the stone floor in the draught. Wings fluttered above us in the high arches. The sound of our footsteps and my grandfather's stick tapping upon the stone echoed through the vast hall.

Some of the stones were larger and darker than others. They had lettering on them, but the words had worn down and this made the stones indecipherable.

'Do you think some of the descendants of the First Ancestors were taller than us?' I asked.

'Doubt it,' my grandfather said.

'But the temple is built for giants.'

My grandfather paused and leaned forward for a rest on his stick.

'This place was built by people trying to reach for something greater than themselves,' he said, as he gazed upwards. 'We will never understand the reason why it was built. But they strived for a connection to something which we can't physically see.'

'The spirit world?' I asked.

'Maybe. There's definitely more to this place. I can feel it. But the meaning has been lost.'

'I don't understand how we could lose the meaning behind what the descendants of the First Ancestors built.'

'Perhaps we lost the meaning because *they* weren't the ones who built this,' my grandfather said.

'Who built it then?' I asked, wondering who or what could have come before the First Ancestors.

'A very good question. And one we should all be asking. But we don't.'

'But I'm asking now,' I said.

'You're asking the wrong person.'

'Who's the right person?' I asked, a little exasperated.

'Unfortunately, the people who've possibly been lying.'

I wondered why the mayor's office would need to lie to us. I stroked Envy for comfort. Sometimes the things my grandfather said made more sense than what we had been led to believe. But then again, some of things my grandfather said sounded quite mad. He frightened me a little with his wild notions. The kind of notions which would get you into serious trouble.

'Let me put it this way,' he whispered, 'I think the temple should be named the Temple of the Long, Long-Dead Ancients. I think this place has been here far longer than we realise. I don't believe the town was built by the people considered to be the descendants of the First Ancestors. There are people who have gone before us, just as there are people yet to come. An ancient civilisation existed here a long time ago. We are a whole new civilisation which rose from the few remaining ancient ones.'

I was gobsmacked.

'I think that's considered blasphemy, Grandad.'

'Yes. It is. Hence why I'm whispering.'

'Why do you think that?'

'Things I've heard down the years,' he said. 'Things I've seen.'

'If people have gone before us and disappeared, doesn't that mean it could happen to us? The civilisation of the future may not know we ever existed,' I said.

'A scary thought. But the most likely outcome.'

'I think I'd like to go home now,' I said, feeling a little uneasy.

My grandfather wrapped an arm around me, but I didn't reciprocate the hug. I think it was supposed to comfort me. But hugs didn't comfort me. I just had someone else's arm around my shoulder.

'Shall we go and treat ourselves to a proper hot chocolate?' he asked.

'I don't think we have enough coupons.'

'I've saved some,' he said. 'We have to treat ourselves now and again. Can't keep drinking that shoe polish we have to make do with from the shop.'

According to my grandfather, most things tasted of shoe polish: tea, coffee, chocolate, soup, gravy, even the water sometimes had a *hint of polish*. It made me curious as to when he had actually tasted the shoe shining liquid.

As we meandered through the temple gardens, I turned to look back at the tower which had been struck by lightning. I couldn't detect any damage from ground level.

'Where should we go?' my grandfather asked. 'The Grand Tea Room?'

'But that's the most expensive place.'

'I'm all about the finer things in life today. I fancy a bit of luxury before I depart and join the spirits in the Forest of Ancients.'

'Grandad. Stop saying things like that.'

'Why? I quite like trees.'

'I honestly don't know if we should be wasting coupons on hot chocolate,' I said. 'What if we need more coupons before the week is out?'

'Why don't you let me worry about that. I want us to have a little treat. The Grand Tea Room it is.'

The proprietor of the Grand Tea Room sat us by a window at my grandfather's insistence. Envy was allowed inside, also at my grandfather's insistence. He had said, if the proprietor wanted any business, she would allow the small dog in and provide a bowl of water. He also informed her that we would be having hot chocolate. Her eyes lit up at that. Cocoa powder was an expensive treat which Eden imported in. The proprietor agreed to a window seat, as long as we took the table closest to the door, which also meant closest to the counter. I presumed she wanted to keep an eye on us. Envy was no bother at all. She got herself comfortable under the table and waited for us to finish.

The tea room had the most extravagant interior in the citadel. I wondered what the room would have been used for in the past. I couldn't imagine it was created for the purpose of sipping hot beverages and eating cake. Candelabra chandeliers hung from the high ceiling, and large ornate mirrors lined the walls. The room smelled divine. It brimmed with the scent of fresh coffee and sweet delights, which sat on display behind glass casing. Most of the townsfolk could no longer afford even small luxuries. Which meant the place wasn't even a quarter full. Which meant, if I whispered, I could ask my grandfather a pressing question.

'Since you're an expert on all things ancient—'

'Sarcasm doesn't suit you,' my grandfather said.

'I'm not being sarcastic. I don't know how.'

'Well, that was sarcasm.'

'Was it? I just wondered what you thought about the building over there,' I said, nodding towards the abandoned building whose porch I had spent some of the morning hiding under.

'Over where?'

'The building I'm nodding to.'

'I can't tell which one you're nodding to,' my grandfather said.

'The one with the columns and small tower on the roof, between the Guildhall and one of the fire-damaged buildings.'

'Oh, the large secret building?' he said, raising his voice.

The few townsfolk who had convened in the tea room all stared in our direction. I could have slunk under the table and disappeared into the highly polished floorboards.

'There's no need to shout, Grandad, I'm not deaf.'

'Yes, but I am. You need to speak up.'

'I don't like speaking up,' I said, thinking how much I hated drawing attention to myself. And I had already drawn too much attention to myself outside the Guildhall.

'But I can't hear with all the background noise,' he said, waving an arm around.

His gesture referred to the clanking of crockery and the constant boiling of water in the copper vat behind the counter.

The proprietor shot my grandfather a look. She must have thought he was destroying the exclusive ambience. The very thing he had told me he wanted.

'If you whisper, I can still hear you,' I said, as I leaned forward. 'So can we whisper, please?'

'Okay,' he said, winking.

'What do you make of it?' I asked.

'Of what?'

'The forbidden building,' I said with some frustration.

'The authorities are hiding something in there,' my grandfather said.

'Are they?'

'We're not allowed in. But they go inside. I've seen them. The building used to be guarded when I was a boy. But down the years, I suppose the next generation became less interested, and the mayor's office no longer felt the need to have guards on the door.'

'I wonder what they were guarding? The door must be locked though?'

'I expect so. But no one would be stupid enough to break in. Not with all the soldiers around the citadel.'

The waitress appeared with our hot chocolates, and my grandfather's eyes flickered with desire, or so it looked to me.

'This is the life,' he said, as he raised the steaming glass to his nose. 'Proper chocolate, and proper milk.'

'We have proper milk at home.'

'Don't you think it's watered down? This is proper milk,' he said, tapping the glass.

'Perhaps they have a cow out the back?'

'Are you trying sarcasm again? Or do you really think they have a cow out the back?'

I don't know what I thought. I just suggested it. I supposed it was possible some cows could live in an additional dairy farm in the citadel.

My grandfather lowered his lips to the glass, then paused.

'Don't tell your mother.'

'What should I tell her?' I asked.

'We went to the citadel. I had my appointment. We visited the temple. And came home.'

'But that's mostly true.'

'There you go then.'

'Apart from the fact we're omitting the tea room,' I said.

'Exactly. It's not lying, just omitting one tiny fact.'

'It is lying. And spending eight coupons on chocolate is more than a tiny fact.'

'Well, I'm going to enjoy this *more than a tiny fact* if it's the last thing I do,' my grandfather said.

'You're not going to die in the tea room, Grandad.'

'According to you I'm not going to die anywhere. Now, can we just enjoy the chocolate. Please?'

My grandfather took a sip and smacked his lips.

'You know,' he began, 'you take after your mother and grandmother in so many ways, but one trait in particular has been strong with all three of you.'

'What's that?'

'Stubbornness. I think it's the red hair.'

'Hair colour is no indication of personality,' I said.

'I beg to differ. I haven't got red hair. I turned out okay.'

'To be honest with you, Grandad, I don't recall you ever having any hair.'

My grandfather's eyes widened.

'Just because you're nineteen now doesn't mean that you can turn into some mouthy madam. And don't say you didn't realise you were being cheeky.'

The chocolate was the best I could remember. The creamy taste remained on my tongue long after we had finished. I would have liked to have thanked the cow.

As we exited the tea room, a small group of soldiers came in. I presumed they had arrived for an early lunch.

'Alright for some,' my grandfather said. 'I bet they're in here every day. The soldiers seem to have plenty of coupons.'

The square bustled with townsfolk. And a large throng had gathered in front of the weird column, which stood at the opposite end of the square from the fountain. A circle of steps led up to the tall tapering column.

A shabby-looking man stood upon the steps and addressed the crowd. His dark hair reached his shoulders, and he had a beard. None of the soldiers had beards and neither did any elderly men. It was not the fashion. Most of the crowd appeared engrossed in the man's diatribe. Curiosity got the better of me and I slid closer.

'Open your eyes. Look around you,' the man yelled. 'It's all lies. What do we really know? Who is the enemy? Why do we have all these abandoned buildings? What was the Temple of the First Ancestors built *for*? Knowledge has been lost. Because of a flood.'

'Lies,' someone in the crowd shouted.

'A major flood set humanity back—'

An elderly man interrupted the shouting man and attempted to pull him down. At the time I had assumed the elderly man was incensed at the unkempt man's disruption of the peace. But looking back, I think he was trying to save the man's life.

My grandfather caught up, just as some of the crowd began to get more vocal.

'Who's he?' he asked. 'He looks of fighting age. Why's he not gone to war? What's he saying?'

'Knowledge has been lost,' I said.

'Well, that's true.'

'He says a flood destroyed past knowledge.'

'Oh dear. In public? He'll get himself arrested.'

As though the soldiers had heard my grandfather, a group of them arrived on the scene. They shoved the elderly man out the way.

The bedraggled man flung his arms around the column and hung on.

The soldiers dragged the man down and proceeded to escort him through the square in the direction where my grandfather and I stood.

The man wriggled and struggled between the grip of two soldiers, while the other soldiers encircled him.

He continued to shout as he passed through the throng.

'She knows,' the shabby man hollered, as he glared at me. 'She's seen them.'

I noted the man's eyes were a piercing blue, as they were a striking contrast to his dark hair and beard.

'What have you seen?' one of the soldiers in the group asked me.

'Nothing,' I somehow managed to blurt out. Although I burned from humiliation.

'What do you know?'

'Nothing. I know nothing about nothing,' I said.

The soldier scowled at me in such a menacing way I thought I might regurgitate the hot chocolate I had just devoured.

'Is this dog yours?' he asked.

'Yes, she's ours,' my grandfather replied. 'What's your problem, young man?'

'The problem, *old man*, is we had word a woman was seen in the citadel after curfew last night. A young woman with a dog.'

'I see. And because my granddaughter has a dog by her side, you assume it must be her? And since all the men have been sent away to fight, apart from your good self, the town is now majority female. What are the chances a woman was spotted? How many must have pet dogs? And why would my granddaughter need to visit the citadel after curfew? She has a perfectly good home.'

'A woman with red hair, I might add,' the soldier said. 'Narrows it down a bit, wouldn't you say?'

'Balderdash,' my grandfather said. 'There are a number of women in this town with red hair.'

'I don't see many, if any,' the soldier said, glancing around. 'And I don't see any who have dogs.'

The shabby man lunged at me, and Envy barked.

'I know you've seen them,' he said. 'I've seen them too.'

I noticed a peculiar and quite unpleasant bitter odour emanating from the man. One I had never smelt before.

'Alright, let's take him away,' one of the soldiers said.

The soldier who had addressed us in an impolite manner squinted at me.

'I'm watching you,' he said.

As the soldiers marched away, I felt sure I would be sick. My grandfather had to hold me up on our short walk to our designated bakery and grocer's shop. We had to collect some essentials before heading home. He must have struggled, what with his stick. My stomach churned as I relived the incident with the soldier over and over again. I berated myself for being so useless. But I hated confrontation. My stomach also churned with the thought of having to attempt to retrieve my book after curfew. But I couldn't think how else I would get it back. And now I was a fugitive. The nightwatchman would lie in wait for me. The soldiers would be looking out for me. Perhaps the ancestral spirits would be, too. I didn't know which prospect was worse.

Chapter 3

The dark Forest of Ancients loomed beyond my bedroom window. I had watched the forest for movement every night. On this night in particular, as the sky turned from violet to indigo, I watched it with more determination. I think I was trying to find an excuse not to go back into the old citadel. To leave it for another evening instead. If I observed anything I would convince myself to stay at home and read. Although I wouldn't have been able to read my favourite book, for I believed that now lay under a bench opposite the Guildhall.

I listened for growling and barking from the dog-headed humans. I watched for lantern light. I waited for dogs as big as humans to skulk close.

The wind intensified as it approached the eleventh hour, and the trees shook with fury. They appeared alive and menacing. Perhaps the spirits of the forest were also angry. Angry at being restricted to the trees. There was nothing to prevent anything from tumbling out of the forest, over the outer town wall, through the fields of sheep, and into our garden, be it spirit or otherwise. We, who lived in the cottages at the outskirts of Eden took that risk every night. It was my job to make sure the hens were locked inside their house, which I had already done that evening. Everybody in the cottages latched their windows closed as soon as the sun died. It was a habit everyone followed. Because what resided out there was terrifying.

Three hours had passed since the curfew. Which meant not a soul remained outside. No one would notice me sneaking through the town and up towards the citadel. But I was still nervous. I left later than I had wanted to. But I had to be sure that by the time I reached the gatehouse on the old bridge the nightwatchman would have drifted off. Up until the previous night, he had always been a terrible watchman. Although I expect he never thought anyone would be so dumb that they would break the law several times a month. Well, he hadn't counted on me.

Envy and I snuck up on the bridge.

A light flickered behind the open door of the nightwatchman's quarters in the first gatehouse. I edged closer along the cold stone wall in an attempt to peer into the room. Envy pinned herself to my heels. I indicated for her to sit as I slid closer.

An horrendous snorting, followed by a whistling sound, came from behind the open door. The nightwatchman dozed in his chair, not watching anything. I have to say, despite my relief, I was most disappointed in him. He was incapable of doing his job.

We scampered across the bridge and entered the old citadel.

Every gas lamp remained lit, which surprised me. Usually, some either had not been lit or had already gone out by the time I ventured into the old citadel. I had the feeling something was afoot. However, other than the lamps outside, no lights glimmered behind the windows of the shops or cafes. All the buildings remained in darkness. All but one.

As I arrived in the square my heart sank. Lights blazed from the Guildhall. A few soldiers loitered around its porch. I detected movement from shadows passing across the windows on the ground floor. Numerous people must have lingered inside. I was never going to retrieve my book tonight. I had had a wasted journey. Plus I felt close to getting caught. A soldier only had to glance in my direction and that would be it, off to prison. Not that anyone in Eden knew the whereabouts of the prison. Rumour had it that the prison was underground somewhere and Eden was built on a network of tunnels which led to the prison. Or it was even inside the hill of the citadel. One thing we did know: the townsfolk sent to prison were never seen again.

I hid in the entrance of a narrow passage between one of the bakeries and the permanently closed tailor shop. Since the townsfolk were mending their own clothes, the tailor's had become redundant. Envy sat behind me, and beyond her lay total darkness. I thought I could stay there until everyone left. Although it was already late. The clock above the Guildhall had struck midnight while we had weaved through the side streets below the citadel. And, for all I knew, the meeting could last all night.

Envy whined.

'No, Envy. Please be quiet.'

She stared at the farthest end of the narrow passage, which led off behind the shops. Her consternation unnerved me, but I couldn't see anything in the pitch-black passage.

She whined again.

If she barked, I was for it.

'Envy. No,' I said more sternly.

She shuffled left to right on her haunches, as though agitated. And she remained fixed on the far end of the passage.

I returned my attention back towards the Guildhall.

Envy grumbled behind me.

I was convinced she was about to bark, so I swung around with a thought to gently smother her muzzle. But a cold hand smothered my mouth instead.

Envy continued to grumble, and I could feel her trotting alongside me as someone drew me back into the passage. But I didn't scream for two reasons. One: someone's hand still covered my mouth; and two: the soldiers would hear.

From the darkness of the passage, I emerged into a courtyard lit by a brilliant full moon and lantern light from some of the windows above. I hadn't realised any of the townsfolk lived above the shops in the citadel. I supposed it made sense that the shopkeepers would live above or at the back of their premises. I wondered if I had ever been seen before.

I tried to catch sight of Envy, but I could only sense her.

'I'm sorry for doing this,' a male voice said. 'But I would prefer it if you didn't scream, as you would alert those soldiers to our presence. And I don't want a repeat of last night.'

My heart leapt into my mouth and my stomach jumped into the vacant cavity where my heart once thumped. I wouldn't have been able to yell even if I had wanted to.

'I'm going to remove my hand now. It's not my intention to frighten you. And I certainly didn't intend to accost you.'

I glanced around to find a ghost with large dark eyes. But he wasn't a ghost. He had definition. The young man was shrouded in a white, or a light grey material. His suit appeared so tight it resembled a second skin. And the tone of his clothing matched his pallor, and his hair. Or at least it appeared that way in the faint light. He was tall and slender, with indistinct facial features in contrast to his black eyes.

'You're a little late,' he said. 'I was worried you weren't coming. But I thought you would want this.'

He removed my book, *Discourse on the Planets and Moons*, from under his arm and handed it to me. Then he knelt to pet Envy, who no longer seemed perturbed by him. In fact, she seemed quite taken by the odd-looking man. I have always considered dogs to be an excellent judge of character. Therefore, if Envy thought he was safe, then so should I.

'Aren't you going to say anything?' he asked.

'Sorry. I'm just … what are you?'

'*What* am I?'

'I mean … who are you?'

'A friend,' he said. 'Is that okay?'

'I don't have any friends,' I said.

'No? You surprise me.'

'How could you be my friend when I don't know you?' I asked, perplexed.

'But we will get to know each other,' he said.

Why did he assume I wanted to get to know him? It reminded me of the old saying: a stranger is a friend you haven't met yet. I had always thought this to be nonsense. A stranger is a stranger, obviously.

'How come you had my book?'

'Ah, there's the question you really want to know the answer to,' he said. 'A peculiar thing happened to me last night. I was minding my own business in the square here, when I saw a young lady with a small dog sheltering under a porch. I went over to say hello. She screamed. Dropped the two items she held. And still screaming, she fled into the night. I was mortified. I didn't realise I had such a terrifying appearance. Anyhow, I retrieved your book. I couldn't save your lamp, as the glass smashed when you dropped it. I shoved that back under a bench. I took your book for safe keeping.'

I considered his version of the previous night's events. But there are always two sides to every story, and his didn't quite match mine.

'You were minding your own business? That's not what I saw,' I said. 'You, and others like you, came from the sky. You were floating all around the square. I was the one minding my own business. I thought you were lost spirits.'

He chuckled.

'Is that what you saw? You may have been a little tired.'

'I was not tired, and I wasn't dreaming. To me it looked as though the citadel was overrun by spirits. Spirits who should have stayed in the forest,' I said, raising my voice a little. And regretting it, in case someone heard and appeared at one of the lit windows.

'I'm not a spirit, as I'm sure you can see. But I am a visitor to your town. I come from a faraway place. To you, I appeared to descend from the heavens—'

'What are heavens?' I asked.

'The heavens are above us. The heavens are home to the stars. Which, I note from your book, is something you're interested in.'

'I've never heard the sky described as the heavens,' I said.

'That's because there's much you don't know. I had a flick through your book today. I had some time on my hands. It's quite basic.'

'Basic? It explains the night sky. How can it be basic?' I asked, annoyed at the man's nerve.

'What do you know of the solar system?' he asked.

'There's a sun and six planets,' I said.

'Six planets? Is that all?'

'And some moons,' I concluded.

'What about beyond the solar system?'

'Well, that's where all the stars are,' I said, thinking how everyone knows there is nothing beyond our solar system other than stars.

'And what are stars?' he asked.

'What do you mean *what are stars*? They're the lights in the darkness which surrounds our solar system,' I said, astounded that the man didn't even know what the stars were.

'Umm, you know no more than what it says in your book, and your book isn't complete,' he said. 'Although I suppose it would never be complete. New things are discovered all the time. But I would hazard a guess there's much you don't even know about the world around you. Never mind everything in the heavens.'

'What do you mean you would hazard a guess there's much I don't know?'

'Have you not heard the saying *hazard a guess* before?' he asked.

'Of course I've heard that saying before,' I said. 'I'm not an idiot.'

'I didn't mean to imply you were an idiot. I wasn't sure if I was using incorrect phraseology.'

He really was a curious man. And I thought *I* was mad.

I clasped my book to my chest, feeling I should protect it from further offence. I had never considered it basic. What else could there possibly be to know?

'Well, thank you for returning my book, and keeping it safe. But I'll be heading on home now.'

'You don't want to watch the stars tonight?' he asked.

'No. I want to go home.'

'But I have a surprise for you.'

'I don't like surprises,' I said.

'You'll like this one.'

'I don't like surprises,' I said again.

'Why not?'

'Surprises mean change. I don't like change,' I said, thinking how standing in a courtyard I had never been in before, and with a strange man, was enough change for me for one evening.

'But you'll like this surprise,' he said.

'And how would you know? You don't know me.'

'You like books. You want to learn. I know that much. That's all I need to know for my surprise to be something I know you'd like. If not love.'

'But I hate surprises. I just told you. That means all surprises. All changes,' I said, feeling exasperated. Why did I have to explain myself to this odd man?

'You're a funny one,' he chuckled.

'Am I? Even compared to you?'

'Ouch,' he said, placing his hand over his heart.

At least I knew in that moment he had a heart. If his heart beat within his chest, he could pass as a human.

'Sorry,' I said. 'But I have my book. That was all I wanted. Plus, the square is teeming with soldiers. I just want to go home.'

I turned to head for the passage, and noticed two other passages also ran off the courtyard. One proceeded down the hill, but I didn't know where I'd end up if I took the unknown route. Therefore I stomped back down the same passage I had been dragged through only a moment ago.

'I take it the soldiers aren't usually in the square this late?' the man asked, as he followed me.

'No. I've never seen them in the citadel at night.'

'Then something has spooked them. Your authorities, I mean.'

'Yes, I guess the mayor must have called a meeting,' I said.

The young man poked his head around the corner of the bakery and examined the square.

'The soldiers could make my surprise more challenging than it needs to be,' he said.

'Why?' I asked.

'Because my surprise is over there,' he said, pointing in the direction of the Guildhall.

'Well, I'm definitely going home then.'

'I wonder if there's another way?' he said, as he disappeared down the passage again.

I could have taken that opportunity to leave. I could have turned around and headed for the bridge. But instead, I waited for him to return. Envy sat by my heels, as though she waited, too.

His shape emerged from the passage, and he held out his hand. 'Come on.'

'Where are we going?' I asked.

'On an adventure,' he said.

I must have looked horrified.

'Don't tell me you hate adventures as much as you hate surprises?'

'I've never gone that way before,' I said, nodding towards the passage. 'I don't like going ways I've never gone before.'

'But there will have been a first time for every way you go.'

I considered this.

'But everywhere I go I was taken as a small child, so I never really thought about it back then,' I said.

'It'll be an adventure. You're adventurous. Don't you break the law every time you visit the citadel after curfew?'

'How do you know about the curfew if you're a visitor from faraway?' I asked.

'Maybe I know more about your home than you know about mine.'

'That's obvious. I don't even know your name,' I said.

'Gabriel,' he said.

'I've never heard that name before.'

'It's an old name. Ancient, you could say.'

I scrutinised this strange young man with a strange ancient name.

'Do you know about the Temple of the First Ancestors?' I asked. 'My grandfather says it should be called the Temple of the Long, Long-Dead Ancients.'

'Does he? I like his thinking. He's half correct. It should actually be called something else entirely,' Gabriel said.

'Like what?'

'It doesn't matter for now. Another time. We have more pressing matters this evening. Are you coming or not?' he asked, stretching his hand out further.

I still don't know what compelled me to do it, but after hesitating a short moment, I accepted his hand.

I had always found meeting new people uncomfortable. I could never understand why I found it so difficult. I preferred my own company. I tried to avoid meeting people as much as I could throughout my life. I had never been a good communicator. The right words rarely seemed to manifest in my mind. Therefore, my mouth had nothing to pass on. I couldn't always understand people, and they didn't understand me. It all seemed like a waste of time. But, somehow, Gabriel made me feel at ease. It helped that he was alone rather than in a group. A crowd of people was always more daunting. Plus, Envy had taken a shine to him. Something about him oozed a calm.

And his large dark eyes were quite hypnotic.

I allowed Gabriel to lead me back through the narrow passage and through the courtyard. Then through a gate which opened onto an alleyway which ran behind the row of shops. I was amazed all this lay hidden behind the square. I only knew of some passageways which linked parts of the old citadel streets. I had no idea a whole other world existed behind the shopfronts and abandoned buildings. Each building appeared to have a gate which led onto the alleyway we sped through. My eyes must have adjusted to the darkness, as one of the gates sat open and I caught a glimpse of an outhouse and small courtyard-like area.

The moonlight bounced off the upper windowpanes on the row of buildings. I realised we were dashing past the back of the Grand Tea Room and one of the large abandoned buildings. We encountered another gate at the end of the alleyway, and this led onto another courtyard. Gabriel guided me down a dark passageway opposite, and we exited onto the square again.

Light continued to glow from inside the Guildhall, and the soldiers remained outside.

We slunk back into the darkness and onto this new courtyard. Gabriel hesitated for a moment and appeared to ponder the blockade before us.

'We need to get up on the wall, as we need to head in that direction.'

'Are you sure you're not taking me to the Guildhall?' I asked. Even I could hear the trepidation in my voice.

'I'm not taking you to the Guildhall, but we do need to get closer.'

Before I had time to protest, Gabriel grabbed me by the waist and hoisted me up onto the brickwork. He did the same with Envy. She stood upon the wall quite content. Gabriel flew up with ease, as though he had wings. I noticed he wore a shroud which was flowing free at the back. It resembled a feather-light robe.

'This way,' he said, as he floated across the brick wall.

We ran behind the hospital, and school, which led on to the fire-damaged buildings and abandoned buildings at the top of the square, and the dreaded Guildhall.

Some of the brick wall had crumbled away in places, meaning we had to leap onto the outhouse rooftops. I wasn't dressed for the occasion. My over-the-knee skirt restricted movement, and the worn-down soles of my shoes slipped on the roof tiles, causing some of them to crash to the ground. Plus, I was sweating under my coat. I considered that if I ever had to leap, run, and climb again, I would wear my little jacket and borrow some trousers from my grandfather's wardrobe. They would be more practical.

While I stumbled and scraped my legs, Gabriel appeared to dance across the walls and outhouses. Even when he had to carry Envy over a precipice, he did it with ease. He was made of lighter stuff than I. It didn't help that I clutched my book under one arm. I suppose I could have left it in the first courtyard, but now I had it back, I didn't want to be without it again.

We leapt over an alleyway, which I could see led onto the square as the gas lamps near the fountain shone down the passage.

I was relieved when Gabriel ceased his graceful dance and we could pause for breath. Or rather I could. Gabriel didn't appear to have any trouble breathing.

He considered the back of the building before us. It was wider than the others and more imposing. It didn't have a courtyard of its own, or an outhouse. It did, however, have a large terraced balcony at the rear. I recalled I had seen this terrace before, when I had wandered down another alleyway between the Guildhall and my favourite abandoned building.

From the rear, the small tower on the roof was more prominent.

'We have to get up there,' Gabriel said, pointing to the balcony.

'I beg your pardon?'

'It's the only way inside.'

'That's the surprise?' I asked. 'Breaking into an authority-owned building? These places are forbidden.'

'How do you know this is an authority-owned building?'

'Because I know where we are, and it's right next to the Guildhall,' I said, a little panicked.

'I see. And you think this building should be off limits to you?' he said, as he raised Envy onto the terrace and climbed up himself.

'It is off limits to me. It's owned by the authorities. And it's forbidden.'

'This building has been commandeered by your authorities for their use alone. But it used to be open to the public, many moons ago. I think you have a right to see inside. You have a right to know.'

'I have a right to know?' I said, as I grabbed his hand and he heaved me onto the balcony.

Several tables and chairs lay spread out upon the terrace. As did some empty plant pots. In the brilliant moonlight, I observed spiderwebs linking the tables to the chairs, and the terrace balustrades to the plant pots. No one had been on the terrace in years, decades perhaps. I imagined at one time it would have been an elegant place to sit in the sun. The buildings at this end of the square backed onto the temple gardens. You would have a fantastic view, overlooking the temple between the trees.

'I had no idea this seating area was up here,' I said.

'Why would you. But this isn't the surprise.'

Three double doors barred our entrance to the abandoned building.

Gabriel ran his fingers over one of the door frames.

'This would have been so much easier if we could've gone through the front door. Damn those soldiers.'

He yanked on a section of frame around the middle door, and a chunk of it came away in his hand.

'Ah ha! I've found our entrance.'

Gabriel tugged at the door, which fell away from the frame, leaving the other half of the double door in situ.

'Finally,' he said, leaning the broken door upright against the wall. 'Now you can have your surprise.'

He offered me his hand again, and led me willingly into the building.

At first, I couldn't make anything out in the darkness. I stumbled into a heavy object, and it scraped across the floor with an ear-piercing screech. I realised it was a table which belonged to another seating area inside.

'It's a pity your lamp broke last night,' Gabriel said, as he disappeared further into the forbidden building.

'Can you see where you're going?' I asked after him, as I felt my way around a second table.

'Yes, sorry. Be with you in a minute. I'm used to the dark.'

Envy stayed by my side, waiting patiently for me to find my way. I knew she had much better vision than myself, and wondered why she couldn't guide me away from the furniture. The floorboards creaked. The furniture creaked. I think even I creaked from the night's excursion. I continued to feel my way past all the tables and chairs, and believed myself to be entering another open space. I banged my leg into something more solid than a table. This too creaked. I reached out to find shelves, and more shelves.

A musty scent lingered in the air. The scent of ages.

My fingers explored the wooden shelves and found small blocks packed in tight. I moved my fingers higher and they fell over the lip of these blocks.

I gasped.

I had discovered paper. I allowed my fingers to run across what I understood to be the spines of books. I felt cloth- and leather-bound volumes.

As I stepped further through this new room, moonlight filtered through from high above, as though the ceiling had a gaping hole.

Light also appeared from below. It was Gabriel with a lantern. He wandered amongst some desks on the ground floor and lit a lamp upon each one. This illuminated the books and documents spread across each desk. Plus, the light shone upon numerous white stone heads. These 'half statues' stood guard next to every bookcase on the ground floor. I wondered why someone had decapitated some statues, discarded the bodies from below the shoulder, and kept the severed heads.

With the place illuminated, I realised I was standing on a balcony. More balconies swept the circumference of the building on numerous floors above me. The middle section of the building was a hollowed-out space. The light which seeped in from the ceiling came through a skylight. But the glass must have been covered with dirt and leaves. I could only imagine what this place would have looked like in its prime. I discovered much later that the best word to describe the middle space would have been atrium. However, I hadn't heard this word at the time. I didn't know how much I had to learn about the world and how much of it had previously been hidden from me.

Gabriel approached. He radiated behind the glow of the lantern. His fair hair turned golden. His pale skin was so smooth it didn't appear real. I assumed, like me, he wouldn't tan. I had to be careful because of my fair complexion and freckles. My grandfather tanned, as did my father.

'Found some matches and a lamp in an office, which was useful. But I was really looking for these,' he said, rattling some keys. 'I also discovered a small kitchen, which must have been an area for the staff.'

He handed me the lantern, and using one of the keys he proceeded to open some of the wooden window shutters a slither.

While Gabriel busied himself, I took the opportunity to explore the building. I shone the lantern over all the book spines on several dark wooden shelves. Each book had a small white label at the bottom of the spine, and each label had numbers on it. I didn't understand what these numbers meant, and I didn't understand what any of the titles meant. I didn't even care. I put the lantern and my own book down on a little table by a bookcase. I returned my attention to one of the shelves, squeezed my fingers into a tiny gap between two books and retrieved one.

Caravaggio it said in gold lettering on the cover. I didn't know what a Caravaggio was. I drew another book out from the shelf, and another, and another.

I had begun stacking them in my arms when Gabriel appeared again.

He stared at me with a little smirk. But perhaps my face was a picture. My mind churned. I was in awe of the place. I had a myriad of questions, but I didn't know where to begin, and therefore no words spilled forth.

'I do believe she likes her surprise.'

I did. And this was unusual. I didn't like surprises. It was a surprise to me to find I adored the surprise.

'Do you know what this place is?' Gabriel asked.

'It's like a gigantic version of Mr Prendergast's shop,' I said, as I placed the pile of books on the table next to my own.

'Prendergast's?'

'The bookshop in the citadel. But he has nothing on this scale. His shop is tiny compared to this.'

'Well, this place is called a library,' Gabriel said.

'I don't know that word.'

'No, none of you do I expect. Apart from your authorities.'

'What does *li-brary* mean?' I asked.

'Think of it as a place of learning. An archive of knowledge. And a house of books.'

'A house of books,' I whispered to myself.

I loved that idea. I loved the place. Gabriel was right.

'What would you like to learn about?' he asked. 'I see you've picked a small selection there.'

'I don't know. I just ...'

'You just grabbed any books,' he chuckled. 'Well, the library—'

'The House of Books,' I said, much preferring that title.

'Yes. The *house* is split into various sections depending on your required area of interest. Or perhaps you would prefer fiction?'

'What's fiction?'

'Not fact. Tales created for people to enjoy at leisure,' Gabriel said.

'Do you mean funny little stories?' I asked. 'Like the ones children make up?'

'Possibly, but on a much larger scale. Fiction is made-up stories about people, or rather characters, from another place or time, or even another world. Readers like to get lost in created stories. They can forget about their worries for a while as they follow the life of another person and their trials and errors.'

'People create stories which are written down? And other people read them for ... enjoyment?'

'Yes,' he said.

This was a wonder to me. It seemed like a waste of time. I had always considered one should be learning.

'I've never heard of such a thing,' I said. 'I've only ever read to gain knowledge. I didn't know there were other options.'

Gabriel chuckled.

'But most are really moralistic tales,' he said. 'The reader can learn some life lessons through a character's journey.'

'But it's made up,' I said. 'How can you learn anything?'

'I understand. This is all new to you. That was kind of the point of my surprise. And here,' he said, spreading his arms, 'you have access to all the knowledge in the world. What would you like to learn about first?'

'I don't know.'

'I suppose it is overwhelming.'

He raised the lantern to a sign which hung from the ceiling.

'Arts. Therefore, this whole section here, will cover the arts. You've picked some art books there,' he said, nodding towards the small table with the pile I had gathered. 'Let's see: Tintoretto, Raphael, Bosh, Botticelli, and Caravaggio. You found the Renaissance section.'

He clambered onto the shelving where I had removed the books and brushed his fingertips over the dark wood at the top of the bookcase. This dislodged a little dust and cobwebs to reveal gold-coloured lettering. The word *Renaissance* glimmered in the lantern light.

'I don't know what that word means,' I said.

'Renaissance means rebirth,' he said, as he climbed back down.

'Oh. What about the other words?' I asked, indicating the books.

'Those are the names of the artists. We should probably start with something you're already reasonably familiar with. I have it,' he said, clicking his fingers. 'I know exactly where you should begin your learning.'

He strolled off along the balcony with the lantern held high.

I collected my book, *Discourse on the Planets and Moons*, from the table and followed.

As we circled the inner building, I noticed ladders leaned against some of the bookcases. We passed signs which read: Philosophy, and Religion. I didn't know what either of those words meant.

'Fiction is back down on the ground floor,' he said. 'We need to go up.'

Gabriel led Envy and I through a double door.

A spiral staircase loomed before us.

We ascended the stone steps. I loved the staircase. It spoke of elegance. I leaned over the edge and gazed up at the wrought-iron railings as the staircase coiled off into the unknown.

'Are you coming?' Gabriel asked.

He was already on the next level.

I sprang up behind Gabriel with Envy in tow. He moseyed ahead with the lantern and continued to read out the signs.

'Geography, history ... there's a lot of history,' he said, as he turned his attention to the lettering above the shelves. 'Classical history, medieval history, military history ... No, it won't be here. We need to go up another floor.'

We headed back to the spiral staircase.

I traced my fingers around the swirling pattern in the wrought-iron railing.

'We're entering the heavens of the library,' Gabriel said. 'Perhaps this is the correct place to find it.'

'To find what?' I asked.

'You'll see.'

More surprises, I thought, as we arrived on the next level.

'Natural sciences. We're getting closer,' he said.

Gabriel was thoroughly enjoying himself, leading me around

and around, up and up, inside the House of Books. I might have even referred to him as smug.

'Science!'

Gabriel hollered the word with such force that Envy jumped and I almost dropped my book.

'Sorry. Didn't mean to startle you. But we have reached our destination.'

Gabriel shone the lantern up and down a few of the aisles and muttered something about *space stuff*.

'Here we are,' he said, as he emerged with a large tome. 'This book will be a great starting point for you. It covers everything, but it will be quite easy for you to digest.'

'Digest? I don't eat books,' I said. 'The rationing is bad, but still. I don't eat paper.'

Gabriel chuckled again. I quite liked the sound of his little chuckle. But not so much that it always occurred after something I had said.

'I mean easy for you to take in all the information.'

I stared at the title. The word *Space* was the only word I understood.

'What does this mean?' I asked, pointing to a word I had never seen before. I tried to pronounce it: 'Encyclo ...'

'Encyclopaedia,' Gabriel said. 'It's like a compendium of all the knowledge in a specific area. This encyclopaedia covers all aspects of knowledge on space. All the planets, galaxies, black holes, star formations, constellations ... all of it.'

'Star formations?'

'Yes, the stars have to form somewhere.'

'What are galaxies?' I asked, puzzled by these new words.

'You share your name with a galaxy: the Andromeda galaxy. Although I assume you don't know where your name comes from? Your parents probably don't even know.'

It was true. I didn't know why I'd been named Andromeda. I never thought to ask.

'How do you know my name?'

'It's in your book.'

Gabriel grabbed *Discourse on the Planets and Moons*, turned to the first page, and read my father's words aloud:

> *To my dearest Andromeda,*
>
> *I pass on to you the discoveries of the night sky. A precious thing which we have relished reading together since you were a small child.*
>
> *With love always, Dad.*

Tears burned around my eyes. I hadn't read my father's message for some time, let alone heard someone read it aloud.

'Your father isn't here anymore?' Gabriel asked.

'I don't know where my dad is,' I said, staring at the floor.

'I'm sorry. I should take you home.'

'I'll be okay. I have Envy for company.'

Envy pawed at my leg, and I patted her soft fur.

'I had another surprise for you,' Gabriel said. 'It's at the top of the staircase.'

Another one. I felt bewildered.

'But it can wait,' Gabriel continued. 'I don't want to overwhelm you anymore than I have. You should go home.'

'I don't have to leave the way we came in, do I?'

The thought of leaping across walls and outhouses made my body ache.

'Good question. Let's go and find out.'

Gabriel placed my book with the *Space Encyclopaedia*, and he gripped them under one arm while carrying the lantern in his other hand.

We jogged back down to the first floor. Gabriel headed for one of the open shuttered windows which overlooked the square.

No soldiers loitered outside. I couldn't tell if any light came from the Guildhall. But I felt tiredness creeping over me. I would have to take a chance.

'I hope the nightwatchman is still asleep,' I said.

'I think I saw a watchman in the square last night. Well, the man watched me, and I watched him. Then he ran back down the hill the way he came.'

'That sounds like him,' I said. 'I told him a tower on the temple had caught fire.'

'He didn't find a fire. He found me. I could frighten him again if you like?'

I smiled at the thought, but didn't confirm either way.

As we headed for the main door, we sauntered past the desks on the ground floor. All the lamps burned bright above numerous open books strewn across every surface, as though the last people in the House of Books had fled in a hurry.

Gabriel unlocked a glass-panelled double door, which opened with a groan onto a foyer. A large wooden desk stood in the middle. It reminded me of the large immovable desk in the foyer at the Guildhall. The main entrance door opposite was of a solid dark wood with engraved panels. At least I would have a more civilised exit.

'Here, take your books,' Gabriel said. 'Don't worry about the shutters and the broken door, I'll deal with all that.'

I had forgotten about the damaged door on the terrace.

Envy and I slid through the entrance door and I swivelled back around to face the House of Books.

'Surely I can't just take the books?' I asked. 'Isn't that stealing?'

'You're not stealing them. You're borrowing them. You'll bring them back when you've finished reading them. That's how a library works.'

'So the faded sign above the door says library? But there's another word before it. I can see an E. I now know the R is in library.'

'That E is a B. The word is public,' Gabriel said.

'Public library,' I whispered to myself.

'You're a member of the public. The public library is for you. You can borrow whatever books you like. It's your right.'

‘I have a right to borrow these books?’

‘Absolutely.’

Gabriel stared at me with a strange look I didn’t know what to make of. My cheeks burned and I turned away. I tucked my hair behind an ear, changed my mind and positioned my hair over half my face. I felt so exposed.

‘I like your hair,’ he said. ‘It’s unusual.’

‘Is it?’ I said, knowing full well my hair colour was not common, and something else which drew attention to me. Which I hated.

‘Yes, I’ve only ever seen that colour once before,’ he said.

Gabriel considered something in the distance with a kind of haunted expression, and then he smiled at me.

‘I think you deserve a lie-in tomorrow morning,’ he said. ‘Get a good rest before tackling the encyclopaedia.’

‘Thank you,’ I said, as I held my new possession to my chest. ‘Thank you for showing me the House of Books.’

‘I’m glad you like your surprise. Meet you back here tomorrow evening.’

Like it? I loved it. A whole new world existed within my world. And it was glorious. I would be going there every night with or without an invite from Gabriel. All the knowledge of the land resided in the giant house waiting for me to devour. The shelves must have heaved with thousands of volumes.

I jogged through the citadel streets in a daze of excitement, despite the encyclopaedia weighing more than an armful of chopped wood. The nightwatchman remained asleep in his quarters. I expected all of Eden must have slumbered. Apart from myself, Envy, and my new strange *friend* Gabriel. Even the soldiers should be home asleep. I hoped.

As it was so late, I didn’t bother to take the side streets. I took the main street. I peered up at a few of the windows in the townhouses as Envy and I sped past. I thought I detected a flicker of light in one and a shadow at the windowpane. But I couldn’t be sure.

Chapter 4

Sunlight blazed through my thin curtains. I yanked on my blanket with the intention of throwing it over my head. But this action disturbed Envy as she lay snoozing at the end of my bed.

My body was heavy but my mind raced from the previous night's discovery.

I peeked over at my writing bureau. I hadn't dreamt it. The *Space Encyclopaedia* remained where I placed it, alongside *Discourse on the Planets and Moons*. The books took pride of place amongst a jar of pencils and pens, candles, dried flowers, and numerous drawings which I had pinned around my writing bureau. Some were of plants, flowers, and birds I had seen in our garden. Other drawings were of ducks, frogs, and toads I had seen by the river. Plus some of my favourite buildings in the old citadel, including the House of Books.

Despite my aching muscles begging for more rest, I discarded my blanket and drew back the curtains in eagerness to begin my learning.

The encyclopaedia had a little dust on it. Perhaps even some cobwebs. Although I think some of the dust and webbing had transferred onto my coat during the evening. Most of the dust had settled between the grooves of the pages at the top end of the book. Dust annoyed me. I would have to clean it off.

When I got downstairs, neither my mother, or grandfather, appeared to be anywhere inside. I thought my mother might be sewing in the little back room off the kitchen, but all the rooms were vacant. I deduced there was no work. My mother hadn't asked me to help her with any sewing of late. But work could be sporadic. Sometimes we had no work for weeks, and we wouldn't have enough coupons to live on. Other times, demand was high, and it would be urgent. I would help my mother with the larger orders. It could be anything from dresses to bed linen. We never knew where these items ended up. They didn't all appear to be required by the citizens of Eden. We would sew into the night if needed. The sewing machine made work easier, but sometimes items required hand stitching, and our fingers would bleed. I was clumsier with the needle and quite often ended up transferring my blood onto an item. My mother only pricked her fingers when she was exhausted. As we had sewn some of the uniforms, I wondered if we had worked on the uniform my father wore. It gave me some comfort to think I might have at least sewn my father's clothes, since I couldn't do anything else for him.

A place had been set for me at the dining table. But the teapot felt cold, and the jar of honey was down to its last dregs.

The cottage sat in silence, apart from the birdsong drifting in through the open windows.

In the kitchen, someone had topped up Envy's bowl with some leftover food, and she pounced upon it.

I dampened a cloth under the tap and ran it over the cover of the encyclopaedia. I noticed the little numbered label at the bottom of the spine was beginning to peel away. The six-digit number read 520.183. I gently scraped the cloth over the label, and then over the top of the pages. The paper was browned from age here. Rust-coloured speckles had formed within the dust.

I made myself a fresh pot of tea and took an egg from a little basket on the kitchen countertop. I would have egg on toast. It made sense, since the hens had laid and the honey was low.

Seated at the table, I gobbled down my toast and poured myself a second cup of tea. With care, I opened the encyclopaedia to a page at random.

I had never seen an image like it. I could never have imagined anything so beautiful. The image captured part of something called the Eagle Nebula. This region of the nebula was known as the Pillars of Creation, due to three colossal pillar-like clouds of dust and gas, within which new stars continued to form.

Gabriel had mentioned star formations. He hadn't mentioned the word nebula. I didn't know what that word meant.

Something called the Hubble Space Telescope took the photo, while it orbited Earth. The nebula was around seven thousand light years away. Even the largest pillar was four light years tall. In comparison, the Earth would be a tiny dot in the humongous dust cloud.

I couldn't understand any of it. What were light years? How could there be a telescope outside Earth? I thought I was supposed to be gaining knowledge, not acquiring more questions.

Envy trotted to the front door, wagged her tail, and sniffed around the gap underneath the door.

My grandfather entered, and Envy lavished him with kisses.

'That's the best welcome home a man could have,' he said, as he gave her a cuddle.

He had to drop the basket he carried due to Envy's overexcitement. The basket contained various root vegetables he had collected from our patch in the allotment.

Once Envy had calmed down, my grandfather retrieved the produce.

'They've come up well,' he said. 'I'll make a nice stew to last the week. Which reminds me, good news, one of the hens has died.'

'Oh no,' I said, wondering how my grandfather could possibly think the death of a hen was good news.

'I'll be adding her to the stew.'

'Which one?' I asked, absolutely horrified that he would do such a thing.

'I don't know which one,' he said, as he joined me at the table.

'Not Ethel? Agatha? Mabel?'

'They all look the same to me.'

'They're not the same. They're all unique,' I protested. 'Unique in markings and personality.'

'Personality? A hen?'

'You haven't spent as much time with them as I have,' I said, thinking how they often waddled over to see me whenever I went into the garden.

'I've got better things to do than talk to hens,' my grandfather said.

'Yes but—'

'This is precisely why your mother didn't want you naming them. They don't live forever you know. Whichever one it is, she's had a good life, and now she's expired. We'll give her a good send-off in the pot. It's what she would've wanted.'

How could my grandfather know what a hen would want in life, or rather death in this instance.

'I don't think she would've wanted to end up in pieces, boiling in a pot alongside bits of carrot and swede,' I said.

'Ah, she expected cremation, did she? I suppose I could roast her over a spit instead.'

'Grandad!'

'Well, when did she give you her funeral requirements?' he asked.

'She didn't,' I said, a little annoyed by my grandfather's teasing.

'You don't have to eat her if you don't want to,' he said. 'But she's going in the pot. There's a war on apparently. We're not wasting her.'

I knew my grandfather was right. We were rationing. We hadn't had meat for about two weeks. And I shouldn't have named the hens. But to me, it would have been like eating Envy. I was sure my grandfather wouldn't want to add her to a big pot.

Thankfully, between my mother's love of baking and my grandfather's love of throwing whatever we had managed to grow into a stew, we did okay foodwise.

'Where's Mum?' I asked, no longer wishing to speak about a poor dead hen.

'She's in the citadel. It's collection day for us.'

My grandfather was referring to the coupons. I had lost track of the days.

'What's that you're reading?' he asked.

'It's a space—' I began, but struggled with the following word again. 'Encyclo-paedia.'

'A what?'

'A book about space.'

'Where did you get it from?' he asked.

'A friend gave it to me.'

'What friend?'

'I saw him the other night, but I met him properly last night,' I said, recalling what a strange meeting it was. Especially as Gabriel had accosted me down a passageway first.

'A *he*?' my grandfather said.

'Yes. He showed me the House of Books.'

'The what?'

'The most magnificent place I've ever seen,' I said. 'It's my favourite forbidden building. Its real name is a library, but I don't like that name so much. The House of Books makes more sense. It's wonderful and vast. There are books from floor to ceiling, everywhere you look. You'd love it too. It's the best place in the world. I can't believe it's been there the whole time and we never knew. But I'm glad I know of its existence now. Thanks to Gabriel.'

'Gabriel?'

'My new friend.'

'Odd name. Where's this Gabriel suddenly come from?' my grandfather asked, as his eyes narrowed.

'I thought he fell from the sky. But he says I imagined that part.'

'Fell from the sky?'

'You remember, the other night when I was in the citadel and the storm came. I told you,' I said.

'Yes, yes. Men don't usually fall from the sky.'

'No, I thought he was a lost ancestral spirit. Remember?'

My grandfather frowned at me.

'When is your next appointment with the doctor?' he asked.

'Grandad,' I exclaimed again.

'Sorry, poppet, but I'm only asking out of concern. Lost spirits and men from the sky. Whatever next?'

'But it's true.'

'I don't think you're getting enough sleep with all your late-night galivanting about. That's why you couldn't get up this morning.'

'I admit I'm tired. But the House of Books exists. How do you think I got this?' I asked, waving the encyclopaedia in front of his face.

'Yes. It's troubling. This friend Gabriel ... he broke into a building we're all forbidden to enter?'

'Yes,' I said, sheepishly.

'Do you think that was wise?'

'Probably not,' I said, thinking about how I regularly ignored curfew, and now I had entered an abandoned building, which meant I had now officially broken two laws in Eden. Albeit two broken laws which led to an incredible discovery.

'What did you say it was called?' my grandfather asked.

'The House of Books.'

'No. The other word. The word you weren't so keen on.'

'Library,' I said.

'Umm, library.'

My grandfather leaned back in the chair, placed his elbows upon the armrests and raised both his index fingers to his lips, so they formed a pointed arch. This was his usual position for deep contemplation.

'I've never heard that word before,' he said, shaking his head. 'This place is a mystery.'

'The library? I just told you what's in there.'

'No, I mean Eden is a mystery. Plenty of odd things down the years.'

'Like what?'

'New names for places and things for starters. Take the omnibus; it was called a people carrier when I was a boy. Then some senior official at the Guildhall said it should be called an omnibus. That was the correct name. As if they had just discovered the word. Found it in a file somewhere. Same with the word *fortress*. Although that one was before my time. When my father was a boy, the townsfolk were informed the old citadel resided within a hilltop fortress, and it was explained to them what the word meant. Up until that point, they had thought it was simply a wall, like the outer town wall. Then the townsfolk began to question who it was the First Ancestors had been trying to keep out of the citadel. A father of one my father's friends had put forward the theory that perhaps some walls were more a case of trying to keep people in. Someone of importance must have overheard, or been informed, as this boy's father was never seen again.'

'The man shouting in the square yesterday … do you think he'll disappear?' I asked.

'I expect so.'

'He said something about a flood setting humanity back?'

'Entirely possible, I suppose.'

'Do you know about any floods?' I asked.

'The town flooded when I was a boy. The river ran through the streets and into the nearby houses. My father told me he thought the town had flooded numerous times in the past. There had been at least one serious flood. There's evidence of water erosion just below the citadel. It's high up in the rockface, on the sheerest side where no trees have shot through to hide the mark. I don't know any more than that.'

'I remember you once spoke of bodies,' I said. 'What do you know about them?'

'I was a child. A group of us were on a school trip to the temple. I can't remember what the teacher was talking about; he would've been prattling away about the First Ancestors I suppose. Things like that are thoroughly boring when you're a child, so a few of us snuck outside and explored the grounds. I don't think there were as many plants and flowers as they have now. The ground has always been uneven though. One of the boys began kicking his feet about in the soil, when he kicked something hard. We all set to uncovering this object and we pulled out a curved piece of bone. We dropped it in shock and ran back into the temple to get the teacher. Well, I'd never seen him so flustered. He babbled on about it being an animal bone. But his face displayed fear. And we knew it wasn't an animal. I think what we found was part of a human hip bone.'

'Why would part of a human bone be there?'

'There were more bones to be found though,' my grandfather said. 'Years later I heard a tale that someone uncovered a skull. We all wondered whether even more bones lay beneath the soil. I don't know how they got there. I just know our authorities covered it up.'

I couldn't understand how beautiful gardens could hold such a dark secret. A horrifying thought entered my mind.

'You don't think they could be the bones of the First Ancestors? Someone murdered them all? Maybe that's why the temple is named after them?'

'I honestly don't know,' he said. 'But I have to assume the bones are no longer there. After the skull find, proving the bones were human, I believe the rest of the bones were removed in order to prevent another accidental discovery.'

I was stunned. My grandfather, as a child, had uncovered human remains. That's how he knew about the bodies in the soil. Also, he'd heard about flooding before, but he had never uttered a word about it. I could understand him not wanting to discuss these things in public, but the privacy of our own home was different. Gabriel thought I had a right to know things. But my grandfather, for all his mad ideas, sometimes hid the truth.

My grandfather eyed the encyclopaedia.

'Keep that book hidden. It's dangerous,' he said.

'It's not dangerous. It's a book.'

'Books which have been kept from us are dangerous. Because forbidden knowledge is dangerous. Tell no one. I mean it. Not even your mother.'

I returned to my bedroom in case my mother came home and found me at the table with a book of forbidden knowledge. I spent the afternoon flicking through the dusty pages, with Envy curled up next to me on the bed. My grandfather's words played on my mind for the rest of the day. With every page I turned over of the encyclopaedia, I heard my grandfather's warning. I knew all about our solar system ... at least I thought I did. But I didn't know we resided in a galaxy, within a universe. My book *Discourse on the Planets and Moons* didn't explain any of this.

During the afternoon I discovered my namesake: the Andromeda Galaxy. I learned we live in the Milky Way and Andromeda is our neighbour. When we look towards

Andromeda, the light we see has taken two and a half million years to travel here. The Milky Way and Andromeda are destined to collide in four billion years. This collision will create a new galaxy.

I learned that the sun was a nuclear star, basically a hydrogen bomb. Although the words meant nothing to me, I knew they didn't sound good. The sun regularly ejects nuclear flames, also known as solar flares, out into the solar system, and these could destroy our way of life. One day, our sun will kill us all.

In an ironic twist, suns have to die for life to even exist. Billions of years ago, a star went out with an explosion and shot forth carbon, amongst other elements. This carbon became us. There is constant death and rebirth in the universe. A supernova created from a dying star creates new stars in the nebula. Our own sun came into existence from a previous star death. All suns die. And they don't go alone.

In around one billion years, the Earth will suffer and then expire at the hands of our nuclear star. The sun will take us with her during her death throes. In a fight to keep her dwindling nuclear fuel, the sun will expand into a red giant. The heat will become too intense to sustain any life on Earth. The giant sun will engulf the sky as she burns down upon a barren planet. Over the next few billion years, she will gorge on Mercury, then Venus.

And there I was, worried about our galaxy colliding with Andromeda in four billion years, when we will already be long dead, thanks to our sun.

I also learned that the Earth and another planet, Theia, collided when the solar system was forming. The rocks which were spewed out during the collision formed our moon, which got trapped alongside the Earth. Good for us though, as the Earth was spinning too fast until the gravitational pull of the moon slowed the Earth's spin down, giving us our twenty-four-hour day. But now the moon is speeding up and drifting away from us. It's moving out into a wider orbit. Only a few centimetres a year. But this will begin to cause havoc. Currently, the gravitational pull of the moon stabilises the Earth's tilt. It's our tilt which gives us the seasons. When the moon drifts further out, this will change. We will no longer have summers or winters. And the Earth will start to wobble. Right now, the moon resides in the perfect position. And it's also in the perfect position for solar eclipses. Its size and distance in comparison with the Earth and sun cause a total eclipse. As it glides away, we will no longer have this wondrous phenomenon.

This all shocked me. I hadn't considered the moon could leave. Things could change. Nothing was fixed. It all sounded terrifying. It all sounded blasphemous. My grandfather was correct, the book was dangerous. And Gabriel was also correct. My book *Discourse on the Planets and Moons* was more basic in comparison. Gabriel signalled trouble. Because I would be in trouble with the authorities, as what I had read was definitely forbidden knowledge. But I couldn't understand why this would be forbidden. Why weren't we to know what was really out there? That the solar system would change? Why had the authorities kept the library hidden from us? More importantly, why did Gabriel want me to know of its existence?

I turned my attention to Venus, our early morning and evening star. I learned that if humans were to land on Venus we would be crushed, boiled, and poisoned in an instant. The pressure in the atmosphere would be too great for our fragile bodies. And the intense heat would sear our skin. Plus, the air was toxic. It's mostly carbon dioxide, with a small amount of nitrogen. Venus's rain clouds contain sulphuric acid. But it's too hot on Venus to rain, so the acid remains in the thick clouds. I thought it odd how Venus was considered our sister planet when she appeared so deadly. It got me thinking about how when the sun expands Earth will become as hot as Venus. No life will remain here. The sun won't have even swallowed Mercury before the Earth will become inhospitable.

I also read up a little on the gas giants and asteroids. I discovered the ice rings of Saturn didn't exist around a hundred million years ago. The ice rings were once an ice moon, whose orbital path clung too close to Saturn. The unfortunate moon was drawn further in and got torn apart. Gravity has kept the broken moon in orbit, but as rings of ice. Something beautiful came from utter destruction.

Jupiter is the most dazzling orb in the solar system after the sun. The dominant gas giant has protected life on Earth for millions of years, as it cleans the solar system of most comets which shoot through. Jupiter's strong gravitational pull draws them away from their original course. The comets then disintegrate into smaller fragments as they're sucked into the gas giant's orbit. Jupiter and its moons are often hit by asteroids. If it were not for Jupiter's influence on most of the loose asteroids, life on Earth may never have got the opportunity to thrive. We would have been battered by everything out there, and life wouldn't have got the chance to evolve. But we can still get hit here on Earth. As some big asteroids have escaped Jupiter's path and carried on towards us. Including the massive asteroid which wiped out something called dinosaurs. The word dinosaur meant nothing to me. And I couldn't find any reference to it anywhere else in the book or the index.

I did manage to uncover one positive thing that afternoon while reading: space dust. Tons and tons of space dust falls to Earth every year. I ached with regret for cleaning the dust from the encyclopaedia. It wouldn't have all been dirt. Some specks would have been beautiful dust particles from the stars. It made me wonder what else I didn't know about even the simplest of things. Perhaps nothing was as it appeared? Perhaps the flying insects came from the stars, too?

Having had my fill of learning about how everything out there was trying to kill us, I went downstairs.

My mother appeared to be rummaging in the garden for herbs. I realised how much I resembled her, as her red hair glistened in the dying rays of the sun.

It wouldn't be long until curfew, and I could leave for the old citadel and the House of Books. And Gabriel.

My grandfather surpassed himself with that evening's stew. Plus he'd managed not to overdo it with the rosemary. I was the last one to finish my plate. My grandfather commented how I always ate slower when he made a stew, and this was obviously to savour the flavour. But truth be told, I just ate slow. However, I scraped the dish clean as I had had nothing to eat since breakfast. I would have eaten anything, apart from Ethel. I had checked on the hen house before dinner and discovered Ethel absent. I refused to have her added to my meal. Envy would get some of the stew, too. Plus the chickens usually got our scraps. But they wouldn't get any of Ethel. I have never approved of eating one's own kind.

I wanted to tell my mother and grandfather all about my new-found knowledge, even if the facts were as frightening as they were fascinating. But I couldn't. My grandfather had told me not to tell my mother about the *Space Encyclopaedia*, and I didn't want her to worry that her daughter had discovered a building in the citadel full of forbidden knowledge. Nor did I wish her to know I had brought a piece of this forbidden knowledge home.

'Mum, why did you name me Andromeda?' I asked.

'Where's this come from?'

'I just wondered. None of the other children had that name in school, and I've never heard it anywhere else.'

My mother shook her head.

'Your dad chose it. He liked it,' she said.

'But where had he heard of it?' I asked, wondering if my father could have discovered the House of Books before I was born.

My grandfather shot me a look. I think he wanted me to keep my mouth shut.

'I'm not sure,' my mother said. 'I just thought he made it up.'

'All names are made up to begin with,' my grandfather said. 'Then people decide they'd like the name for their children, and it continues on.'

'But no one else has my name. That's my point. It hasn't continued on from anyone.'

'Well then, you're extra special,' my grandfather concluded.

'Don't you like your name?' my mother asked.

'I don't dislike it, I'm just curious.'

'You'll have to ask your dad then. When he comes home,' my mother said.

She sipped her tea and stared at the photographs of him in his uniform on the mantelpiece.

My grandfather shot me another look. One of disappointment I thought.

But I couldn't understand why my father had named me after a galaxy, and one which was set to collide with our own. How did he know about it? He must have discovered the House of Books. What else had he known? Did he get into trouble for what he knew? Was that the real reason he was sent off to fight? He may have been sent away because he knew too much.

Envy sprung up from her position in front of the log burner and began whining and pacing around the sitting room.

A mass of wings flew over the cottage as the birds fled from the forest.

'Not again,' my mother said.

The ground began to shake.

All three of us fled the table. My mother darted for the tall dresser, where she leaned upon it to keep it upright against the wall. The crockery on the dresser clanked against the glass display window.

My grandfather grabbed his wedding photo and the urn which contained my grandmother's ashes from the sideboard.

'Damn these bloody quakes,' he said.

I grabbed the rest of the framed family photographs from the mantelpiece above the log burner, including the two of my father. Then I leaned against the grandfather clock.

Something smashed behind the kitchen door, and Envy barked.

The poor girl was terrified. I couldn't do enough to comfort her. She must have thought the world was ending every time we had an earthquake.

The earthquakes were worse the closer you lived to the forest. Therefore, the cottages bore the brunt of the vibrations. Sometimes the earthquakes manifested from the forested hill on the other side of Eden, and we would have little of the pandemonium. The earthquakes appeared to intensify month on month.

No one knew why the Earth was angry. With every earthquake I thought the ground would open and swallow the town. It would be as though Eden were never here. The earthquakes were another reason I had the feeling Eden held a secret. We had never had them in my childhood. They began around the same time the men had to go off and fight in the war.

The ground ceased moaning and Envy stopped pacing.

I placed the photographs back on the mantelpiece and gave Envy a reassuring cuddle. She had got herself into such a panic she'd overheated, and she panted in my ear.

My mother and I went to check on the kitchen. The teacups and saucers we had used earlier and left on the worktop lay broken across the tiled floor. The fragments made the kitchen a perilous place for paws. I commanded Envy to stay back as I collected the debris.

'We'll have no crockery left if these earthquakes continue,' my mother said.

'But that's three teacups we don't have to wash up tonight,' my grandfather concluded, as he inspected the mess.

My grandfather was at the far end of our garden smoking his pipe when I ventured outside with the shattered crockery. We had been storing all the smashed items in our little outhouse, along with all kinds of paraphernalia. We may never use the items again, but we didn't know if we would ever be asked for broken glass or crockery for the war effort. Some of the things the posters asked for were weird. One poster requested animal bones. These could be reused for fertiliser, glue, and something called explosives. What they wanted to explode I didn't want to know.

My grandfather always turned to tobacco after a good earthquake. I assumed it calmed his nerves.

'Light's on in the forest again,' he said, nodding towards the treeline.

'Forest spirits?' I asked.

'Balderdash. Do you still believe in them?

'I don't know what to believe anymore.'

'I will say, I doubt forest spirits require lights,' he said. 'And they're noisy spirits, if the earthquakes are anything to do with them. There's something in there anyhow.'

'Maybe the dog-headed people go into the forest after dark to collect something?'

'Whatever it is, the authorities have never wanted us snooping in there.'

'They're hiding something in there?' I asked.

'I'd bet my life on it,' he said.

My grandfather inhaled deeply from his pipe and spluttered.

'I don't know what they're putting in this tobacco these days, other than straw. Whatever it is, it has a hint of the shoe polish about it.'

Not a single star glistened above as I left the cottage with Envy. Thick clouds smothered my view. I had left the encyclopaedia at home, as I still had so much more to learn from it. I would return it to the House of Books once I had devoured the complete tome.

After the earthquake, I had gone to my room to read a little more. I received several shocks. Firstly, in school we had learned that a man named John Montague had discovered the four moons of Jupiter. My new book told me otherwise. It was a man named Galileo Galilei. I thought this was even more of an unusual name than Gabriel. Also, it said he had discovered the moons in 1610. Which was impossible. That was the future.

I didn't understand some of what I had read that afternoon and evening. The word *dinosaur* was just one of many baffling words I had encountered. Plus, as if I hadn't been lied to enough in school, I learned that scientists down the centuries discovered Jupiter had at least eighty moons. Not four. Saturn had eighty-two. A planet called Uranus was discovered in 1781. And Neptune in 1846. Our solar system had two asteroid belts, not one, and the farthest one from Earth was called the Kuiper belt. At one point, we had even had nine planets. The ninth planet was discovered in 1930 and named Pluto. But Pluto received a downgrade in 2006 when it was decided Pluto was another dwarf planet within the Kuiper belt. I only thought there were six planets. And 2006 was the far-flung future.

As I was about to close the book, it fell open to the first page, which had a label glued onto it. The label read: Stonburh Council Library Service. Underneath this were numerous date stamps. The last date stamp read 25.02.2027. I hadn't noticed this page before as I had only flicked through the book. Over the page from this was a copyright page. This stated the book was first published in 2022.

As I rambled through the town, I thought about my schooling. Could it be the teachers had lied on purpose, or perhaps they didn't know either? But an even worse thought struck me. What if the *Space Encyclopaedia* was lying? Why would my book *Discourse on the Planets and Moons* lie? Why would the authorities lie? Was Gabriel lying? I didn't even know who he was. Again I wondered why he had shown me the House of Books? The building has stood in the citadel my entire life. The authorities have never opened it up to the townsfolk. They have never explained what was inside. Were they all lying to me?

The night turned gloomy and I was grateful for all the gas lamps in town. It had begun to drizzle by the time Envy and I reached the slope of the gatehouse bridge.

The nightwatchman wasn't in his quarters. A lantern flickered on a table next to an empty chair. For a moment I wondered if he was observing me from somewhere else so he could catch me breaking curfew again.

Envy looked at me as if to say: 'Aren't we going to cross?' She couldn't have sensed him nearby. She would have wanted to turn back if she sensed any kind of threat. We stepped past the gatehouse. Then I broke into a sprint.

I struggled for breath by the time we reached the square. I felt relieved to find the place void of soldiers, and the Guildhall in darkness, which meant I wouldn't have a repeat of the previous night. Things were back to normal in the citadel after curfew.

The front door to the House of Books opened with ease.

I slipped through the foyer and entered the main body of the building. I found no sign of Gabriel, but he had lit all the lamps upon the desks again.

I placed my damp coat over the back of a chair and glanced up at the wonderous balconies heaving with books.

The only problem with books in my mind was all the dead trees. Dead trees lingered in abundance everywhere. In every home there resides a dead forest of various woods. A forest of drawers, wardrobes, dressers, and floorboards. The House of Books was a forest of paper and shelving.

I caught sight of Gabriel leaning over the balcony of the first floor, right above the door. I scowled at him for spying on me. He must have noticed, as he chuckled.

'How are you getting on with the *Space Encyclopaedia*?' he asked, as he disappeared behind a bookcase.

'Can books lie?' I asked.

'Lie? You think the encyclopaedia is lying to you?'

Gabriel's voice travelled along the first floor, but I couldn't detect exactly where he was.

'A man called ... some unusual name, discovered the moons of Jupiter in 1610,' I said. 'But that can't be right. The book is lying. Or, when you enter this building, you're somehow transported into the future.'

'I like that idea,' he said.

Gabriel appeared at the far end of the balcony and headed towards the spiral staircase. When he emerged on the ground floor, Envy rushed to him.

'So the book is lying?' I asked. 'Or is it a made-up story, like that fiction you mentioned?'

'No. It's not fiction. And it isn't lying. Books do sometimes lie. Books have been written specifically to misinform, cause agitation and upset. The writer may exaggerate the facts, or omit facts. Whichever suits their agenda. A writer can spin a lie as the truth and get away with it, if no one is bothered to investigate the so-called facts the writer has put forward as truth. But the book I gave you is one of truth. Or rather, scientific truth as it was known at the time of writing. It has no need to lie.'

'Then ... are you lying?' I asked, thinking perhaps I should be seriously concerned about Gabriel's intentions.

'How could I lie about all this,' he said, raising his arms in the air to indicate the House of Books. 'Creating this place, and all the books, would be a lot of effort on my part, just to lie to you.'

This was true. But it left me stumped. Perhaps I was too

tired to think straight. But I wouldn't get an early night now I had returned to the House of Books.

'Well, someone is lying to me,' I mumbled.

'Yes, they are,' Gabriel said.

I watched Gabriel making a fuss of Envy. He couldn't have malicious intentions, Envy would've sensed it. I loved that he was so affectionate with her. She appeared to adore him. She melted under his belly rubs, the little flirt.

'I asked my mum why they'd named me Andromeda. She said my dad liked the name. He must have heard of the Andromeda Galaxy somehow.'

'Not necessarily,' Gabriel said. 'The Andromeda Galaxy is named after a princess from Greek mythology. Maybe you were named after her.'

'What's a princess? What's Greek *myth-ology*?'

'Great questions,' he said, grinning. 'Our first stop this evening will be the Classical History section.'

Gabriel withdrew a thick book from the shelf and flicked to the back pages.

'Andromeda, page one six four,' he muttered to himself.

Having found the page, he handed me the open book. A beautiful image caught my attention on the adjacent page to the text. It was a painting by someone called Titian. Plus a smaller image of a statue nestled within the page of text. The statue stood outside somewhere. I had never seen another statue, other than the three damaged ones in the citadel fountain and the weird severed heads in the House of Books.

'Andromeda and Per …'

'Perseus,' Gabriel said.

'Who's Perseus?'

'You'll have to read to find out. You can do that tomorrow.'

Gabriel slid around the other side of the bookcases and reappeared with another large tome.

'You should look at this too. Broaden your mind about other ancient cultures and civilisations.'

He offered me a book entitled *Civilisations From Around the World: Ancient to Medieval*. But I remained confused about Greek mythology and the painting.

'Who's Titian?' I asked.

'He was a Renaissance painter. Like the painters whose work you busied yourself collecting last night. Would you like to learn more about Titian's work? We could go to the Renaissance Art section.'

Gabriel didn't wait for me to respond. He was off. Envy followed him. As did I.

He dropped another heavy tome into my hands: *The Complete Works of Titian*. Gabriel held the lantern high as I flicked through the most beautiful pictures I had ever seen. Even in the lantern light the colours were striking. Every painting featured at least one person. None of the art in my home looked like this. The little art we did own was mainly botanical. We had a painting of horses that I had always liked. But that was the only picture I could say gave the impression of movement.

'Is there anything else you can recommend I learn?' I asked.

'I think these three heavy books will be enough for tonight. But there's something I think you should know.'

'Are you leaving?' I asked, suddenly worried that I wouldn't have anyone to point out specific books I should be reading.

'No,' Gabriel said. 'Although I may have to hide somewhere else during the day.'

'You've been hiding in here?'

'Yes, and someone came in earlier.'

'Who?' I asked.

'A soldier. Luckily, I was on an upper floor when he came in. As he worked his way up through the li— House of Books, I crept along the floor ahead of him. I thought the floorboards would give me away. But sometimes they creak for no reason.'

'So, as far as he knows, no one is here?'

'Unfortunately not. For two reasons.'

Gabriel led me into the seating area, the one we – or rather I – had stumbled into from the terraced balcony.

'We left evidence behind,' he said.

'When I walked into the table and moved it?'

'And footprints,' he said. 'We left evidence in the dust.'

'Space dust,' I corrected him.

But Gabriel ignored my comment.

'We've left shoe and paw prints throughout the building,' he said. 'You can't really see it now in the lamplight. But when the sun comes blazing through those doors, it's obvious. I think he must've noticed them.'

'What can we do?'

'There's nothing we can do. If they suspect someone has broken in, they'll lock this place up like a prison and keep guards at the entrance. He hasn't returned since, but I'll look out for him tomorrow.'

'What was the second thing?' I asked. 'You said there were two reasons why you might have to leave.'

'Yes, the second reason is on the top floor, hidden amongst the shelves.'

The sign hanging from the balcony read: Local History Archives.

Gabriel led me to the far corner.

Blankets lined the floor and a crumpled pillow sat slumped against a bookcase. I would have referred to the corner as a snug. A lantern nestled between some leather-bound volumes on a shelf. Numerous books sat in small piles on the floor next to the makeshift bed, although I noted there were more books in the piles than gaps on the shelves. I presumed some of these books had been moved from elsewhere.

'You've set up a bedroom here?' I asked.

'Not me. That's the problem. Someone else. But I don't know who. I located this earlier when I had to keep moving to escape the soldier. He must've discovered this too. I watched him come down this aisle.'

'But this means someone else in Eden knows about the House of Books,' I said. 'Or do you think this stuff could've been here for years?'

'I don't think the blankets and pillow have been here long,' Gabriel said. 'They're not covered in dust or cobwebs like everything else.'

'The footprints could also be from this person,' I said. 'Not just us.'

'That's possible. There'll be footprints everywhere because there's dust everywhere.'

'Space dust,' I corrected him once more.

'Not all dust comes from space,' Gabriel said. 'Some dust is ... quite disgusting.'

'By the way,' I said, 'I don't like the fact I'm going to collide with the Milky Way. I hope my dad named me after the Andromeda in this Greek myth-*ology* book.'

'I expect he did.'

'It doesn't explain how he knew about a Greek princess. Unless he'd been in here himself,' I said, wondering if my father could really have discovered my favourite place before me.

'He could've heard the name through someone else,' Gabriel said.

'I suppose I may never know,' I said, thinking I might never see my father again.

Gabriel said he'd wanted to show me the other surprise. But the cloud cover made it pointless, which meant his surprise had something to do with the sky.

The clock above the Guildhall rang its elegant chime and then gonged twice as Envy and I meandered down the cobblestones.

The drizzle had continued all evening and some of the stones were treacherous.

I gasped as we arrived on the bridge.

The nightwatchman stood under the nearest gatehouse, holding his lantern aloft.

'Where've you been?' he asked, approaching us.

'Nowhere.'

'*Nowhere?*'

I had to think.

'My dog ran off earlier and we couldn't find her. I'm sorry it's gone past curfew, but I wouldn't have been able to sleep if I hadn't found her.'

'And you thought she'd be in the citadel?'

'That's right,' I said, relieved that I could be this good at lying.

'What have you got there?'

'Just ... some books.'

'You went out looking for your dog while carrying some books? Heavy-looking books too.'

I hung my head. I wasn't good at lying.

'Funny,' he began. 'When I saw you cross the bridge earlier tonight, you were with your dog, but without the books. Can you explain that?'

He had spied on me.

'I know where you've been,' he continued. 'You know it's forbidden. You've broken the law.'

'I don't know what you mean?'

'You know full well what I mean. I'm arresting you.'

'You can't arrest me. They'll send me to prison,' I exclaimed, on the brink of tears.

'That's the point. You've broken curfew twice ... that I know of. *And* you've been inside one of the forbidden places.'

'But ...'

I slumped forward, clutching the books to my chest as my tears fell.

Envy leapt at my face and pawed my legs. She barked and whined for me to explain the cause of my distress.

The nightwatchman grabbed my shoulder and I winced.

'I'm putting you in the lock-up for tonight. You'll go before the mayor tomorrow. Then it's prison for you.'

He dragged me towards the nearest gatehouse. Both gatehouses were used as lock-ups. Some of the tiny windows on the upper floors had bars across them. If anyone was caught breaking curfew, they would be locked up for two days and nights without food or water. Keeping them inside a gatehouse above a river appeared especially cruel, I thought. In the past I had seen some of the imprisoned townsfolk peering through the bars. I felt sorry for them. I would often wonder if everyone else around me had noticed them too but they just pretended it wasn't happening. I now wondered if they would pretend I wasn't temporarily imprisoned above them while they meandered below?

Envy took offence at the nightwatchman pulling me away. She flung herself at him and began yanking on his trouser leg.

'Get off, you stupid dog,' he snapped.

Envy manged to yank him away from the gatehouse. The nightwatchman stumbled and dropped his lantern, which smashed. But light still shone from the nearby gas lamps.

He turned to kick Envy.

'Don't you hurt my dog,' I hollered.

Enraged, I heaved my books upward with force and aimed for his chin. He received a full face of *Civilisations From Around the World: Ancient to Medieval, The Complete Works of Titian,* and *Greek Mythology Retold.*

He lurched back with a stunned appearance, tripped over his own feet, and landed with a thud upon the stones.

I watched him lying there. He was still, but breathing. He looked like he was sleeping. What had I done? I had hit someone of authority in the face, that's what I had done.

Envy and I scurried all the way home.

Chapter 5

How could I ever visit the House of Books again? My world had expanded, and now it was crushed. I had learned I didn't walk in dirt, but space dust. I had learned a telescope floated around the Earth. I wondered if I could I ever soar amongst the stars. I doubted I could ever leave Eden. But Eden lied. It held a secret. I contemplated whether more hidden treasures could lurk under my nose. The old citadel which I thought I knew crumbled away from me. I still loved it though. It was all I had ever known. I didn't blame the citadel. I blamed the authorities. The mayor. The liars.

I couldn't live without the House of Books.

I struggled to sleep that night. When I did nod off, I woke with a jolt and my interaction with the nightwatchman tormented me afresh. My stomach churned. I had found the most precious place in the world. But the nightwatchman had destroyed my happiness.

I wanted to stay in bed all day. I wanted to curl up and disappear. But my mother came into to check if I'd remembered I had my doctor's appointment. I had forgotten about my morning appointment. I was too distraught. I told her I felt unwell, but she assumed I didn't want to see the doctor, not that my heart was broken.

Not only was I in no mood to go, I felt exhausted. Both my mother and grandfather offered to go with me. But I wanted to be alone. I wanted to retreat inside. I had Envy of course. But she didn't want to talk about the weather. I craved silence. And Envy was a comfort.

Before I left the house, I noticed one of my new acquisitions had a large blemish on the cover. The nightwatchman's chin had left an imprint. I removed the stain with a damp cloth. I wanted no remnants of him. The destroyer.

Envy sat on my lap while we rode into the citadel. I think she knew I needed consoling. I wrapped my arms around her and buried my face in her soft fur. I was also anxious about being recognised. Even if the nightwatchman couldn't get me into one of the lock-ups, then the daywatchman, or a soldier, would. The nightwatchman must have told someone. I wondered if he had still been lying comatose on the bridge when the daywatchman arrived to start his shift.

I pulled the cord on the omnibus, which rang the bell to alert the driver I wished to get off at the second stop in the citadel.

The doctor's office sat above the candle shop, on one of the steepest streets leading up to the square. And the entrance to the clinic lay down a narrow side passage. A small shiny bronze plaque on the wall next to the door read: Doctor Hartnell and Doctor Troughton. I would be seeing Doctor Hartnell. I had only ever seen her.

'You'll have to wait here, Envy,' I said as I stepped inside.

I meandered up the stairs to the waiting room on the first floor, where the receptionist greeted me from behind her desk.

I sat by the window and watched some women queueing outside a bakery across the street. The bakery nestled below the wonkiest of all the skewwhiff buildings in the old citadel.

The townsfolk all referred to it as *the crooked building*. I had a drawing of it around my writing bureau. I had always loved the structure, but it always looked as though it might fall in on itself at any time. Luckily, the doctor's office didn't have the appearance of sinking into the candle shop below.

The waiting room had a cosy feel, like sitting in someone else's home. Three comfortable sofas framed a low table. A carved stone fireplace dominated one wall, not that it appeared in use anymore. The receptionist and I were the only two people in the waiting room.

I considered the art upon the walls. It resembled the kind of botanical art we had in the cottage. There was nothing like Titian. I had never seen anything like Titian anywhere. I had never seen art with people in it before.

Doctor Hartnell's door swung open.

'Miss Woburn,' she said, as she smiled at me.

Doctor Hartnell was one of the best dressed women in Eden. Her clothes didn't have the appearance of once belonging to someone else. The deep blue of her skirt suit remained vibrant rather than faded.

Her consulting room had the same welcoming feel as the waiting room. Its main feature was another carved stone fireplace. More botanical art hung on the walls. She had some plants, and a small bookcase, which was quite sparse. She only had a few medical manuals spread out amongst some ornaments.

Doctor Hartnell indicated for me to sit as she consulted some paperwork she had removed from a file.

A ticking clock sat upon her desk. This annoyed me. The ticking came courtesy of the swinging pendulum below the clock face. The clock itself was pretty enough. Like a magpie, I was already drawn to the gilded clock. It didn't need to tick to get my attention. The grandfather clock in the cottage didn't tick as loud as this. I didn't mind the tick of our grandfather clock, it felt soothing. Plus, I had grown up with it and hadn't ever thought about the gentle ticking. Besides, the clock stood in the sitting room. Perhaps if it stood at the end of my bed I would have had more of a problem.

'The last time you were here we discussed how you were feeling stressed?' Doctor Hartnell said.

'I don't think I said I felt stressed. You said you thought I was stressed,' I said.

Doctor Hartnell returned her concentration to the file.

'Do you feel stressed today?' she asked, without glancing up.

If I didn't feel stressed before, why would I feel stressed today, I thought.

'No, I'm just tired,' I said, staring at the irritating pendulum.

'You've not been sleeping?'

'Not last night.'

'Is there something bothering you?'

Of course there's something bothering me, I thought. The nightwatchman has ruined my life. One of the abandoned buildings in the citadel had turned out to be the most wonderful place in Eden, and the moment I find it, it gets taken away from me. I'll never see the House of Books, or Gabriel, again. That was what I wanted to say, but instead I said: 'I'm not feeling very well today.'

'Oh, in what way?'

In the way that I hate the world. In the way I wish someone would just take me to a place where people don't ask endless questions, I thought.

'Does that thing not stop ticking?' I asked.

'The clock?'

'Yes, it's frustrating. How do you listen to it all day?'

'I don't think it's that loud,' she said.

'It is that loud,' I said, thinking how I could barely concentrate on anything else.

Doctor Hartnell studied me with a curious expression, then she rose from her desk and retrieved a manual from her small bookcase.

'I believe you could be suffering from something called post-traumatic stress disorder,' she said as she returned to her seat.

'I don't know what that means. I thought you said I had a condition? Now I have a disorder?'

'Basically, a traumatic incident will have triggered your stress. Has anything—'

'What traumatic incident? Do you mean the war? My grandad thinks the war has upset me, what with all the change it's brought. And what with Dad gone,' I said, thinking how much I hated change, and surprises, and my father not being around. So many years had passed, I could barely picture his face whenever I recalled a memory of him. The memories I mustered were like looking at blurred photographs.

'Having a father sent off to war could be a possible trigger,' Doctor Hartnell said.

'But I don't know if I feel *stressed*.'

'How do you feel most of the time?' she asked.

I wrung my hands. How did I feel most of the time?

'Lost,' I said, staring at the floor.

'Lost?'

'Like I don't belong here. I don't understand the world and the world doesn't understand me,' I said.

I thought about how much Envy understood me. I wondered if Gabriel understood me, too. After all, he knew I would love the House of Books.

Doctor Hartnell said she would look through her manuals for another possible reason for how I was feeling. She told me to come back and see her in a few days, so I made an appointment with the receptionist. I think Doctor Hartnell thought I was now depressed. Perhaps I was.

I trundled up the hill towards the square with Envy. I had considered catching the next omnibus straight home. But my heart ached, and I wanted to gaze upon the House of Books.

I sat on a bench in the square staring at the elegant façade. I was the only one who knew what secrets lay hidden within. I even knew the faded letters above the door had once read PUBLIC LIBRARY, many moons ago. How many moons ago, I couldn't say. The fire-damaged building to the right of the House of Books also had grand columns, but they had been blackened from the blaze. I couldn't even imagine what that building had once housed. I knew what lingered in the building to the left of the House of Books: the mayor and all his officials.

I thought of Gabriel. He would expect to see me later that evening. How could I let him know about my confrontation with the nightwatchman? He would assume I was no longer interested in learning. Although I still couldn't understand why Gabriel was so insistent that I did learn all this forbidden knowledge. It was as though he was trying to get me into trouble. For what purpose, I couldn't fathom. Gabriel was a stranger to Eden, and that meant he should be hostile. But he didn't appear malevolent. Plus Envy liked him. If the House of Books was filled with the truth, then I wanted to know everything. I just didn't understand why Gabriel wanted me to know. There were still mysteries in Eden, and Gabriel was one of them.

Some soldiers stood outside the Guildhall, while others loitered around the square. They were keeping an eye on the queues for the shops and the omnibuses. The townsfolk mooched about me. No one noticed me. The townsfolk didn't seem to notice anybody. Even the soldiers appeared only half interested in their task. No one saw a young woman sitting on her own. They didn't see Envy lying by my feet. It was as though I didn't exist. I was happy with that. I didn't want to be bothered.

The clock above the Guildhall began to chime.

As the clock struck twelve and the little mechanical men appeared, I rose from the bench and helped myself to some water from the square's drinking fountain. It had a cool but metallic taste. I held my palms out like a bowl, allowing the water to flow into my hands. I bent down towards Envy. She lapped up the revitalising water.

I glanced across at the soldiers. Most spoke amongst themselves.

Envy followed as I slid past the soldiers and veered off around the side of the Guildhall, towards the Temple of the First Ancestors.

I pinned myself to the side of the Guildhall ... and waited. I don't think I even inhaled. I half expected a soldier to appear. But no one materialised.

I continued on to the gardens and darted into the treeline which ran along the back of the Guildhall. I glanced up at the windows in the Guildhall for movement. The sunlight reflected off the glass, which meant I couldn't peek inside. But I wondered if those inside could see me. It was a chance I would have to take. I retreated as far away as I could from the windows of the Guildhall, and I deliberated the terraced balcony at the back of the House of Books.

Envy and I had to get over the back wall, into the alleyway, then over another wall and up onto the terrace. Then we would be in. It sounded easy enough.

I hoisted Envy up on the wall with relative ease. But I found it more difficult getting up there myself. I scraped my shins as I scrambled onto the brickwork. Once again, my skirt made the ascent arduous.

I fell into the alleyway at the back and commanded Envy to jump into my arms. I was already sweating and we had another wall and a balcony to deal with.

I checked the Guildhall windows for movement again. But I could still only find the reflection of the sunlight from my angle.

I raised Envy onto the wall next to the balcony and she trotted onto the terrace, seeming to understand my plan.

I scratched my arms upon the next wall, receiving a nice graze just below the sleeve of my blouse. I eventually rolled myself onto the terrace. If anyone had watched from a nearby window they would have had a good laugh. It must have looked undignified.

I tried the middle door, which remained unlocked and broken.

Gabriel was right. The sunlight beamed through the glass, highlighting all the footprints and pawprints. It was clear the space dust had been disturbed.

I headed into the main body of the House of Books. The skylight, despite being smothered in dirt and leaves, allowed a reasonable amount of illumination to filter down, albeit a dulled light.

The House of Books looked and smelled magnificent. Space dust danced in the air before me, and the scent from the old books spoke of history eager to be devoured.

I peered over the balcony and the floorboards protested my presence.

I couldn't locate Gabriel on the ground floor amongst the desks. I couldn't detect anyone else, to my relief. I considered Gabriel might be hiding on the top floor, in case someone entered. He hadn't opened any of the window shutters, not even a slither. I presumed this was so no one outside would notice a difference. I also recalled how he appeared to have no trouble seeing in the dark.

I took the spiral staircase and emerged on the upper floor at the section entitled Local History Archives.

'Gabriel,' I whispered.

Envy darted off along the balcony and vanished behind a bookcase.

I followed her trail and found Gabriel tickling Envy's belly as she lolled on the floor.

'Are you mad?' Gabriel asked.

'My doctor thinks so.'

'Sorry?'

'Nothing,' I said, but inside I was beginning to think I was actually mad. I certainly felt as though I was going mad, even if I wasn't already mad. I no longer understood my world. I no longer knew what was real.

'I wondered who it was,' Gabriel continued. 'What are you doing here in broad— You're bleeding.'

'I had a challenge getting up here.'

I think Gabriel smirked at me. But the corner behind the bookcases lay in shadow, and I couldn't be sure.

'Anyway, I had to come today,' I said. 'I got caught last night.'

'Did you?' he said, as he sprang from the floor. 'Are you okay?'

'Yes. But I won't be able to visit during curfew anymore. They'll be waiting for me.'

'Who caught you? How did you get away?'

'The nightwatchman. Envy helped us escape. But I also hit him in the face with the books,' I said, cringing.

'Oh. Wow. You don't strike me as the violent type.'

'I'm not normally. But he was going to put me in one of the lock-ups for the night and have me presented to the mayor today. Then they'd put me in prison. Then I'd never see my family or Eden again.'

'I've gotten you into a lot of trouble. I'm sorry. I never should've brought you here.'

'But I love the House of Books,' I said. 'It's the best surprise ever. And I hate surprises.'

Gabriel appeared to radiate from within the shadow as he chuckled.

'Since you haven't enjoyed any surprises previously, I can see how it would be the best surprise. I'm glad you still like it.'

'I adore it. I always will.'

I meant it. Even if I could never see the House of Books again, it would always be my favourite place.

'Your love has made you brave,' Gabriel said.

'Well, I thought they'll expect me to come back again tonight. But they won't expect me in daylight. My grandfather had said no one would be stupid enough to break into a forbidden building. Seems I am stupid enough.'

'Ah, stupidity over bravery,' Gabriel said. 'You know, you shouldn't put yourself down.'

A clinking noise came from somewhere below. A door opened with a groan. We both froze as footsteps echoed across the ground floor.

'Who could that be? I asked, in a whisper.

'Someone must've seen you.'

At least two mumbled voices ascended from the ground floor.

'Wait here,' Gabriel said.

'But I want to see who it is.'

'Are you stubborn as well as brave?'

'Apparently,' I said. 'It's due to my red hair.'

'Hair colour is no indication of personality,' Gabriel said, with another smirk.

I don't know if I smiled on the outside, but I smiled internally at his reply. It was the exact same retort I gave my grandfather in the Grand Tea Room only a couple of days earlier.

We tiptoed towards the balcony. But the floorboards responded to our steps and we hesitated.

'What was that?' a male voice asked.

'Probably nothing. Old building isn't it,' another male voice said.

The double doors at the far end of the ground floor swung open, and I realised the men were heading for the spiral staircase.

Seizing our opportunity, Gabriel and I withdrew as far back

into the corner as we could. The floorboards announced most of our steps. But as the men still lingered on the staircase, I assumed they wouldn't hear.

A door opened close by.

'Is this the right floor?' asked one.

'Think so.'

My stomach flipped.

The men stomped across the upper floor, but on the balcony opposite.

'This is it,' said one of the men.

'How many should we take?' asked the other one.

'She didn't specify. I suppose we should get as many as we can. We can get more later if need be. Anyway, the mayor will have to confirm whether or not she can have these books.'

I wondered who this *she* was. Whoever she was, the mayor had the final say.

A thudding sound echoed through the atrium. As though numerous books were being slammed together.

The thudding ceased and the men stomped towards the staircase.

Gabriel and I slid closer to the edge of the balcony once their footsteps disappeared.

The men emerged on the ground floor. They were soldiers and they each carried a large cardboard box brimming with books. They stormed through the foyer and out the main door.

My heart sank. I wondered if they would return to take more books. I wondered if it was all my fault.

'That's a relief,' Gabriel said. 'They just came to get books.'

'And take them away for good,' I said mournfully.

'They might just be borrowing them. It is a library after all. Let's see what they removed.'

I wish I could have been as upbeat as Gabriel about the removal of the books. But I had a feeling the books the soldiers took would never be returned.

We scampered round to the opposite side of the balcony. The sign above the bookcase read: Health and Medicine.

'Curious,' Gabriel said. 'Maybe a lot of people are getting sick?'

'They must need a lot of books as they said they could come back later.'

'Do you know anyone who's sick?' he asked.

'No. But then I don't know anyone,' I said.

'Perhaps people are coming down with a mystery illness?'

'Everyone looks okay to me. From what I've seen of the townsfolk in the citadel today.'

'I've noticed a few gaps on shelves as I've been exploring the library,' Gabriel said.

I winced.

'Sorry, House of Books.'

'Gaps where?' I asked, wondering if soldiers had stolen books before.

'Military history has an entire vacant shelf. But I suppose that makes sense as you're at war.

'I don't know what military history is.'

'You won't want to know. It's men having to fight other men because men more senior to them have ordered them to. It's men being slaughtered in their thousands. We should stick with the positives for now. How did you get on with Greek mythology?'

'I was too upset to read last night.'

'Understandable. Although we can now spend the whole afternoon studying anything you want.'

'Something positive,' I confirmed, thinking I needing cheering up. My appointment with Doctor Hartnell, and now the removal of the books, had left me feeling quite low. 'What about the other surprise?' I asked. 'The one on the roof?'

'No point. It's daylight,' Gabriel said.

'I couldn't see it last night because of the clouds. But I also can't see it now because it's daylight?' I asked.

I had already gathered it was something to do with the sky. But now I was confused as to why daylight interfered with the surprise.

'That's right. It's the wrong time,' Gabriel confirmed.

'But I'll have to leave before curfew.'

'Some other time then. It's not going anywhere. It really needs to be dark outside.'

'But last night—'

'Minus clouds,' he said.

Instead of seeing this most mysterious of surprises, where the sky had to meet Gabriel's exact requirements, he handed me a *General Knowledge Encyclopaedia*. I spent the afternoon learning about evolution. All life on Earth began in the deep ocean, by a volcanic vent spewing out heat and chemicals. These were the *building blocks of life*. Water was our planet's gift, and remains so for all animals. We are completely reliant on it.

Seven million years ago apes climbed down from the trees of African forests and became the first 'hominins'. Human-like species have been evolving for millions of years. And one million years ago, a new branch of hominins appeared: Homo sapiens. All the other hominins became extinct, leaving us to flourish without competition. Humans have existed for two hundred thousand years, although this is nothing compared to the age of the Earth.

I came across the dinosaurs again. But this time I got to see what they looked like. I was horrified by the monsters. Gabriel chuckled at my revulsion when I first saw the images.

This book, too, stated they were wiped out when an asteroid slammed into Earth. The monsters who survived the initial hit died due to the change in the atmosphere as the planet became hostile to life. A giant rock from space killed the monsters. Which was a relief.

I learned about all the magnificent animals and mammals

who inhabited the world. I had no idea I lived on such an incredible planet. The land and water teemed with all kinds of life. And yet every living creature on Earth evolved from a single-celled organism. These single-celled organisms are our oldest ancestors.

I landed into the final alleyway with an awkward thud. Having spent the most wonderful afternoon in the House of Books, it was time to go home before the omnibuses ceased running and the curfew came into effect.

All the scrambling over walls had left me dishevelled. I brushed the dirt and space dust from my attire. I was tucking my blouse back into my skirt when a soldier appeared at the entrance to the alleyway.

'You. What are you doing down here?' he bellowed.

'Nothing,' I said, although it was barely audible.

He approached at speed.

'What have you got there?'

'Nothing,' I said, a little louder.

'Let me see your hands.'

Envy growled, I supposed she didn't like his tone. I didn't like it either.

I removed my hands from the waistband of my skirt and showed him my palms.

'What have you put down your back?'

'Nothing,' I said again, getting a little fed up at having to repeat myself.

'Turn around,' he said, gruffly.

He didn't let me turn around in my own time. Instead he grabbed me and ran his hands down my spine. He wouldn't find a book. I hadn't taken one.

Envy barked at him.

'Where've you been then?'

'Nowhere,' I said, realising my palms had begun to sweat.

'You've done nothing and you've been nowhere?'

'Yes,' I confirmed, wondering whether I was going to be sick, or pass out, or both.

'You can't come down here,' he said.

'But it's not blocked off,' I said, noting my armpits were damp now, too.

'It's illegal.'

I wondered how it could be illegal to walk down an alleyway. I opened my mouth to respond but no words came forth.

'You've got no business being down here. Do you see other townsfolk down here?'

'My dog ran off,' I said. 'I just followed her. She must've heard something.'

'Good excuse. If only you'd thought to say that when I asked you a moment ago,' he sneered. 'I know who you are.'

He may have known who I was, but I didn't recognise him.

'Who am I?'

He grinned. It wasn't a pleasant smile. It mutated into menace.

'The nightwatchman sends his regards.'

An intense heat shot through my body, and I thought I was definitely going to faint. This soldier knew I had hit the nightwatchman. Did all the soldiers know? This soldier wouldn't bother with the lock-up. He would take me directly to the mayor. Then the mayor would confirm that I should go to prison. I was in serious trouble.

'Some books have gone missing,' he said. 'You wouldn't know anything about that, would you?'

I stared at the ground. I had lost my bravado.

'What, nothing to say? I'll find out where you live. Your family will be punished. I assume your father is fighting? I can make sure he won't come back alive.'

I couldn't understand what any of this had to do with my family, or my father stuck in the town of Frontline. And how could this soldier control what happened in the war?

'You're coming with me,' he said.

He seized me by my grazed elbow. His grip felt like a hot iron on my skin. I winced as he hauled me out of the alleyway and into the square.

Envy barked and attacked his legs. But he ignored her. He was focussed on his mission.

I loved Envy, but having her always with me gave me away.

Most of the townsfolk had dispersed from the square, as the shops were closing. The remaining townsfolk, who stood in a queue for the next omnibus, all swung around to stare in my direction. It was obvious I had done something wrong.

I wanted to die. I'm not a troublemaker. I prefer being inconspicuous. I prefer being left alone. But now I had become an enemy to the authorities. All I had ever done was sit in the old citadel after dark. And now I read at the House of Books. But I hadn't killed anyone. I had never hurt anyone. Okay, I had smacked the nightwatchman in the face. But I was provoked.

I hung my head as more soldiers approached us.

Envy continued to bark and whine.

One of the soldiers kicked her away and she yelped.

I wanted to pick her up and give her a reassuring cuddle. But the soldier retained a firm grip on my arm.

An ornate black and gold carriage arrived in the square.

The white-haired man from the Guildhall rushed forward as the horses came to a halt outside. Then he drew open the carriage door.

I thought someone was going to exit the carriage. But it appeared he opened the door for someone who was leaving the Guildhall.

The mayor appeared on the steps of the Guildhall with two soldiers flanking him. If Doctor Hartnell was the best dressed woman, then the mayor was the best dressed man in Eden. As he strolled towards the carriage, his black suit appeared to glisten in the late afternoon sunshine. His buffed shoes reflected the sky like two obsidian mirrors. His grey sideburns, which poked out from under his top hat, were neatly trimmed.

The mayor turned to me.

'Hello, my dear. Are my men treating you well?'

The soldier released my arm and I rubbed my elbow, which throbbed.

'No,' I said, somehow compelled to tell the truth, despite feeling intimidated by coming face to face with the mayor.

'I'm sorry to hear that,' he said. 'Can I give you a ride home?'

'No thank you,' I said, wondering why the mayor would offer me a ride home. Wasn't I about to be sent to prison? Or, if he was offering me a ride, perhaps the prison was exactly where he would take me?

'Some other time then,' the mayor said. 'Take care, my dear. Get home safely.'

He touched the brim of his top hat in that goodbye gesture all gentlemen performed.

He entered his carriage with no acknowledgement to the driver, and the horses hauled him away.

'Best get on home, then,' the soldier said. 'Your lucky day today.'

How could I be lucky? Why did the mayor seem to think I might not get home safely? Perhaps it wasn't the mayor who sends people to prison. Perhaps it was someone else in Eden. And this person would be waiting for me on my journey home.

Chapter 6

If my ignorance was darkness, then Gabriel and the House of Books were the light. Now I had the House of Books, I couldn't let it go. I had to visit every day despite fear of capture. I would have to be cunning and bold. But that person didn't sound like me. I wondered if I had become more adventurous. I must admit I felt a thrill at sneaking into the so-called library and reading forbidden books. But those books would lead to my end. I had got caught too many times already. I had no idea why the soldier let me go after the mayor spoke to me. However, I had become obsessed with the House of Books. And no one, not even a soldier, would stop me from visiting it. Or rather, breaking into my favourite place. I had to concoct a plan.

When my grandmother passed, I had inherited some of her scarves. She had been an elegant lady. I never saw her without a hat or scarf, and gloves when needed. The older generation always had impeccable style. Most of the townsfolk today seemed to forget about hats and gloves, and only wore them when it was cold, rather than as a smart accessory to enhance an outfit. The current style for hats and gloves were basic and woollen. Only the more mature townsfolk wore their old refined hats. The younger townsfolk no longer bothered with items made with care and fine detailing. Everything about Eden today was just functional, even the clothing.

I hadn't worn any of my grandmother's scarves before, through fear of ruining them. However, a thought struck me that morning that now I had a use for one. I knew Envy wouldn't approve of my plan, because it didn't involve her, but I had no choice.

Alongside the abrasion on my arm from leaping over walls, the flesh around my elbow had turned black and blue from the soldier's grip. Luckily the weather had cooled since the previous day, and I could wear long sleeves. I opted for a little jacket over my blouse.

I stood before my swivel mirror, pinned my hair up, wrapped the scarf around my head and tied it in a small bow at the top. This was the way the women who tended the allotments wrapped their hair. I never thought I would have a use for the style myself. I also borrowed a pair of my grandfather's trousers, which I belted tight and tucked the hems into my winter boots. I thought the trousers would look better with boots.

I glared at my reflection. I had never concealed my hair before, and I had never worn trousers. Even I didn't recognise the woman prepared for another round of breaking and entering. I hoped when I went into the old citadel the townsfolk and soldiers would assume I had come from the fields.

I had to assume I was on the verge of being arrested. I had broken the law several times. If anyone was looking for the red-haired young woman with the dog, they wouldn't find her, not today.

I grabbed one of my mother's shopping baskets, another essential component of the plan.

Envy wagged her tail as I proceeded towards the door. Her face changed to one of bewilderment once she sensed something was wrong. It broke my heart to leave her behind, but she would be safer with my grandfather. I didn't even tell him where I was going. I don't think I needed to.

I hopped on the next omnibus, and for the first time I was truly alone. I had never gone into the citadel without family, or Envy.

I sat downstairs, as the weather had decided it was no longer spring and it would wake us up with a little autumnal chill instead.

Due to the dreary weather, a dim eerie light filtered through the skylight in the House of Books. I went straight to the top floor when I arrived. Gabriel wasn't lurking behind the shelving where Envy found him last time. He didn't appear to be anywhere on the top floor. The crumpled blankets and pillow remained, and it reminded me that this person could come back at any time, whoever they were.

A sneeze echoed up from the cavernous space on the ground floor. I hoped it was Gabriel.

I found him, sitting in shadow and engrossed in a book.

'How can you see in the dark?' I asked.

'Ah, there you are,' he said. 'What have you done with your hair? Where's Envy? What's that for?' he asked, pointing at my basket.

'Which question would you like me to answer first?'

'Sorry,' Gabriel said, chuckling.

'This,' I said, raising the basket, 'is to hide books in. I've covered my hair, and I've come alone because I'm too recognisable. Unfortunately, having Envy is the equivalent of carrying a big sign which reads: *yes, it is me. I am the one you're looking for. Red hair. Small dog*. I wish I could blend into the background.'

'I see,' Gabriel said, nodding. 'You need to blend in when you're breaking the law.'

'I want to blend in all the time.'

'No, you don't,' he said, half laughing.

'Yes I do,' I said, a little offended that he found my shyness amusing. 'How would you know how I feel?'

'You shouldn't want to disappear amongst everyone else.'

'Well, I do.'

I glared at Gabriel. Not only did I have to explain myself to the soldiers, but I always seemed to have to explain myself to Gabriel. I wondered why no one could just accept me as I was. I was someone who wanted to explore the House of Books. I wanted all the knowledge in the world. But I was also someone who usually preferred being alone. Plus I hated being stared at. Which Gabriel was now doing.

'Have any soldiers come in this morning and taken any more books?' I asked.

'No, they haven't,' Gabriel said with a sniff.

'That's good. You're risking it being on the ground floor though.'

'I know, but curiosity got the better of me. I started looking at the books and maps left—'

'Maps?'

'Yes. Books and maps which have been left on the desks,' Gabriel said. 'Most of them must've come from the local history archives upstairs, as they're about this area. Eden, I mean. I suppose it makes sense that people would've been interested in local history. But the town and surrounding area is the subject in almost every book and map on every single desk, as though—'

'As though people were looking for something?' I asked.

'Maybe.'

'What are maps?'

'I'll show you. We should take some of the books and maps upstairs. But don't take too many, just in case someone does come in. Otherwise they'll notice the desks are bare.'

'Shall we open a window shutter?' I asked, as we retreated to a desk on the top floor.

Gabriel pulled a face.

'We don't have to open it fully,' I said, wondering if he was part bat or some other nocturnal creature.

'It's not safe,' he said. 'We'll light a couple of lamps in the corner.'

Gabriel flicked through another book, while I considered a map. I never knew large scrolls of paper with aerial views of the land existed. It struck me as a novel idea. Something about the layout of the map I scrutinised seemed familiar. And yet the place names were strange. I had never seen Eden from above, but I could imagine it would look something like the town I stared at. The map was entitled *The Parish of Stonburh*.

'This is Eden,' I exclaimed. 'There's the old citadel hill. The citadel wall is marked, too. Even the fire station. But there are four bridges over the river, and the river has a name. The River Chiltern.'

I traced my finger along the river and through the town, past where I knew the allotments lay, and down the winding lanes which led to my cottage.

'I live there. That's where the cottages are. That's my lane. Where's all the forest? Some of it's woodland. But the fields just continue. I don't know the names. Barton Woods, Sharpenhoe Fields, Pegsdon Springs, Hexton Hills, Sundon Nature Reserve, and Bluebell Woods. There's no outer wall. And what does SC mean? There's an SC marked near the river.'

'I don't know,' Gabriel said, as he loomed over my shoulder.

'It's near this village called Sol ...'

'Solstice,' Gabriel said.

'I don't know that place.'

'That's because you've been led to believe nothing really exists outside Eden. Apart from some other isolated towns, whose people you've never met.'

'But we're fighting those people. Although it's true, I don't know anything beyond the cottages where I live.'

'You live there?' Gabriel said, pressing his pale digit to the exact spot.

'Yes. The abandoned buildings are shown here, I think. That one has a cross on it, and that one is the manor house. But this must be the future. They've cut down all the forest.'

'Why do you think it's the future?' Gabriel asked.

'Because the Forest of Ancients has been here for thousands of years. And that man Gallilee—'

'Galileo Galilei.'

'Yes, he discovers the moons of Jupiter over three hundred years from now,' I said.

'In 1610 I believe.'

'Are you saying I'm correct? The House of Books transports us into the future? To a time when the forest is gone?'

I wanted to see what these future people would do to the old citadel. I scrutinised that section of the map, but between the small writing and the subdued glow of a lantern I found it hard to discern some of the lettering. Everything appeared squished in on the citadel hill. I could make out the letters PL, where the House of Books stood. The future people must understand it's a public library. I was glad it remained.

The temple had a cross on it, to match the crosses above all the weird abandoned buildings scattered around the suburbs of Eden. Or the Parish of Stonburh.

'Do you think there's a larger or clearer map of the old citadel anywhere?' I asked.

'Could be. Wait here. I'll check the desks downstairs first.'

The lantern flickered as though a gust of wind had forced its way through the forest of paper and shelves in the House of Books. I wondered if someone had entered by the main door. If they had, they would find Gabriel on the ground floor searching for a map.

Darkness swallowed the skylight.

I had an overwhelming sense of foreboding.

Light flashed outside and the sky bellowed. I thought the House of Books might collapse with the shaking.

Rain pelted off the skylight. Washing away the space dust.

Another flash of light sent a shockwave thorough the House of Books.

A beautiful but haunting song rose around me. Multiple voices overlapped to create eerie notes of harmony. Tiny orbs of light floated before me, while spectres danced around the skylight. I watched them in awe. I thought about the first night I had seen them, and how Gabriel appeared to me when I was huddled in the doorway of the Guildhall. But then, the next night, when Gabriel reappeared, he no longer resembled a spirit, despite his pallor. I wondered if I had been confused about him ever being an ancestral forest spirit. Perhaps it just happened that he arrived on the same night as the storm and the spectres. Anyway, why would a forest spirit introduce me to the House of Books?

Screams erupted from the square.

The third flash illuminated the entire House of Books. This revealed shadow figures slinking along every floor.

I realised that all the window shutters had sprung open. The skylight was clear of debris.

Some of the shadow figures lurked nearby. They slid between the shelves, seemingly oblivious to my horror.

The scent of aged books vanished.

I dashed along the balcony for the spiral staircase and darted around the shadow figures. One passed through me as I descended the staircase and I felt a surge of energy.

Gabriel stood in the doorway at the bottom of the staircase.

'What's going on?' I asked.

'I don't know,' he said, staring at the skylight.

He appeared more interested in the dancing spectres than the wandering shadow figures. But the wandering shadow figures perturbed me. Their darkness made them more menacing. They appeared indifferent to my presence. It was as though they weaved between the bookcases in another time.

One came from behind and walked through us while we remained in the doorway.

I felt relieved I had left Envy at home. She would have been petrified.

I couldn't believe how different the House of Books appeared in the blazing light. It was alive.

I slid along the shelves on the ground floor. The books were free from dust and cobwebs. Vivid colours burst from the spines.

I headed for the foyer and drew open the main door enough to peer upon the square. A bitter acrid scent, spliced with drops of sulphur, hit my senses.

I couldn't glance out much further than the door. Some of the townsfolk had huddled together under the porch. They didn't notice me, as they all faced the rainstorm and the shadow figures and spectres.

Gabriel snuck up behind me and I considered him for a moment.

'Where do you come from?' I asked. 'You told me you were a visitor to Eden, from faraway.'

'That's right.'

'But where exactly? What are you doing in Eden? Should you even be in Eden?'

'It's a long story,' he said.

The illumination faded in the House of Books as the spectres disappeared through the skylight and the shadow figures fell into the darkness.

I took several tomes from the House of Books that day. I didn't like removing more than one book, but the authorities were confiscating the dusty volumes. I had to accept the House of Books wasn't for me alone. It was after all a public library. It should be for the entire townsfolk of Eden. Therefore, I had a right to borrow more books. Although Gabriel had instructed me not to take too many books from the desks on the ground floor, I thought how no one truly observes what's right before them, or not before them. No one would notice a few items missing. But I would have noticed. The desks wouldn't have looked quite right.

Two of the books I took were on architecture. One book covered the work of Sir Christopher Wren. The other was a compendium of architects. I only took those books because the buildings on the covers intrigued me. I had never seen those façades before and I wondered where they were located.

As I flicked through the books, I realised some of the buildings reminded me of the old citadel. Had these architects designed some of Eden's magnificent structures?

Another of the books I had taken had lain open on a desk. I recalled the page number and slammed the book shut. I would read those pages in the evening. The book was entitled *Ancient History of the British Isles*. The cover showed two neighbouring islands. I considered there must have been a reason the previous townsfolk scoured through those books before they fled.

Prior to that, I collected a book from the third floor, on animals. I had decided animals were my next favourite thing to the House of Books and night sky. Gabriel said I should take the *General Knowledge Encyclopaedia*.

I wanted to understand the world and my place in it. I hadn't gained this knowledge in school. I hadn't obtained it from Eden. I certainly hadn't acquired it from the authorities. I wanted the truth. And the House of Books would provide.

I covered the volumes in some brown paper I had found in

the bottom of the shopping basket, and I snuck out through the front door.

No one witnessed me leaving the House of Books. Everyone in the square had a dazed appearance. Some of the townsfolk remained clustered together down passages. They watched the sky as though the storm could return at any moment, bringing with it the spectres and shadow figures.

I caught sight of a man with half a face standing in the doorway of the Guildhall. I blinked and he vanished. I questioned whether my disorder might cause me to imagine weird phenomena. I concluded I was as confused by the escaped forest spirits as the rest of the townsfolk, and it had left me on edge.

Envy leapt upon me as I opened the door of the cottage. Her kisses landed like punches. I'm not sure if she was displaying her love, or her anger at being discarded. Or whether it was a combination of both.

She entangled herself within my lower limbs and tripped me up as I tried to step over the threshold. I realised I couldn't ever leave her again. She was a menace.

I managed to get the heavy basket of books inside, next to the little table by the door. Then Envy bounded along the path in a playful disposition. I felt such a terrible guilt for deserting her earlier. The least I could do was take her for a walk around the lanes and up to the abandoned buildings and allotments.

After a good forty minutes of play and wandering I turned for home, and Envy trotted alongside me.

We were yards from our cottage when Envy paused and glared at the forest. She barked once, wagged her tail, and bolted towards the outer wall. She startled the sheep as she charged through the field. They bleated in protest and bunched together for protection. But she wasn't interested in them. She scampered along the stone barricade leading to the location where the river enters the forest through a damaged grate in the wall.

'Envy, get back here. Where are you going?'

She ignored me. She was on a mission.

She sniffed around the grate by the grassy bank. Her nose had gone into overdrive.

To my horror, she nudged herself through the grate and disappeared.

'Envy,' I hollered.

I had no visual on her through the grate, and I couldn't hear any movement.

I couldn't fathom what had come over her. As she was a dog, I couldn't say she knew the forest was forbidden. But I had never taken her in there. She must have had some sense it was prohibited for her, or whatever dogs think.

'Envy,' I called again.

She responded with a mischievous bark. But it came from somewhere much deeper in than I could observe.

I loved her, but she had gone mad.

I lowered myself to the grassy bank. The river splashed upon my clothes as I slithered along to get my head through the damaged grate. I was glad I wore my grandfather's trousers as I crawled along the wet grass.

'Envy, come on, this isn't funny.'

She didn't even have the decency to respond that time. Somehow this was a game.

I glanced around at the dense forest. I never thought I would ever go beyond the wall. Not only because it was forbidden. It meant change. Somewhere else I had never trodden before. I could get lost. Worse, I could meet a dog as large as a human.

What was Envy thinking?

Gabriel had got me into trouble. Envy must have felt it was her turn. But I couldn't bear it if I never saw her again.

I forced the rest of my body through the broken grate and stood on the wrong side of the outer wall. The river didn't mind entering the Forest of Ancients. I believed I wouldn't get lost if I stayed in sight or at least earshot of the flowing water.

I brushed wet grass from my jacket and trousers, accepted my fate with the spirits and monsters, and stepped into the dark forest.

The first thing which captured my attention was the birdsong in the canopy. The birds sounded happier here. This was their true home. Bluebells had shot through the woodland floor. They dominated the ground with a stunning carpet of vivid blue. Bees hummed and flitted about the bluebells and other wild flowers, which came up to my knees. The scent of the forest awakened my senses. The fragrant flowers, the fresh long grass, the earthy bark of the tree trunks, and the softer aroma of the leaves. The green of the forest under the canopy struck me as the most vibrant green I had ever seen. It gave me a sense of calm. This was more than the Forest of Ancients. This was the 'Forest of Beautiful Lies'. Despite what I had been told, I couldn't imagine any evil existing in this haven. At least not during the day.

A breeze teased the leaves, sending light and shade spiralling along the ground. The wind rose and the forest spirits spoke.

The river gushed over large rocks and crashed down weirs. One weir flowed under a crumbling stone bridge.

The forest floor rose to a steep incline either side of the surging river.

I could detect no sign of Envy, and presumed she had climbed higher. I called for her several times, but no response came.

I clambered up a hill that led to a plateau. I imagined if it were not for the trees it would provide a fantastic view of the town and old citadel.

In amongst the trees ahead, I thought I saw huge upright stones. As I got closer, I realised my eyes had not deceived me. I meandered through the dark grey stones, which were laid out in a wide circle. I wondered why these stones were grey, when all of Eden was made from a honey-coloured stone. Some of the stones had fallen against thick trunks, where they had been ripped from their original position by the force of the roots. Some lay flat on their fronts or backs, depending on which way they had fallen, but most remained in the earth, strong and resilient.

It appeared the ancestors had placed a large circle of stones in the Forest of Ancients, but I couldn't comprehend the purpose.

A shadow moved in the corner of my eye. I thought it was Envy and I called her. But again I received no response. I wondered if the little madam was getting her own back on me for leaving her behind earlier.

A twig snapped somewhere to my right. I turned to find Gabriel standing by one of the upright stones.

But it wasn't Gabriel.

However, the man appeared as ashen as Gabriel. He slipped away once he realised I was watching him. I wondered if he and Gabriel were the same kind. Like Gabriel, the man was more defined than I thought a spirit would be. He was more human. Perhaps these men were not spirits at all, but they lived in the forest.

A rustling came from beyond the stones and Envy scampered into the circle.

'Where've you been?'

She barked a joyful little greeting and wagged her tail against the wild flowers.

'We're going home. You've gotten me into a lot of trouble if we get caught.'

She barked twice, as if to say: 'I know, but wasn't that fun? I found a new place.'

I slid down the hillside towards the river as Envy trotted beside me.

I considered why she might have run off. Had she seen or sensed the man and mistook him for Gabriel?

Not only was Gabriel as much trouble as Envy. I now knew for certain that he must come from the forest. But perhaps somewhere much deeper in the forest, since he had said he came from a place far away. These humans looked slightly different. Probably because they dwelled permanently in the forest. Therefore, I had been half correct in my initial thinking of Gabriel being a forest spirit. But why had Gabriel hidden this from me? Or did he have a much bigger secret?

Chapter 7

Envy snuggled into the nook of my waist as I lay upon my bed. I propped one of the books I had taken – *Ancient History of the British Isles* – up on my pillows.

The first page had a label glued onto it, just like the *Space Encyclopaedia*. The label also had numerous date stamps. I hadn't even begun to read the other books I had taken recently, but I presumed they all had this label with the words Stonburh Council Library Service printed at the top. All the books had a small six-digit numbered label at the bottom of their spines. The six-digit label on *Ancient History of the British Isles* was 941.371.

The relevant pages, which I had made a mental note of in the House of Books, were about somewhere named 'Doggerland'. At first, I thought it was a land for dogs. I have to say, a land occupied by dogs sounded appealing. I could have definitely lived somewhere surrounded by the giant furballs, although I had never heard of this place. And I was about to discover why. These pages explained the events which destroyed it. Up until eight and a half thousand years ago, mankind could roam across a piece of land which linked a place called Britain to somewhere the book referred to as mainland Europe. This connecting land was called Doggerland. But now, according to this book, it resided under the North Sea.

I had never read the words *Britain*, *Europe*, or *North Sea* before. More odd words were to follow throughout the text. The book implied it was telling a story from the distant past. But the date stamps told me this was a book written in the future.

A set of cataclysmic events caused Doggerland and the people who lived there to disappear. A period of global warming meant the ice sheet which covered North America melted, creating a giant lake, which buffeted against an ice dam. Eventually, the ice dam burst, causing millions of cubic metres of water to flow into the Atlantic Ocean. The sea rose by around a metre. A sudden cooling occurred over Britain and northern Europe, as the Gulf Stream, which brings warm ocean currents from Central America, adjusted its course to sit below Europe. This left Europe to freeze in a mini ice age. The people began to migrate south. But for those who remained in Doggerland, or were passing through at the time, the worst was yet to come.

Due to the rise in sea level, a huge landslide on the coast of northern Europe created a mega tsunami, which wiped the land from the face of the Earth.

The people of Doggerland died abruptly. The violence of the gigantic wall of water turned land to sea in seconds. The force of the water shattered the fragile bodies of mankind and animals alike. They had nowhere to run. The once fertile valley became a death trap.

I considered all the death upon a piece of land which now existed under a sea. I assumed a sea must resemble a large river.

It seemed these people didn't know what was coming. They couldn't plan for it. One disaster led to another. They must have thought the world had turned against them.

This all happened eight and half thousand years before the book existed. But the First Ancestors were not even around two thousand years ago. Again, I concluded the House of Books transported me into a future realm.

At some point I had dozed off before turning down the lamp.

I woke with a jolt as Envy sprung from the bed and began pacing my bedroom.

It was another earthquake.

I heard my mother moving about downstairs. She had probably got out of bed to hold the dresser against the wall. Or she was already downstairs in the back room. I thought I had heard the sewing machine as I had drifted in and out of slumber. I should have gone downstairs to help once I had heard the quake, but instead I lay there pondering the tsunami. Such a strange word. The story of the tsunami, and now the earthquake, got me thinking about how dangerous Earth was. And how fragile life could be.

My grandfather was listening to the wireless when I came downstairs for breakfast, but I knew it was already on when I was upstairs, as it came blaring through the floorboards. Reports on the wireless remain the same every hour. We get an update on the progress of the war, and how our men are faring in the town of Frontline. Progress is slow. The men are faring well. But today was different. The report announced that the mayor would deliver a speech at four that afternoon in the square. I thought I was going to be sick. He was obviously going to inform the townsfolk of my folly in the House of Books, and how much of a bad citizen I had become. This explained why I hadn't been arrested yet. He was going to make an example of me in front of everyone. My mother stated she couldn't recall the mayor ever giving a speech before, and she concluded there must be some extraordinary news about the war effort. Perhaps the war was over? Either way, he had information to pass on. I hadn't thought of that. My sickness subsided in an instant. Relieved, I placed another piece of toast on my plate.

I decided I would pay a visit to the little bookshop in the citadel that morning. Curiosity had got the better of me again, and I had to know if I wasn't the only one who didn't know things. Books were another item which Eden imported. I wondered whether the books available at Prendergast Books had been approved by the mayor's office. Whereas the books in the House of Books were obviously not acceptable reading.

Once again, I disguised myself and grabbed a shopping basket. But this time, I told Envy she could come with me.

She bounced around me as though she had springs instead of paws, while I attempted to walk in a straight line up the lane.

Half of the moon remained visible in the clear sky. I had always found this a pleasing spectacle whenever it happened, but now it had an ominous presence. I thought about the moon slipping away from us a few centimetres a year, and I shuddered at this future havoc.

If anyone had missed the announcement on the wireless, then the garish posters which smothered the omnibus I caught assaulted the eye. The poor omnibus was plastered in orange posters with light blue text. As stated over the wireless, the posters declared that the mayor would give a speech at four in the square. I presumed it was as late as four because the children would have finished school and the mothers would come back to the citadel to collect them once they had finished whatever work they did.

The posters hurt my eyes. Reading the text felt as though the words jumped around the advertisement. I don't know if it was the blue text on the orange background, but the colours jarred. I felt nauseous again.

I thought Envy and I would have the omnibus to ourselves for the entire journey, until a small gathering of women boarded on the main street. It appeared only a few townsfolk wished to go to the citadel.

More posters lined the main street. There were even some across the townsfolk's front doors. I wondered where all the paper had come from. Most of the war posters in the citadel were faded and tattered. These newer ones screamed their luridness. I didn't mind orange, but it was too much. I was vexed to find that the lurid posters had even destroyed the beauty of the gatehouse bridge and the old citadel walls.

I alighted one stop before the square and strolled a few yards up the hill towards Prendergast Books.

I told Envy to be good and wait outside. But I wondered if the little minx thought it might be fun to seek out another lone adventure. If she had any sense she would stay put, otherwise that would be her last time in the citadel.

The bookshop had a double-fronted dark green façade. The little bell above the door jangled as I entered. I enjoyed the sound. I felt like going out and coming back in again just to hear the jangle. All the shelves were painted the same dark green as the shopfront. I had always felt welcome in the shop. Not just because the elderly shopkeeper was approachable rather than intimidating, but the shop itself drew me in and embraced me. I was always happy to pay a visit when I had to purchase an additional book for school, or when I would go browsing with my father.

Mr Prendergast glanced up from his ledger.

'Ah, hello ... Andromeda, isn't it?'

'Yes, Mr Prendergast.'

'Haven't seen you in a while. Mind you, I haven't seen many customers in a while.'

'No. I suppose the coupons don't really cover books, since they're not considered essential,' I said.

Mr Prendergast nodded.

'Plus, after yesterday's storm, and the other ... things,' he said. 'The citadel is quiet this morning. Are you after anything in particular?'

'I'm going to browse animals,' I said.

'Let me know if you need anything.'

I moseyed over to the Wildlife section and examined the titles. It appeared to be the usual cats, dogs, horses, birds, fish, insects.

I slunk over to astronomy. Mr Prendergast had one copy of the updated edition of *Discourse on the Planets and Moons*. I compared the updated edition to a similar book on the solar system he had. Both books still claimed Jupiter had four moons. As far as Eden in 1273 was concerned, this was the truth.

Mr Prendergast had nothing which went beyond what I already knew previously to discovering the House of Books.

'Do you have anything on larger animals?' I asked as I approached the counter.

Mr Prendergast peered at me over his glasses.

'Larger animals?'

'You know: lions, tigers, elephants, that sort of thing.'

'I don't know those words,' Mr Prendergast said, glaring at me.

'Do you have anything about disasters? Like' – I tried to pronounce the word as best I could, as I had only ever seen it written down – 't sun amis?'

'Pardon? Are you making up a new language?' he asked.

'No. Why would I need to do that?' I said, feeling flattered that Mr Prendergast thought I had the capability to create a new language.

'What are those words then?'

Well, if he didn't know, he didn't know, and I wasn't going to explain it all to him.

'Doesn't matter,' I said. 'I just thought I'd enquire for a little experiment. Sorry for confusing you. Bye for now, Mr Prendergast.'

As I suspected. No tomes existed outside the House of Books which held the kind of knowledge I currently accumulated. For some ridiculous reason, we were not to know about all the wonderous animals, never mind the vastness of space. What purpose would it serve to hide those things from us? I wondered if I would ever work out why the authorities had kept the library hidden. I might be thrown in prison before I ever had a chance to discover the truth.

Envy sat wagging her tail as I exited the bookshop.

'See, you can be good.'

She didn't respond. She appeared more interested in where I would take her next.

I was grateful most of the townsfolk had stayed away from the citadel that day. But soldiers lingered everywhere. We would have to go the long way around. I checked that no one watched us. I decided to use the same route which Gabriel had uncovered on the first night we snuck down the narrow passages and alleyways, which meant another undignified entrance to the House of Books. Presuming it was still a house filled with books and it hadn't been cleared out by the soldiers.

Gabriel was sitting at one of the desks on the ground floor.

'I could've been anyone. Don't you care if you get caught?' I said, leaning over the balcony.

'I see you've come in disguise again. Cunning.'

Envy whined at me; she wanted to go downstairs and greet Gabriel.

'One of the books I took home yesterday had been left open on a desk,' I said as I approached Gabriel, and Envy leapt all over him. 'Last night I read the relevant pages.'

'Intriguing. And?'

'I didn't really understand it. There were place names I didn't recognise, and it stated that a piece of the land and all the people were lost from a great tragedy. Just swept away in a torrent of water. It was called a t-sun—'

'Tsunami,' Gabriel said.

'You know what that is? How do you know how to pronounce something I've never heard of?' I asked.

'What was this book called?'

'Something about ancient history of some islands. And that's another thing, it stated this happened over eight and a half thousand years ago. But the First Ancestors—'

'Weren't around then?'

'Exactly. What is this place?' I asked.

'The library? Or your citadel?'

'Both,' I said, feeling quite apprehensive as to what I might be about to find out.

'I think deep down you know,' Gabriel said. 'You even told me your grandfather has questioned things. He said the temple should be called the Temple of the Long, Long-Dead Ancients? I have something to show you, but we should probably go upstairs.'

Huddled over a small desk on the top floor, with only one lantern for illumination, Gabriel unfurled a map. I recognised the layout immediately. It was of the old citadel. The Guildhall remained the Guildhall. The building next door was named Public Library. Next door to that stood something called the Theatre Royal. This was a fire-damaged building in my time.

Framing the right side of the square were three university buildings. But in 1273, one of these was another fire-damaged building. The remaining two were the school and the hospital in my time. At the furthest end of the square facing the public library was something called Assembly Rooms. In the present day this was another large abandoned building, which stood adjacent to the Grand Tea Room. Framing the top left side of the square were two buildings called Stonburh Museum and Stonburh Art Gallery. Again, these buildings were also abandoned in my time.

The fountain even had a name: the Angel Fountain. I didn't know what angel meant. The weird column opposite the fountain was a war memorial. Several buildings called public houses were scattered throughout the citadel.

The square had a name: King Aethelwulf Square, which was the strangest name I had ever encountered. In the centre of the square, a small circle illustrated something called the Statue of Aethelwulf, King of Wessex. I realised this was the exact position of the broken stone block.

In place of the Temple of the First Ancestors sat something called Stonburh Cathedral. There were no gardens. The cathedral had grounds, but no markings to indicate any flower garden.

'Who's this King A Ethel woman?' I asked.

'A man. A king is male.'

'Ethel's a man?'

'Aethel*wulf*,' Gabriel said with a cough.

'I don't know what the word means.'

'Aethel means noble. And wulf means wolf. Therefore, the name means noble wolf.'

'What's a wolf?'

'A wolf is a large dog. Wolves are the ancestors of all dogs.'

'It must be wolves who roam the forest. And Ethel means noble?'

I felt terrible. I had had a noble hen. She had died only the other day and ended up in my grandfather's stew. Plus, Envy's ancestors were wolves. I wondered if she was noble.

'What's a *cath-edral*?' I asked.

'A place of worship. That's the other thing I have to show you.'

Gabriel produced a thin book. It said *Stonburh Cathedral* on the cover, and in smaller lettering it said *Guide Book*. It was the temple in its prime. The windows had glass panes. Small upright stones surrounded the cathedral in the foreground of the cover picture.

'Stonburh is a weird name,' I said.

'Not when you break it down. Ston is short for stone, in this instance. And burh means fort, or stronghold in an old language. Therefore, stone fort. Which makes sense, since the citadel sits within a fort or stronghold made of stone.'

'I suppose that does make sense when you know. How do you know these things? You seem to know everything about everything.'

Gabriel chuckled.

'My secret. For now,' he said.

Sometimes Gabriel could be tiresome.

I browsed through the book and recognised the temple's pillars. Robed people made from stone lined the cavernous space. Chairs adorned the temple floor. This area was called a nave. I studied a map of the layout of the cathedral. It had four different chapels, a font, a pulpit, an altar, a choir, two transepts, a presbytery, a cloister, a chapter house, and a crypt. Plus, tombs were dotted about the floorplan. It also noted the windows, such as Rose Window and the Great War Memorial Window. The cathedral even had a prison. But it must have been a cell for one person as the square on the map was miniscule.

Once again, most of the words meant nothing to me.

'This is a place of ... what did you say?'

'Worship. People built great cathedrals to get closer to God, who they believed had created them. To enter a cathedral was to enter God's House. He who resided in the heavens.'

'Amongst the stars?' I said, recalling that Gabriel had mentioned heavens before to describe the sky.

'Yes, something like that.'

'And these people are long dead? The House of Books is from their time?'

'Yes,' Gabriel nodded.

'Then my grandfather was correct? People have gone before us. They were here years before the First Ancestors. Why did they disappear?'

'Could've been a natural disaster. Or a war. Either one of those could be catastrophic, depending on how bad they get. The Earth can be a terrifying place. Volcanic eruptions, earthquakes, tsunamis. Like the tsunami from thousands of years ago.'

'Volcanic eruptions?' I said.

'Have you read anymore of the General Knowledge Encyclopaedia?'

'I haven't even got anywhere near completing the space one,' I said, suddenly feeling overwhelmed. I wanted to know the truth about everything, but at the same time it was too much to take in.

'The general knowledge book will cover volcanoes,' Gabriel said. 'I'm sorry, Andromeda. Your authorities have taken everything from you, including the opportunity to understand your own world. There have been – and always will be – natural disasters. Droughts destroy crops and animals, and people struggle to survive. Floods cleanse the land of every living thing. Plus, wars are frequent. Catastrophe is around the corner. Peace is not the norm.'

'You sound like my grandad.'

'History will be repeated if humans don't learn from the past. Or forget the past. Or, in your case, have it removed for them.'

'Why have they lied to us?' I asked. 'They said the descendants of the First Ancestors created everything for us? I just don't see the purpose of all these lies.'

'I don't know either. I don't recall ever …' Gabriel sniffed, and rubbed his nose.

It terrified me to discover people could be erased. I didn't even know things like that could happen until the previous evening. I was exploring my world and the universe through books. But mostly it appeared frightening. I had learned space was trying to kill us. I had learned that the planet was trying to kill us, too. The North Sea must house the spirits of those people who died at the hands of a giant wave.

'Don't look sad,' Gabriel said.

'But I'm so confused.'

'You're gaining new knowledge every day.'

'Why do you want me to know all this?'

'Don't you want to know the world?' he asked.

'Yes, but I don't understand why you've shown me all this. I wasn't sure if you were trying to get me into trouble,' I said.

'Why would I want to get you into trouble? That's the last thing I'd want to do,' Gabriel said, looking wounded.

'But, why have you come to Eden? What do you want here?'

'My coming to Eden was an accident.'

'Was it?' I asked, a little surprised. I wondered how you could visit a town by accident.

'Yes,' he said. 'Then I discovered ... Anyway, I told you before why I've shown you the library: I believe you have a right to know your real history. You should know the real world.'

I felt a bit embarrassed having doubted his intentions again. He always seemed sincere enough. Although he may have wanted me to know the House of Books, I didn't really know him. But I had also become quite fond of him in a way. It wasn't just books, which drew me to the House of Books. I was putting all my trust in Gabriel. I hoped he wouldn't prove me wrong.

'Are there any other citadels like mine?' I asked.

'Walled cities?

'If that's what they're called.'

'Yes, let's have a look.'

Gabriel examined the history shelves and removed several books from world history. Then we retired to the corner of the top floor.

Gabriel showed me a book on historical walled citadels. I was stunned to find that numerous walled citadels existed. All in places I had never heard of, of course: Croatia, China, France, Italy, England, Russia, Morocco, Portugal, Spain, Ethiopia,

Uzbekistan, and Estonia. It got me thinking about what my grandfather had said about his childhood, when another child's father had questioned whether walls were built to keep people in. I wondered if the outer town wall had actually been built to keep us in, rather than keep the giant dogs and dog-headed humans out.

'Why were walled citadels built?' I asked.

'Unfortunately, throughout history, there are always people who want in, and walls were built to protect the people of the city.'

'They weren't built to keep the people in?'

'Not usually,' Gabriel said.

But I wondered if Eden had been the exception.

Gabriel sneezed and this brought on a cough.

'Are you okay?'

'Space dust, I think,' he said, sniffing and tapping his chest. 'It gets everywhere.'

Gabriel skipped through the pages of the walled citadels book and showed me a map featuring a few large islands.

'What's this?' I asked.

'It's a map of the world.'

'Is it?' I said, gobsmacked. 'I thought the world was one giant piece of land.'

'These are continents, which have countries in them. You're here,' Gabriel said, pointing to one of the smallest of the islands.

'On that tiny place?' I said, wondering why, if the other islands were so big, mine had to be so small.

Gabriel chuckled.

'Yes, it is small compared to some others. But it's your home.'

'I live in the British Isles? The islands created from a tsunami?' I said, a little fearful that the rest of the isles could be swept away under a torrent of water.

'That's one way of putting it,' Gabriel said. 'Nature does like to change things. Nothing lasts forever.'

'I'm realising this. And I don't like it,' I said.

'All the more reason to enjoy life. The world can change in an instant.'

'So this is the real world,' I said, staring at the map. 'This is the truth. Well, part of the truth anyway. What year is it really?' I asked.

'What year do you think it is?'

'It's 1273.'

Gabriel pondered this.

'I would add another thousand on to that, at least,' he said.

'A whole thousand?' I said. I don't know why, but I hadn't expected the true year to be so distant. 'I think I'd like to talk about something else.'

'What else would you like to learn?'

'I'd like to learn more about the world. All the different lands and civilisations. I didn't realise any of this existed. And what's that?' I asked, pointing to a long monster which was on the cover of another book Gabriel had brought upstairs.

'That's a dragon. From Asia.'

I must have looked petrified.

'They don't exist,' Gabriel said. 'They're a mythological creature. Mythology is made-up stories, like the stories in your Greek mythology book.'

I was relieved to hear it.

'Where's Asia?' I asked.

'That's here,' Gabriel said, pointing to the map.

'And they tell stories about these creatures?'

'They're not the only culture to do so. Europe also has dragon mythology,' he said, pointing to the European continent. 'But the dragons are different. Asian dragons are more like serpents in appearance, but with feet. They slither through the sky or a river. European dragons have wings and breathe fire.'

'That's even worse,' I exclaimed.

Gabriel chuckled again.

'They don't exist,' he said.

'But if they don't exist, how come Asia and Europe have them in their mythology? They must've both seen something like that?'

'You've seen the dinosaurs now. Who's to say these different cultures didn't separately come across dinosaur bones. Then they created dragons in their respective mythologies?'

'Do you have a logical explanation for everything?' I asked.

'There's always a logical explanation for everything,' Gabriel said, with another cough.

We spent the afternoon pouring over text and images of other citadels, countries, and cultures. The differences. The similarities. The religious beliefs. All the various mythological stories. It was the best afternoon of my life. The world was an incredible place and I was uncovering it all with Gabriel as my guide. I realised how much I enjoyed spending time with him. He was an enthusiastic teacher. Most of all, I felt comfortable in his presence. Despite having had doubts about his intentions, Gabriel wasn't wicked. Even if he was still a mystery.

As I was leaving, Gabriel dropped the book on the cathedral into my basket, along with another, much chunkier, book. He said that book should provide a deeper understanding of the cathedral and why it was built.

I left the House of Books feeling as though I knew everything about everything. Which is impossible, as you can never know enough in truth. Even if I lived to be two hundred years old, there still wouldn't be enough time to learn all of the world's history. But in that moment, I believed I knew more than anybody else in Eden.

The townsfolk had begun gathering in the square around a wooden platform which had appeared next to the fountain. Or rather, the Angel Fountain, with the three damaged statues.

A few of the townsfolk surveyed the sky.

As the clock struck four, the doors of the Guildhall opened. The mayor stepped out, chaperoned by a soldier on either side. The white-haired man followed carrying a small box.

They sauntered towards the raised podium.

I indicated for Envy to sit in the alleyway, while I joined the back of the crowd. I placed my basket upon the floor, as the books were quite a weight.

I pulled my scarf further over my ears when a soldier glanced in my direction.

'Dear people of Eden,' the mayor began. 'I do not want you to fear. However, I must be honest with you. Our way of life is under threat. The enemy from the north draws ever closer. This war, which we have been forced to participate in, is far from over. Yesterday, we witnessed one of the enemy's tricks. They are rising. Who knows what more the northern region are capable of. We must be prepared. The enemy possesses weapons we do not have. We have heard of attacks coming from the air. How do we know this? The people of faraway towns have sent word to us. They have been attacked by poisons released in the air. A type of gas.'

A murmur rose from the crowd.

I thought of Gabriel. If the people in faraway towns had been attacked, perhaps Gabriel had come to Eden to escape. Now I had seen a map of the British Isles, I had to assume it was the people of the north of these islands carrying out the attacks.

'We have reason to believe we will be attacked any day now,' the mayor continued.

This caused the murmuring to rise further.

Although I felt relieved that the mayor's speech was nothing to do with me and my law breaking, the relief was short-lived, knowing Eden would be attacked.

'Yesterday was a trick. Their practice run,' the mayor said. 'Therefore, every household will be issued with gas masks. Every citizen must always carry their mask with them. Is that clear?'

'What about the shapes we saw in the rain yesterday?' one woman asked.

'A trick, as I said. An hallucination brought about by a poison in the air.'

'They sent rain with poison?' asked another woman.

'The people of the northern region are unfortunately more advanced than us in their offensive capabilities.'

I wondered why the people of the northern region would be more advanced than us. Plus, if we were not as advanced in our weaponry, then we wouldn't be as advanced as them in anything. Therefore, what did we have that they could want?

'Are you saying we're not safe here?' an elderly man asked.

'We are safe, when we follow the rules,' the mayor said. 'We are safer in Eden than out there in the world. The enemy will kill us if we leave the town.'

I was still puzzled as to why anyone would want to poison us in our town, and now they would kill us if we tried to leave, too.

'But you said they can send things through the air that can kill us here?' the elderly man said.

'Then we must be cautious and stay inside our homes,' the mayor said. 'If we have to go out, we must bring our gas mask from this day forward. Or, even better, wear it at all times when outside.'

This all sounded terrifying. And it meant a drastic change. Which I hated.

'How will we get these masks?' a woman asked.

'One person from every household must come to the Guildhall tomorrow morning and collect a mask for each family member. However, all the children will be given theirs at school tomorrow.'

This meant either my mother or grandfather would have to come in. I certainly couldn't go inside the Guildhall. Even with a scarf on my head, it would be too risky.

'What about the people who haven't come into the citadel today?' someone else asked.

'There will be an announcement every hour in tonight's news report for those who have not been able to come in personally today,' the mayor said. 'You can collect for elderly relatives or neighbours if they have no one else.'

'And these masks will stop us breathing in poison?' an elderly woman asked.

'Yes, I will show you.'

The mayor clicked his fingers at the white-haired man who stood behind him. The man retrieved an item from the box he still clutched and presented it to the mayor.

'This is the mask you shall wear,' he said, as he held it aloft.

It was the most unusual-looking thing I had ever seen. The mask had two large clear eyes and a protruding round snout.

The mayor placed it over his head, and it covered his entire face.

Three things entered my mind. One, this might actually help with sneaking into the citadel as everyone would look the same wearing a mask. Second, Envy wouldn't get one. How were we supposed to protect beloved pets and best friends? Third, Gabriel wouldn't get one either. He would be exposed to these poisons. As far as the authorities in Eden were concerned, Gabriel didn't exist. I realised how much I cared about him.

Chapter 8

When I got home, I explained the gas mask situation to my mother and grandfather. My grandfather offered to come into the old citadel with me in the morning. He would collect the masks while I visited Doctor Hartnell for my appointment.

I wanted to tell him all about the ancient tsunami and show him the book. I wanted to introduce him to the British Isles, where we lived. I wanted to tell him about other walled citadels, about dragons, about different beliefs across the world. There was one god for some, and a myriad of gods for others. I wanted to tell him I had seen a map of the world, and all the land masses. But it would have to wait, since I couldn't risk saying anything in front of my mother. I still felt it was for the best that my mother remained in the dark with regards to the House of Books. It's not that I didn't trust her. My mother wouldn't have said a word to anyone outside our cottage. I just didn't want to concern her.

My mother had said she didn't like the idea of any of us having to visit the citadel. She had heard from a neighbour about the incident with the light and dark shapes in the storm.

The citadel didn't sound safe anymore. She was shocked I had even gone in after such an event the day before.

But we had to go in. We wouldn't be able to get the extra food we needed otherwise. We could only grow so much.

I sat up late into the night reading the guide book on the cathedral. I also commenced with the heavier tome that Gabriel had said should give me a deeper understanding of the cathedral. But the writing was too small. Even with the combination of light from my lamp and some candles, I struggled. The pages were so fine I could see the text for the following page through the page I currently read. Plus, it appeared confusing. I didn't know what the words meant. The first word was Genesis. Then it went on and on in a language style I couldn't get to grips with. The book had numerous mentions of light and water, and firmament. But I didn't know that word. I couldn't relate to any of the text or the people. Well, that's a slight lie. I came across Eden. Eden was a garden. Where this garden was, I couldn't say. Adam and Eve lived there until they were banished. I gave up after this point. I couldn't see how Gabriel would think I could understand any of it.

My grandfather, Envy, and I stood at the top of the lane waiting for the omnibus, which approached in the distance.

'You were right, Grandad, about everything,' I said.

'Everything? Was I?'

'Yes. The authorities have lied. People have gone before us. More ancient than our ancients. I read a passage in a book about the ancestors of the people who were here before the First Ancestors. That's how ancient they are.'

'I knew it. I have been lied to my whole life,' my grandfather said, bitterly. 'I wonder why they lied?'

'I've got books to prove it. The Temple of the First Ancestors is a building called a cathedral. Stonburh Cathedral to be precise. Stonburh was the name of the town back then.'

‘Stonburh Cathedral? Never heard those words before.’

‘It’s a house for a god. This god person lives in the sky and he created everything that we see around us,’ I said. ‘I read more about the cathedral last night. They used to bury their dead in the ground. Which I find odd, considering they believed there was a man in the sky. He resided in a place they called heaven. Heaven is where they would all go after death. You would’ve thought they would have burnt their dead so their souls could float to the heavens. The grounds outside the temple were where they buried their dead. That’s why you found bone. The temple even has bodies under the floor. The larger floor stones with worn-away lettering have the bodies underneath.’

My grandfather laughed.

‘What’s so funny?’ I asked, thinking it was disrespectful to laugh about dead people.

‘It was a place of reverence, rather than a place for sacrifice,’ my grandfather said. ‘I thought it felt too peaceful.’

‘Yes. I’ll tell you more on the omnibus.’

We sat downstairs so we were inside, away from the prying ears of the driver, should he be eavesdropping on conversations. I never had the impression any drivers did, not out of malice anyway.

I filled my grandfather in on all things global. On all the wonderful cultures, including our own past culture, and one which we knew nothing about. Apparently, I jibber-jabbered all the way into the old citadel. My grandfather said he didn’t think I had ever spoken so much in one sitting. It must have been my excitement. We arranged to meet in the square, and I trotted off to Doctor Hartnell’s clinic with Envy. I was feeling quite happy, I suppose this was due to all my excitement about discovering what the temple really was, or had been. I wasn’t at all worried about anything Doctor Hartnell might have to say to me.

'That's a pretty scarf,' Doctor Hartnell said, as she ushered me into her consulting room.

'It was my grandma's,' I said, while I adjusted it around my hairline.

Doctor Hartnell had a manual open upon her desk, and a notepad, where it looked as though she had made some notes.

I glanced across at her small bookcase. To my shock, it was now full. Not only was it full, it burst with books from the House of Books. The little numbered labels ran across all the spines. My mind raced back to the day of my last appointment. After I had seen Doctor Hartnell, I went to the House of Books, and two soldiers came in to steal some volumes from the Medical section. The books were for a *she*, they had said. Doctor Hartnell had been the *she* the soldiers had referred to.

The clock pendulum swung back and forth on her desk, and I clenched my teeth.

'We've discussed before how you feel anxious,' Doctor Hartnell began, 'and you told me last time you feel that no one understands you. And you don't understand them. You said you felt lost, and in the wrong place at the wrong time.'

'Umm,' I said, still distracted by the now heaving bookcase. Not to mention the clock.

'You must feel rather isolated in the world?'

'I suppose so,' I said, turning my attention back to her and wondering how much Doctor Hartnell knew about Eden.

'Do you find it hard to form friendships?' she asked.

I thought of Gabriel. Other than Envy, he was my only friend.

'Usually,' I said.

'Would you say you don't like social situations, and you try to avoid them?' she asked, reading from her notepad.

As much as I can, I thought. But it's a bit awkward avoiding the citadel during the day when you keep asking me to make appointments.

'Yes,' I said.

'Do you prefer routine, compared with change?'

I thought about Gabriel again. Until I met him, surprises and change were difficult, if not challenging.

'Mostly routine,' I said. 'I don't like change.'

Doctor Hartnell nodded, and studied her notes again.

'Did you struggle with subjects in school? Have difficulty learning new things?'

I pictured all the glorious shelves in the House of Books, heaving with knowledge.

'I like learning new things,' I said.

'Would you say you struggle to understand how people feel? What about their intentions? Do you find interactions confusing? Do you misunderstand people?'

She hit me with four questions at once and didn't expect me to be confused?

'Sometimes,' I said.

'You found my clock annoying,' she said, glancing up from her notepad.

'It is annoying,' I said.

'What about other noises? Are they annoying too?'

'It depends on the noise,' I said.

'Ticking is annoying?'

'Yes.'

'Would you say you're distracted by noises other people don't appear to notice? Like the background sound of my clock?'

'That's a background sound? But it's right there on the desk in front of me,' I said, astounded that such a noise wouldn't be considered irritating to anyone else.

'I see. Are there any other noises you find annoying?'

I found lots of things annoying, I thought, including Doctor Hartnell now. I didn't really know her, but now I knew she stole books from the House of Books. Plus, I didn't like the fact she was asking me all these personal questions.

'People talking loudly,' I said. 'People stomping about in a room above or below me. The sound of the wireless coming from another room. People hollering across the square to one another ...' And people telling me lies, I thought.

'So it's the noises people make?' she said. 'People are the problem?'

This was true, I realised. I adored birdsong. I loved the hum from the bees. I delighted in the clip-clopping and neighing from a horse. I cherished Envy's playful bark. But I also enjoyed the Guildhall clock chime. The bell on the omnibuses. The little bells above the shop doors in the citadel. I just didn't like the constant ticking clock in the doctor's room.

'People are annoying,' I agreed.

She smiled, but I thought she was about to laugh.

'I believe you have something called autism spectrum disorder.'

Now there was a new name for the thing I had. It had a different name before. Why did it need a name? Couldn't I just be me?

'I thought you said I had a stress disorder?' I said. 'Now I have a spec-trum disorder?'

'We're learning things all time about illness: conditions ... and learning difficulties.'

'I don't have learning difficulties. I can learn things.'

'That's why it's called a spectrum. Because even people with autism can be anywhere within the spectrum,' she said, as she consulted the open manual.

Perhaps I felt insulted. Perhaps I had just had enough of Eden and all its secrets. I really was in the wrong place at the wrong time. This world wasn't made for me. Not with all its lies and its autism spectrum disorder. I hated that she implied my head wasn't right. That I had a *thing*.

And I snapped.

'How do you know this all of a sudden? You never knew

any of this before. You've learned all this since the other day? Where have all these books come from? Have you stolen them from the library? Yes, that's right, the library. Don't think I don't know.'

Doctor Hartnell gawped at me. I couldn't discern her expression. It could have been one of fear, concern, or embarrassment.

I didn't stay to find out.

As I stormed through the square with Envy in tow, I realised I shouldn't have said it. Now she knew that I knew about the House of Books. She would inform the mayor that I had confirmed it. I had already gotten into too much trouble over the past few days. Now I could have gotten my whole family into trouble.

The wooden podium which the mayor addressed the crowd from the day before remained erect. I wondered if he planned another address at some point.

Envy located my grandfather sitting on one of the benches in the square. Her nose and eyesight were impeccable.

My grandfather had three canvas bags lying across his lap. He had removed one mask from a bag for a closer inspection. This didn't deter Envy from attempting to claim a comfy spot on my grandfather's thighs.

'How did you get on?' he asked, while trying to keep the masks from falling on the ground.

'Have you tried a mask on?' I asked.

'No,' he said. 'They don't look comfortable.'

I glanced around the square. Quite a few people had already collected their masks for their family. But no one was wearing one.

'I think the mayor advised we should wear it when in the citadel,' I said.

'Did he? I bet he's not wearing his while he's sitting in his office, dictating.'

‘I probably shouldn’t bring Envy into the citadel anymore. If there’s an attack, how would she survive without a mask?’

‘Best to leave her at home in future,’ my grandfather said, nodding.

‘She won’t like it. She went mad the last time I left her,’ I said.

I considered her sweet round face as she grinned away. At least that’s what it looked like whenever she panted. She had overheated in her enthusiasm to smother my grandfather with her love.

‘You still haven’t answered my question,’ my grandfather said. ‘How did you get on?’

‘I have a disorder. On a spectrum. I think she was trying to say the disorder makes me peculiar.’

‘How do you feel about that?’

‘I wish people would stop asking me how I feel. And stop telling me how they think I’m feeling,’ I said, thinking how I had never been good at explaining how I felt, even when I was asked directly.

‘Sorry. You were happy earlier. Your mother and I, we just want you to be happy.’

‘Well, I’m not happy.’

I turned away from my grandfather. Envy pawed my leg and grumbled. She sensed I needed comforting. She leapt into my lap and snuggled herself under my chin.

I hate—’

‘You hate?’

‘Nothing,’ I said.

We sat in silence for a moment as the townsfolk ambled past.

‘I hate the lies,’ I said. ‘It’s wrong to lie about our history. Lying is unjust. I hate having to discover things too late. What’s the point of having authorities if all they do is lie? I hate everything and everyone.’

My grandfather drew me close and kissed me on the forehead.

❧

We continued to sit upon the bench and watch the townsfolk collect their masks and their shopping, and leave via the omnibuses. No one appeared to want to linger, apart from my grandfather and me.

'Would you like to meet Gabriel? I asked.

'Is he here?'

'He'll be in the House of Books. I think he lives in it at present.'

'A bit dangerous, should he get caught,' my grandfather said.

'I don't think we'd be able to go through the front door. But I don't know how you would get over the wall at the back?'

'I wouldn't. Not with these legs. Can't you ask him to come out?'

'He doesn't go outside,' I said, thinking how I hadn't seen Gabriel outside since I first met him. 'I've only ever seen him outside after dark.'

'Scared of being seen is he?'

'Don't know. Maybe. I thought he was terrifying the first time I saw him, so perhaps that's why. I think you'd like him though.'

'Not saying I wouldn't like him,' my grandfather said. 'If you like him, and Envy trusts him, then I'm sure he's okay. Just weird.'

'But apparently I'm weird. And you like me. Don't you?'

My grandfather laughed.

'That must be why I love you then, poppet.'

A soldier with a walking stick shuffled towards the wooden platform. Most of his face lay hidden beneath bandages. He had pulled his hat low. Only the top right side of his face poked above the wrappings. Even his mouth was obscured by the bandage. He wore gloves and the collar of his coat concealed his neck. An elderly man, who I presumed to be his father, helped him up on the podium. The soldier appeared to have lost the full use of his legs.

'Has he come back from the war?' my grandfather asked.

I shrugged. I couldn't understand how my grandfather expected me to know.

'I'm here to tell you …' the soldier began to say, in a strange garbled voice, before he faltered.

He gripped the wooden beam before him, but he seemed not to have the strength to support himself. The elderly man propped him up as the townsfolk gathered. The other soldiers watched.

'I've seen what's out there,' the soldier continued. 'I've seen who it is who fights us. I've watched friends die. I almost lost my life. I should be dead. My body is broken.'

The soldier struggled to speak, as though his tongue had come loose in his mouth. I was surprised the citadel soldiers hadn't tried to arrest him. They appeared as intrigued as the rest of the townsfolk.

'I've been allowed to come home because I cannot fight anymore. But your husbands, sons, and fathers, are still out there. Fighting for you. I cannot show you the horror of the war as I saw it. I can only show you what the enemy has done to me.'

The soldier turned and nodded to the elderly man, who helped him unravel his bandages.

'This is what they did to me,' he said.

An audible gasp travelled through the throng.

Half his face was gone. His head had a caved-in appearance. He had a vacant socket where his left eye belonged. He had no nose, no left cheekbone, most of his lips had gone too.

I think a woman screamed. But the rest of the townsfolk fell silent.

My stomach churned as a dizzying heat came over me. I was glad I was sitting on a bench.

The citadel soldiers appeared equally horrified. It was as though none of us had considered what was happening to the men of Eden, hundreds or perhaps thousands of miles away in the town of Frontline. Some were dying a brutal death. Others were surviving horrific injuries. They weren't faring well at all.

Also, I realised that I hadn't imagined a man with half a face standing in the doorway of the Guildhall the day Eden swarmed with shadow figures. He had been real.

A strange hissing sound interrupted the silence. All the townsfolk glanced around to locate the noise.

The injured soldier's one remaining eye darted about the scene.

'Gas,' he shouted, as he raised an arm to shield his face.

A dark mist slunk along the ground and rose to meet my face.

Something soft smacked me around my mouth.

It was Envy's tongue.

I opened my eyes to find three pairs of dark eyes looming over me.

'There she is,' my grandfather said, as he wafted a book over my face.

Gabriel beamed, while Envy continued to smother me.

A shelf dug into my back, as I sat propped up against a large bookcase on the ground floor of the House of Books. My grandmother's scarf lay across my legs.

'What happened? How did we get inside the House of Books?' I asked.

'That'll be your friend Gabriel,' my grandfather said, patting Gabriel on the back, which caused Gabriel to cough.

'I still don't understand,' I said.

'There was a gas attack. You passed out,' my grandfather said.

'But you're okay?'

'I put the bloody mask on.'

'What about Envy?' I asked.

'I shoved her face under my jacket.'

'And you brought us inside?' I asked Gabriel. 'How did you—'

'I was peering through a window shutter. I saw you sitting on a bench. I saw the wounded soldier. I saw the gas hit.'

'You were spying on me again?'

'Good job I was,' he said, with another cough.

'But the gas didn't affect you?'

'I'm quite special, you know,' Gabriel said with a grin.

I tried to raise myself from the floor, but my head spun, and I slumped back against the bookcase.

'You need to rest, poppet,' my grandfather said.

'I feel sick.'

'That'll be the gas you ingested,' Gabriel said.

We were huddled in one of the furthest corners from the main entrance. The floor felt cold on my derriere.

My grandfather contemplated all the balconies.

'So, this is the great House of Books,' he said. 'What should I read first?'

'There's a big map of the old citadel and one of the whole town and surrounding area on a desk over there,' I said.

My grandfather and Gabriel helped me stagger over to the desks. My grandfather studied the Parish of Stonburh map.

'There's no forest,' my grandfather said. 'Some bluebell woods. Mostly fields. But no forest.'

'I've been in the forest,' I said.

'When?' he asked.

'A few days ago.'

'How? Why?'

‘Envy ran off, as though she caught the scent of something. She went through a rusted grate in the wall, where the river flows into the forest. I went after her. I ended up quite deep in the forest, but it was daylight. It was beautiful. I wondered how it could be full of monsters after dark. It didn’t seem like a place for evil spirits. It was a place of peace. I felt drawn to it. I felt as though I belonged. Which was odd, since I’d never ventured in there before. I came across large upright stones, laid out in a circle. Having seen a map of the town from centuries ago, I know this to be a place of high importance or even worship for the true ancient ancestors. The stones have been left undisturbed in the forest. I could have stayed there all day. I was captivated by its magnificence. But then I saw ... found Envy, and left.’

‘You really have been exploring Eden,’ my grandfather said. ‘Inside and out. Good for you. Are you saying the true ancestors really did live within the forest?’

‘The land would have mostly been forest at the time of the people who built the stone circle,’ Gabriel began. ‘They were here long before the people who built the cathedral. Thousands of years of history lies here. The ancestors who built the stone circle were known as pagans. They believed in multiple gods. They had sky gods, land gods, river gods. The pagans were more in tune with nature. Their respect for all the gods was a respect for nature, which surrounded them. For nature gave them life. The stone circle would have been a place of great importance. A place to worship. A place to gather as a collective group of people. Either no trees grew on the plateau originally or those ancestors had begun to clear parts of the land. The stone circle would have been a prominent construction on a plateau free from trees.’

‘They cleared the land to build a stone circle?’ I asked.

‘They cleared some of the land to grow crops and keep animals. They became farmers and settled in communities.

Life was safer for them that way. Prior to becoming settled communities, people had moved around in smaller groups. They were hunters. That was a dangerous life. It made more sense to live in larger numbers and raise families, and have easier access to a food source.'

'This stone circle was created as a place for the true First Ancestors to gather?' my grandfather asked.

'Yes. They would have celebrated life there. Mourned their dead there. Paid respect to the gods there. It's possible there was another sacred place to the pagan ancestors where the cathedral sits today. That's another prominent spot on a hill, and the river runs directly below it.'

'They didn't build the cathedral?' I asked, wondering how many different ancient people there had actually been.

'No,' Gabriel said. 'Outside influence had brought a new religion in long before the cathedral was built. The new religion eventually swept the land and took over from paganism. In some areas, the people who followed the new religion built churches, and later cathedrals, on top of, or next to the sacred places of their pagan ancestors.'

'Oh, but I like the cathedral,' I said. 'Now I'm not so sure. I didn't realise it might have destroyed something else.'

'You can still like the cathedral. Just know that an older religion was practised here long before the new religion arrived. While some pagans converted to the new religion, for others, the old ways never died. Some refused to accept the new religion, and they continued to practise their sacred rituals. They never conformed, not even when more unpleasant invaders arrived. These invaders built your cathedral. They terrorised anyone who refused to accept their authority. Even those of the same religion. They persecuted and intimidated the population as they took their land from them. They now owned everything. They proved this by building their huge religious houses. They even built their giant cathedrals on top of more humble cathedrals and churches too. I expect, to some, the new buildings were as terrifying as the invaders.'

'This is disappointing news,' my grandfather said. 'Even the cathedral people eradicated the history which came before them.'

'But some of the people who came later must've had respect for the true First Ancestors,' Gabriel said. 'I noticed the village in the map is named Solstice, and I wonder if they named it after what they thought the stone circle was used for.'

'Used for?' I enquired.

'Stone circles resemble giant sundials. They could have set specific stones up so the sun shines through them on summer solstice, and shines through other stones for winter solstice. This enabled them to know what time of year it was.'

'How?' I asked.

'Because the sun appears to pause at the peak of summer solstice, and again during the peak of winter solstice. If they marked the *pause*, by using the stones, then they would know, for example, that after the peak of summer solstice, the days would begin to get shorter and shorter, right up until winter solstice.'

'What does solstice mean?'

'Solstice means sun stands still,' Gabriel said. 'There must be books in here about the pagans. I'll go and see.'

Gabriel left the table and headed for the staircase.

I thought 'sun stands still' was the most beautiful phrase I had ever heard. But Envy interrupted my reverie by growling.

The main door burst open and I initially thought three snarling dog-headed monsters stormed inside. But I think my vision was still a little blurred. I realised they were soldiers when they began speaking.

'Caught in the act,' one said.

'Likes to steal things which don't belong to her,' said another.

'Balderdash,' my grandfather said. 'Why are you accusing my granddaughter of stealing?'

'This building is forbidden to you.'

'Why should it be?' my grandfather asked. 'What is it the authorities don't want us to know?'

I realised I couldn't sense Gabriel. Only my grandfather appeared to confront the soldiers.

'Your granddaughter steals. Your granddaughter breaks into private property.'

'She has no shame,' another soldier concluded.

'You idiots,' my grandfather roared. 'I showed her this place. I've been taking the books.'

'Grandad?' I said.

'She wouldn't be in here if it were not for me,' my grandfather continued. 'If you want to punish someone, punish me.'

Why was my grandfather lying? To protect me? The soldiers appeared to consider what he had said.

One soldier moved forward.

'Alright, old man. If you insist it's you we should be arresting, then you're coming with us.'

My grandfather was pushed or punched to the ground.

Envy barked in fury, but she too got pushed away, and she yelped.

I tried to stand, but slid from the chair.

'Grandad!'

'Don't worry about me,' he said.

I slithered along the floor towards my grandfather.

'Where are you taking him?' I asked.

'Where we take all criminals.'

I managed to grab his ankles and I clung on.

A soldier forced my grandfather's head down, which enabled him to lean in close to me.

'Don't worry, Andromeda. I have lived my life. You need to live yours. I do this for you. Free yourself. Free Eden. Live.'

Chapter 9

Live, my grandfather had said. But I wanted to die. They had taken my father off to fight in the war. Now they had taken my grandfather to prison. He sacrificed himself for me. But that was futile. What could I do? What life could I have? The authorities knew I was the real thief. They would arrest me eventually. All my grandfather had done was prolong the inevitable. I wondered if they tortured people in prison. I convinced myself I had heard that before. From whom I couldn't recall.

I remained on the cold floor with my arms outstretched. I could no longer reach for my grandfather. He had gone.

How would I explain to my mother what happened to him?

Envy licked the tears from my face. But new tears formed to replace them.

I sensed Gabriel was near me, but I couldn't see him.

I didn't know if it was my broken heart, or the effects of the poisonous gas, but my body wanted to sink into the floor and stay there forever. My eyes wanted to close and never open again. To be entombed in the House of Books, haunting the balconies, and reading day after day forever, was my wish in that moment.

I woke in the darkness. Envy lay next to me.

The ground beneath me felt soft. I realised I lay upon the makeshift bedding in the snug, on the top floor of the House of Books.

The memory of my grandfather being dragged away returned to torment me.

Gabriel lit a lantern.

'Where did you go?' I asked.

'I couldn't risk being seen. I'm sorry.'

'Why not?' I snapped. 'Why can't you be seen? Why can't you go outside? Why aren't you like a normal person? What do you want from Eden? What do you want from me?'

Gabriel looked at the floor. I sensed I had wounded him again. He may have had a secret, but he wasn't a liar, unlike the authorities.

'Sorry,' I said, 'I know I'm a fine one to talk about being a normal person.'

I thought about how Doctor Hartnell had explained autism to me; did that make me odd compared to the rest of the townsfolk? I thought Gabriel was odd, but how did everyone else see me? Thinking about Doctor Hartnell reminded me of all the books in her office, which were stolen from my favourite place.

'He's gone for good, you know,' I said.

'We'll get him back.'

'How?' I asked. 'People don't ever come back. They get sent to prison and no one ever sees them again.'

'We'll find a way.'

'There is no way. That's how it is. They've taken him away for good,' I said, on the verge of tears and knowing it was all my fault my grandfather had gone.

'I'm sorry. I never should have shown you the House of Books. I shouldn't have interfered in your life.'

'But I love the House of Books,' I said. I just hated that my love for the House of Books had gotten my family into trouble.

'Do you know where the prison is?' Gabriel asked.

'No one knows where the prison is. I told you, people go in and never come out again. There's no one who can tell us,' I said, knowing my grandfather would die somewhere horrible.

'You said before that you think it might be underground,' Gabriel said, 'but it could be somewhere deep in the forest.'

I glared at Gabriel. It made sense. But the forest was vast.

'What are you thinking?' I asked.

'I'm wondering if I could locate it.'

'On your own?'

'No, I'd need help.'

'From whom?' I asked, wondering if now he might tell me about his people: the forest people.

'Don't worry about it,' he said. 'Get some rest tonight. Or would you like me to take you home?'

'What time is it?' I asked.

'The clock struck nine a short while ago.'

'It's been an hour since curfew,' I said. 'We can't leave.'

'We could try and sneak out. We could try another bridge. But you'd have to go home the long way around.'

'Eden has nightwatchmen on all the bridges. And I don't know what to say to my mum,' I said, thinking not only would I have to explain to her that my grandfather will never return home, I might also have to tell her about the House of Books.

'She'll wonder where you both are,' Gabriel said.

'I know. I don't know what's worse. Her worrying where we are, or her knowing Grandad is in prison because of me,' I said, as the tears began to sting my eyes again.

'He wanted to go,' Gabriel said.

'Because he didn't want me to go.'

'Exactly.'

'Why couldn't you risk being seen?' I asked again, more calmly. 'Why do you even stay in the House of Books? Who are you hiding from?'

'I'm not hiding.'

'You are hiding. You must be. You won't go outside during the day. I've only ever seen you outside after dark. You didn't want those soldiers to see you. But you might have frightened them if they had seen you, they might've thought you were a forest spirit, like I did the first time I saw you. Then they would have run out, and they wouldn't have taken my grandad away. You're hiding from someone and you won't tell me who.'

Gabriel stood and went over to the nearest window and pulled the shutter back a little.

'Clear night,' he said. 'I wanted the surprise to be special. Now it'll probably be more like a consolation prize.'

'I forgot about the surprise. But I see you've changed the subject.'

'I think we both need to think about something else for tonight. There's nothing we can do for your grandfather in the present moment.'

Gabriel was right, of course. I couldn't think straight. My worrying about my grandfather was causing me to feel nauseous.

'Would you like to see the other surprise?' Gabriel asked. 'It's at the top of the staircase and out on the roof.'

'You want me to go out on the roof?' I said, alarmed.

'Then into another building. It's not far.'

We climbed the spiral staircase to a door which brought us out onto the roof.

Envy trotted across to the small tower.

'She knows where I'm taking you,' Gabriel said, chuckling, until it turned into a cough.

He unlocked the door on the tower, and we found another wrought-iron spiral staircase. Only this one was narrow. Envy had no problem bounding up.

I ascended before Gabriel and emerged in a large octagonal room lit by moonlight coming through eight tall windows. Something ominous lay in wait in the middle of the room.

Gabriel appeared with the lantern, the light from which highlighted a monster. It was the length of a man and looked like a giant rifle pointing towards the sky.

Gabriel mounted some steps to reach one of the tall windows.

He pulled the sash window down, exposing the room to the elements. The night sky poured in, and the indigo heavens gleamed with a multitude of stars. When he clambered away from the steps, he manoeuvred the monster through the open window.

'I hope I still have this in focus,' Gabriel said.

'What?'

'The telescope.'

'That's a telescope?'

'Yes. Would you like to see a planet?' he asked. 'Here, look through this lens.'

I managed some hesitant steps towards the monster. Envy followed.

'You won't see anything just hovering before it,' Gabriel said.

I don't know what I thought would happen. Perhaps I thought a real monster hid inside the monster, and it would punch me in the eye when I peered through the lens. It felt like such an odd concept: peering through an object to observe the night sky.

'Can you see anything?' Gabriel asked. 'Is it still in focus?'

'I'm trying to concentrate.'

'Do I need to adjust the settings?'

'Gabriel, be quiet,' I said, thinking how I have never been able to concentrate when someone was nattering in my ear.

'Sorry,' he said.

'I can see a really bright ...'

'Yes?'

'I think it might be Jupiter,' I said.

'Good. That is Jupiter, and his four largest moons. The Galilean ones.'

'Named after the man who discovered them?' I asked.

'That's right.'

'The four moons, which were the only moons I thought Jupiter had?'

'Right again.'

'One of the four stars is larger than the others,' I said.

'That's Ganymede. Ganymede is the largest moon in the solar system. It has its own magnetic field. Because it has a magnetosphere, when the solar winds hit Ganymede, it causes an aurora at both poles, just like on Earth.'

I must have looked confused.

'Ah, you haven't read up on auroras yet ... An aurora is one of the most mesmerising spectacles you can see on Earth. Ribbons of green and blue, sometimes purple, and even red, stream through the darkness and dance across the sky. Wouldn't it be incredible to see one on a moon?'

'You want to see an au-rora on a moon?'

'Not just an aurora,' Gabriel said. 'Wouldn't it be amazing to stand on Ganymede and see Jupiter filling the sky, with all its swirling storm patterns? Or on Saturn's moon Enceladus, which orbits a path within the rings of ice.'

Now I really was confused.

'I think it would,' Gabriel continued. 'If you had an opportunity, would you like to go to Ganymede?'

'Why would I want to go to Ganymede? It's become apparent I don't even know Earth. I don't know our moon. I read the other day our moon has some of the highest mountains in the solar system. I didn't know we had mountains on our moon. I didn't know anything.'

'Fair point.'

'Space fascinates me but ... it's terrifying at the same time,' I said.

‘Are you no longer interested in space beyond Earth’s moon?’

‘Yes, I always have been. But there’s so much on Earth I don’t know. And ...’

‘And?’

‘My grandad could be inside the prison now. That’s it. The rest of his life will now be spent in prison. He doesn’t deserve that. My dad’s gone, and now my grandad. I don’t know if I should tell my mum about the House of Books. But the authorities might assume she does already know. They might take her away, too. Then I’ll have lost all my family.’

Envy fell asleep in my lap, as Gabriel and I sat upon the blankets in the snug and read until the early hours. I believe Gabriel deliberately distracted me, as he jumped from one subject to another. He showed me pictures of the auroras. He explained how the mesmerising light display was due to Earth’s magnetic field deflecting radiation from space. Radiation was another danger lurking in space. I felt relieved the magnetic field offered us this protection.

Gabriel also thought I should know about Eastern and Western philosophy. We spent most of the night reading about various philosophers. Eastern philosophy began in the countries of India and China. It started with the great Eastern religious founders: Buddha, Lao Tzu, and Confucius. Western philosophy started with the ancient Greeks, including Pythagoras, Socrates, and Plato. Like me, the first Greek philosophers were interested in cosmology. A photograph in the Western philosophy book depicted a bust of Socrates. This reminded me of one of the half statues on the ground floor. I thought it odd they were named busts. After that I don’t recall anything. I think my eyes could no longer stay open.

When I woke in the early hours, Gabriel had gone. Perhaps he didn't ever really sleep in the House of Books. I had just assumed he did.

A slither of moonlight came through an open shutter, and the light bounced off a glass of water on a small table. I gulped some of it down. It had a metallic aftertaste. I recognised it as the water from the square's drinking fountain. I wondered where Gabriel could have found the glass. Then I recalled he had found a kitchen on our first foray in the House of Books. He had also left a bowl of water for Envy. But she seemed more interested in nestling into me as we lay in the snug.

Gabriel materialised once the sun rose. But he had a weakened appearance.

'Are you sick?' I asked.

'I'm fine,' he sniffed.

'But your eyes look red.'

'I'm just tired.'

'Didn't you sleep?'

'Things on my mind,' he said. 'Do you need breakfast? I have some bread I salvaged from a bakery. It's yesterday's bread. But it should be okay.'

I rummaged in my pocket for some coupons I thought I might have.

'I should have enough coupons to purchase something,' I said.

'Like what?'

'Maybe a small jar of jam for the bread.'

'Sounds good,' Gabriel said, nodding.

'Have you been living off bread alone?'

'Mostly.'

'That must be why you're not well.'

'I'm fine.'

He was lying. He did not look fine at all. He had been coughing and sneezing on and off for at least two days, and he thought I wouldn't notice he was sick. He had the sort of pallor which would usually leave you no choice but to call for a doctor. However, I no longer trusted Doctor Hartnell. Plus, I couldn't alert anyone to Gabriel. If Gabriel was actually hiding from someone, it might be because he was in trouble with his authorities, just like I was. Therefore, I had to protect him. I didn't want Gabriel to be taken from me, too.

I left Envy with Gabriel and ventured outside to purchase the jam.

A couple of soldiers watched me with intent while I took long strides across the square wearing my grandfather's trousers and grandmother's scarf. I thought of the soldiers who dragged my grandfather away. I couldn't recall their faces. It could have even been these soldiers who gawped at me now for all I knew. I don't believe they noticed which alleyway I had sprung from. I would have to go back to the House of Books the long way around, as it appeared they were spying on me. I jogged away from them towards the shops.

When I returned to the House of Books with some jam, Gabriel and Envy lay snuggled together on the makeshift bed. My arrival on the top floor awoke them both. Gabriel's eyes appeared worse.

'Do you need medicine?' I asked.

'I probably just need some sleep.'

'I'll have to see what medicines we have at home. How do you feel? Do you have a headache? Do you feel hot? Cold?'

Gabriel chuckled.

'I'm tired,' he said. 'Don't worry about me.'

'But I am worried.'

'I can tell. Thank you for your concern. However, we should eat. We'll both feel better with some food inside.'

We tore small pieces from the loaf and dunked them in the

jam jar. It would have looked uncivilised to any prying eyes. But I was hungry, and already used to eating insufficiently at times, with little to no variation. The war rationing had made me grateful for the simple things. The sweet jam was a little treat. Until I thought of my grandfather again. I wondered what he would be eating for breakfast. If he would be eating anything at all. I wondered if they would starve him. He was an old man. Perhaps the prison guards would consider him almost dead, and therefore not worth keeping alive. If they hadn't considered starvation, I wondered if they would shoot him, just to get it over with? Then what would happen to his body? Would they cremate him in a proper ceremony? Or would they dump his body somewhere?

As I strolled around the heaving balconies, a book lying face up on a small table caught my attention. I hadn't noticed it before and wondered if Gabriel had placed it there. The book had gold lettering against a black cover. It was called *The Truth*. The cover material felt odd to me. When I rubbed my hand one way the cloth cover appeared smooth. When I ran it the other way the cloth felt rough, and it caused me to grit my teeth. The texture disagreed with me. But I found the book intriguing. It was a slim book. I would've said less than two hundred pages.

I returned to Gabriel and the snug. I was about to examine the weird-looking volume further when the House of Books plunged into a gloom as the skylight disappeared in the darkness. A flash of white and a bellowing roar brought another deluge outside. The eerie song arrived with tiny orbs of light. The House of Books came alive once more. Shadows moved on every floor and the spectres floated above.

I considered the shadow figures. Were they the real ancestral spirits? Had they all come back to haunt us because they had lived here in the past? Were the ancestors of the First Ancestors angry that their history had been eradicated? Therefore they had risen from the dead?

Gabriel grabbed my hand.

'I want to show you something.'

We sped from the House of Books into the torrential storm. Aside from the shadow figures and the dancing spectres above, huge dark shapes hung in clouds. The bitter acrid scent spliced with sulphur hit my nostrils again.

I still clutched the book. Envy had followed, but I sensed she wasn't keen to be outside.

The townsfolk scarpered through the square screaming and darting for shelter.

Between the gas attack, the earthquakes, and the storms which brought forth shadows and spectres, and now larger dark shapes, I think everyone had gone mad.

The old citadel swam within an ocean. Shadows dashed through me. The orbs of light floated through the deluge.

I paused at the fountain.

The three figures had a new lease of life. They were no longer damaged and decayed. Their faces now obviously tilted skywards and they bloomed. Their arms were raised and each figure held hands with their neighbour to form a circle. Each figure wore robes and had wings protruding from their backs, which spread outwards and formed an outer circle. These were *angels*. The fountain glowed through the pouring rain, as though it were a bright summer day above the statues.

The whole citadel shimmered a golden hue through the storm.

I turned to face the broken stone block, and found it unbroken. The statue of a man stood upon the block. He also wore a robe, and he had a strange-looking hat atop his head. It looked like a band with several crosses on it.

Gabriel pulled me away. He too radiated with a renewed vibrancy. It was as though the arrival of the floating spectres had healed him somehow. I considered he must be linked to them, even though he appeared human.

We hurried past the Guildhall and into the temple gardens. But the temple flower gardens had disappeared.

Within the golden light a lush grass had sprung all around. Stones sat upright in the ground, marking the final resting places of the long since deceased. Those ancestors before my ancestors. I thought again about the burials. In a way it did make some sense. They wished to be buried outside the house of God, while their bodies nurtured the earth.

The Temple of the First Ancestors sang.

My heart soared as we dashed through the huge open door and the voices from a choir intensified.

Light beamed through the stained-glass windows. Statues of robed figures appeared all around. Shadow figures sat within the pews. Voices rose and fell in harmony. The organ played. Spectres swooped above. It seemed they wore the same attire as the statues. Their light shone down along with the tiny orbs. Their arms stretched out towards the heavens, and large wings unfurled from their backs.

Gabriel guided me through the nave, and we passed all the things I had read about in the cathedral guide book: the font, the pulpit, and the altar, behind which a giant cross with a naked man hung. I stopped to behold the man and knew this to be the man named Jesus. He was either dying or dead. He had suffered multiple injuries. Large nails protruded from his palms and feet. His head lolled under a crown of thorns which pierced his flesh. Blood dripped from his forehead and into his eyes. Blood seeped from the open wounds across his torso and the vicious wounds from the nails which pinned him to the cross. I had never seen a dying man before. I thought again of my grandfather. He must be dying now. Not upon a cross, but perhaps upon a dirty floor. I was about to cry. But Gabriel yanked me away.

As we approached the choir of shadow figures, the huge rose window loomed above in the north transept. A rainbow of colour danced across the stone floor as the voices from the choir reached a crescendo. We left the choir behind and sped through the presbytery, aisles, and chapels.

A bell, much louder than the bell inside the clock tower above the Guildhall, rang out. More bells began to clang within the heavens. I cowered into Gabriel, having never heard such a cacophony. He explained the huge bells were situated high up in the main tower. They were rung in celebration. It was supposed to be a joyous event. Not a terrifying one.

I wanted to be inside every building in the citadel when the angels came. I wanted to behold historic Eden, or rather Stonburh. I wanted to know what everything had meant in the past. Other than the authorities, why did no one in Eden appear to know our true past? Why had the true past been hidden from us? What was so terrible about it that our authorities had kept it hidden? It didn't appear terrible to me. It appeared magnificent, like Gabriel. He was something special.

As curfew took effect and the few remaining stragglers of townsfolk left the citadel, Envy and I vacated the House of Books. As I hadn't brought a basket in with me the day before, I tucked my new book, *The Truth*, into the band of my trousers.

I fancied a stroll rather than taking the last omnibus.

Envy and I danced through the old citadel streets. We floated over the river via the gatehouse bridge. We skipped past the fire station and through the main street with townhouses framing us on both sides.

The gas lamps illuminated the streets. Cosy lights glowed from inside homes.

The townsfolk had also lit bonfires on the wide pavements. Smoke was also rising from behind the houses, so I presumed they had also lit bonfires in their gardens, too.

My elation ended when I glanced up and saw a shadow behind a window.

The shadow stared down at me.

Two soldiers appeared from a doorway and Envy growled.

'The mayor would like a word,' one said, as he grabbed my arm.

'But I don't want a word with him,' I said, as I struggled against his grip.

'So, you run this town, do you?'

This was it. I was going to prison for sure now.

'But … my dog?' I said.

'Get out of here,' the other soldier yelled at Envy.

She trembled and peered at me with pleading eyes.

'It'll be okay,' I said. 'Go home.'

She whined.

'I said get out of here,' the soldier bellowed again, as he kicked her in the side.

She yelped and bolted a short distance, before turning back to plead with me once more.

'Go, Envy. Go,' I begged her.

She sprinted through the street. Heading for home, I hoped. A home I would never see again. I would never see Envy again. Or my mother, and father. If my father ever returned from the war, I wouldn't be there to greet him.

Chapter 10

The soldiers ushered me through the mayor's private residence. I had never set foot in one of the townhouses before. The mayor's home was one of the largest of the townhouses. I should have realised someone important resided within. Or should I say, someone full of their own self-importance.

His hallway had an air of opulence matched only by the Grand Tea Room. More paintings lined the entrance hall than we had in my entire cottage. Even more paintings lined the staircase. Every one of them sat within a gilded frame. They didn't depict simple flowers or homely settings. The paintings were of women. As the soldiers led me up the staircase, I noticed that all the women let their hair flow. They wore robes or long flowing gowns. Some were of lone women, while others depicted groups of mostly women. Some of the groups may have even danced. They reminded me of the Renaissance paintings I had been studying recently. The mayor had paintings the likes of which I had only seen in those books. If those books were forbidden, then the paintings were forbidden. But not for him.

We reached the first floor. I came face to face with a painting of a woman swaddled in gold, playing an instrument I didn't recognise. She had long red hair like me.

A soldier tapped on a door.

'Enter,' the mayor said.

I followed the soldiers into the most sumptuous room I had ever seen.

The mayor stood before a roaring fire, which spat and crackled within a stone surround. Plush red curtains draped two large windows. A huge patterned rug lay under a desk. One of the walls lay hidden behind large floor-to-ceiling bookcases. The three remaining walls featured more Renaissance-style artworks within gilded frames.

Two busts perched precariously upon plinths. They faced each other from either side of the room, although I now stood between their stare-off.

A male voice sang from one corner of the room. It came from what looked like a bell on its side. The sound was not too dissimilar to the harmonious choir I had heard earlier in the cathedral.

'Take a seat my dear,' the mayor said, as he indicated the chair in front of his desk.

The chair wasn't like any other chair I had ever sat in. It too had a gilded frame, and seemed far too luxurious for someone of my low status.

'You can leave us,' he said to the soldiers.

I removed my scarf. The room felt warm, and the mayor knew who I was. I couldn't hide from him. I wondered why he hadn't had me arrested sooner. Perhaps he had wanted to make sure he had the right woman? Now he knew he did.

He progressed towards me, but then stopped to draw back one of the heavy-looking curtains, and he peered outside.

'Do you know why the townsfolk have lit bonfires?' he asked.

I shook my head.

'To drive the evil spirits away,' he said. 'Superstition and fear rule their minds.'

I think he sneered as he turned away from the window and took a seat at his desk.

'Can I offer you a drink? I have tea, coffee ...'

'No thank you.'

The mayor poured himself a light brown liquid from a decanter into a thick cut glass. The glasses we had in the cottage were only thin, and easily broken. My grandparents had had a large glass bottle, similar to this decanter, but my grandmother had kept flowers in it. It used to sit upon the dresser in the sitting room, until it fell and smashed to pieces during one of the earthquakes.

My eyes wandered over to one of the bookcases briming with red, green, brown, and gold bound volumes. None of them had the little white label on their spines. Therefore these books were not from the House of Books.

I got distracted by the singing voice in the corner, as it had changed from male to female. The female voice soared above a distorted hiss, which was also coming from the strange-looking bell.

'Do you know what that is?' the mayor asked.

I shook my head.

'It's called a gramophone. It's playing a musical recording made in ... the nineteen forties, I think.'

He smiled at me. But I didn't recognise it as friendly. I sensed the falseness. I wondered if I was getting better at reading people.

'You're not going to ask how I could possibly have a recording from the nineteen forties? A date which, to you, must be in the future?'

'No, sir.'

'You're not going to ask what a musical recording is?'

I bit my lip.

‘Of course, I know why you don’t ask these questions,’ he said. ‘You already know.’

I stared at a beautiful painting above the fireplace. It featured a woman with a fair complexion and long flowing red hair. Red hair wasn’t common. Not in Eden anyway. Yet the mayor had at least two paintings of women with red hair. This woman was swathed in green. The whole painting gave the impression of having stepped into a forest and stumbling upon this woman before the dog-headed humans and other monsters arrived. I would say her features appeared more handsome than delicate. As were the two faces either side of her at the top of the painting. The three female faces reminded me of the painting outside the room, with the woman in gold. I assumed both paintings were by the same artist. Maybe both paintings featured the same woman.

‘It’s glorious, isn’t it. It’s from the Victorian period. *La Ghirlandata* it’s called. Painted by one of the Pre-Raphaelites. Have you heard of them?’

‘No,’ I said, thinking it was a shame I hadn’t discovered the painting sooner. If I had seen it in a book in the House of Books, I would have taken the book home, propped it up on my writing bureau, and left it permanently open on that page.

‘You haven’t got that far into your studies yet?’ the mayor said, leaning across the desk, as though he could see inside my brain and obtain what I really knew. ‘You’ve perhaps only covered the Renaissance?’

I think the mayor’s tone had an element of what my grandfather referred to as sarcasm. I sank into the chair. I was out of my depth, and the mayor knew it.

‘It was painted by Dante Gabriel Ros—’

‘Gabriel?’ I said, suddenly interested.

‘Yes. Dante Gabriel Rossetti. Have you come across him in some other capacity?’

‘No. I just know the name Gabriel.’

I could feel my palms moisten. How did the mayor know

about Gabriel? He had my grandfather, and now he wanted Gabriel, too.

'Gabriel is a biblical name,' he said, nodding.

I must have looked confused.

'Meaning from the Bible,' he clarified. 'Have you heard of the Bible?'

'Yes,' I said, sheepishly, thinking the mayor probably already knew I had a copy of the Bible from the House of Books. I thought about the peculiar tome which mentioned the Garden of Eden. Was that supposed to be a real place?

'Gabriel is an archangel in the Bible,' the mayor continued.

'Gabriel is an angel?' I asked. He must have thought I was slow, but I didn't mean the Gabriel in the Bible. I meant my Gabriel.

'Archangel,' he said. 'The two women at the top of the painting are angels, too. But not archangels.'

I considered all this. The floating spectres were possibly angels, and Gabriel was possibly an archangel. He came to Earth and showed me the House of Books.

'Do you know about angels?' the mayor asked.

'Not really,' I said, beginning to panic, wondering how much he did actually know. He must have discovered Gabriel. Perhaps it was the mayor who Gabriel was hiding from?

'But you do know some things you shouldn't know,' the mayor said.

I squirmed in the chair. The mayor probably thought I felt uncomfortable from his line of questioning. I was uncomfortable. *The Truth* dug in under my ribcage. I stretched my stomach and breathed in, trying to get the book to loosen further down under the band of my trousers.

'Who showed you the library?' he asked.

'No one,' I said, thinking that maybe he didn't know about Gabriel specifically. Was it just coincidence that he had mentioned the name Gabriel because of the painting?

'You entered the building all alone, of your own free will?'

'Yes,' I said, as the book dislodged from under a rib, and I breathed with ease.

'Your grandfather—'

'How is he?'

'He's fine. Your grandfather has never been in trouble before. He may have almost found himself in trouble when he was a child, but nothing came of it. For him.'

'What do you mean?' I asked.

'He discovered something.'

'The piece of bone?'

The mayor's eyes flared.

'So, your grandfather has spoken of this with you?'

I could have grabbed *The Truth* from the band of my trousers and smacked myself in the face with it. But instead I stared at the rug, as the voice on the gramophone transitioned into a different female. If my grandfather had not been condemned to die soon, he more than likely was now, and because of me.

The mayor leaned back in his chair.

'I cannot decide whether your grandfather is an old fool, or a very brave man,' he said.

Neither could I, I thought. It seemed he sat somewhere between both, depending on how upset I was with him. Or with myself. Or with the lies of Eden.

'Would you like to see your grandfather?'

'Is he here?' I asked.

'No, my dear. He is somewhere usually no one can visit. I am offering you a chance to see him.'

I wanted to see my grandfather. I also craved the complete truth. Not just a book about the truth. Although at what cost, I couldn't say.

I stood in the doorway of the mayor's townhouse, while bonfires raged around me.

A gentle clip-clopping announced the arrival of the mayor's ornate horse-drawn carriage in the main street.

A soldier strode ahead to open the door for me.

I stepped inside. The mayor followed.

I thought I might be dreaming. My body moved, but my brain yelled at me to stop. Something else controlled my limbs.

We sat in silence during the carriage ride through Eden. The little curtains were drawn back. A comforting amber glow radiated from behind the windowpanes of most of the townhouses.

We flitted past the last of the townhouses and turned off the main street. Then we sped along the winding streets of the more modest homes.

We headed for the side of town where my cottage lay, but we turned off before the cottages and the horses thundered onwards for the outer wall.

The driver steadied the horses and I heard him step down from the carriage. The outer wall stood before us and water sploshed below. I peered down from the carriage window. We had stopped on a little bridge. The wall directly in front of us had a gatehouse, not unlike those on my favourite bridge leading into the old citadel, only on a smaller scale.

The driver spoke with a nightwatchman.

The gatehouse door opened and the driver returned to his seat atop the carriage and cracked his whip.

My body was flung back into the lavish furnishings of the coach's interior as we hurtled into the dark forest. The trees swallowed the carriage. Branches appeared to beat the roof when we got too close. I could hear the river and assumed we followed the exact snaking path.

The mayor glared at me as though he knew my thoughts. He knew he had me. It was a game to him. He knew I knew it was the end for me. He knew I had ventured into the House of Books. Now he dragged me through the forest. Which was forbidden. Which meant it was a one-way journey. He was transporting me to my death. He may well let me see my grandfather. But then I would die. He toyed with me in the same way a cat plays with a mouse. But the poor mouse is never a willing participant in the game. The mayor had won.

I wondered if Doctor Hartnell had conversed with him. Had she served me up as mouse of the day?

The forest no longer appeared inviting. I was convinced the dark leaves hid a myriad of beasts. It didn't ring with pleasant birdsong. The darkness caused it to whisper and jeer in the wind. It had devoured my grandfather.

I thought about the large dogs which could rip your head off. I wondered how anyone knew of them really. If someone had gone into the forest years ago and lost their head, how would we know? They wouldn't have survived to tell anyone about it. Perhaps the tales of giant dogs and dog-headed humans were just that, tales. Perhaps the tales had not originated with the townsfolk. Perhaps they had originated from the authorities. They didn't want us to venture into the forest. My grandfather was right. I should have always questioned the things I had been told.

Rain spat and then pelted off the roof of the carriage. I reflected on my actions that evening and concluded I hadn't thought it through properly.

The carriage jolted to a halt.

Flaming torches hung from sconces upon the wall before us and lit an entrance gate. Above the torches I observed an imposing dark stone building of sharp edges and twisting turrets which disappeared into the rain clouds.

The driver cracked his whip, and may have cursed as he did so. Even the horses didn't want to enter this sinister black fortress. They trudged through the gateway.

We arrived in a torch-lit courtyard. How such a monstrous place rotted away within the forest was beyond me.

Through the rain I noted that the windows were not really windows, but the narrowest of openings amongst the fortified walls. My heart sunk to know my grandfather deteriorated behind one of those tiny slithers, open to the elements.

I thought I detected the voices of tormented souls within the rain. As though a thousand men wailed behind those appalling excuses for windows.

The carriage door sprang open, and a man in a tall hat and wearing a dark uniform with lots of buttons appeared. He nodded at the mayor before turning his attention to me.

'Come on then, I haven't got all night,' he said.

I resigned myself to my fate and stepped out into the driving rain. My boots squelched in the muddy ground of the courtyard.

'Follow me,' he said, as he led me to a wide door.

The carriage driver cracked his whip and the horses drove the mayor away at speed. I presumed the poor horses couldn't get away fast enough.

The rain ran down the back of my neck and chilled my spine. At least I was heading inside. But inside to what? A monstrous stronghold and a tiny cell with a miniscule window?

Another man stood by the door, another sat behind a desk, and another lingered by an internal door holding a set of keys. They were all wearing the same uniform as the man who ushered me inside. It was navy, and the jacket had an excessive number of gold buttons down the front. This was obviously the uniform of a prison guard. I noted that every prison guard was of fighting age, but like the soldiers in the citadel, none had gone to the town of Frontline. Or perhaps, like the injured soldier from the square, they had returned?

The guard who had collected me from the courtyard approached the guard with the keys.

'Take her to the stars,' he said, before turning to wink at me.

How did he know I liked the stars? What else did he know about me?

The guard with the keys directed me through a labyrinth of dank corridors which lay in utter darkness, other than the lantern he held aloft. I crossed my hands over my lower abdomen and held *The Truth* in place under the band of my trousers. The last thing I needed was for the book to drop through a trouser leg.

The tormented voices I had heard through the rain rang louder in the corridors. The cries and whispering came from behind every bolted wooden door we passed.

Black eyes stared at me through small barred openings at the top of each door. The dark stone walls and floor glistened with damp in the lantern light. A steady drip, dripping of rainwater from the ceiling accompanied the cries.

The guard handed me over to another guard.

We climbed stone steps within an icy tower and exited onto another labyrinth of equally grim corridors. I was passed over to another guard and he led me to more stone steps, and another labyrinth of corridors.

On each floor I was handed over to a new guard. The prison was more expansive than I could have imagined. There were innumerable men behind those doors. Why weren't they fighting? I considered how all the townsfolk could be imprisoned within the walls and there would still be room. I also considered that if anyone ever managed to escape from a cell, they would never find the way out of the warren of despair. Freedom from the cell would be futile.

Another guard waited for me at the end of the passage. He turned to face me as I approached. In the flickering light of his lantern, I realised half his face was gone. I stared at the horror for a short moment, before a combination of sickness and knowing it was rude prevented me from staring anymore.

I followed the man with half a face. He struggled to climb

the next set of stone steps with his walking stick, while holding his lantern. He stopped for a short rest every few steps, but onwards we climbed, past wide wooden doors on every level. I wondered if we had now arrived within the rain cloud. I also wondered if my grandfather had been expected to climb hundreds of steps like this injured man. I wondered if all the guards were damaged from the war in some way.

My thighs stiffened first, followed by my shins. I was relieved when the man with half a face paused at the top of the steps, until he gave me such an odd grin, with what remained of his mouth, that I knew it to be malicious. I no longer felt any sympathy for him.

'Your floor,' he said.

He unbolted the wide door which stood before us, and we entered a small corridor.

I was confronted by four cells.

Someone shuffled behind the first door on the left. From the darkness of their confinement, I sensed that they watched me.

The man with half a face held his lantern aloft and unlocked the first door on the right.

'Welcome to your new home,' he said, as he nudged me into a dark cell.

I examined the tiny slither of a window. My only source of light came from the torches far below and the lantern currently held up to the small barred opening at the top of my cell door.

The cell had a small bed in one corner and a bucket in another. Straw covered the floor.

'Night, night,' the man with half a face said, as he locked me in.

He disappeared with the light and bolted the outer door in the corridor.

'Andromeda? What are you doing here?' a croaky male voice asked.

It was my grandfather. He occupied the cell opposite mine.

He shoved his bony fingers through the bars of the little opening in his door.

'Grandad,' I said, with a sob.

I broke down. I couldn't hold my guilt inside anymore. I was relieved they hadn't killed him yet, but it broke my heart to know he had been marched through that maze and dragged to the top of this damp tower.

'If this is your idea of a rescue mission,' he said, 'I'm afraid it won't work.'

'Grandad, I'm sorry.'

'You're sorry the rescue has ended in disaster?'

'Sorry you're in here because of me.'

'And now you're in here regardless of my actions. Why are you in here?' he asked.

'The mayor wanted to see me, and—'

'That bastard. If I ever get out of here alive—'

'How are they treating you? Did they beat you?'

'A little,' he said. 'It's good to see you on your feet. Last time I saw you, you were a bit groggy.'

'The gas knocked me out.'

'Yes, but it should've killed you. That would've been the intention if the enemy dropped the gas.'

'You don't think the enemy dropped the gas?'

'No. The gas wasn't poisonous,' he said. 'We would've all died that day if it was. It simply knocked people out temporarily if they breathed enough gas in. What would be the point of that?'

Someone else stirred in the darkness. They were in the cell adjacent to my grandfather. The cell door juddered a moment, as though someone leaned upon it. I had the feeling someone else watched my door with intent.

'Think about it,' my grandfather continued. 'A gas attack hits the day after they said there would be an attack imminently. Odd how they said we should expect one, and what do you know, gas everywhere. Call me suspicious.'

'Are you saying our authorities did that to us?' I asked, thinking that the lies we had been told were bad enough, but gassing the townsfolk on purpose appeared extreme.

'Aren't you suspicious? You should be,' my grandfather said. 'Especially since it was your friend who carried us inside, and the gas didn't have any effect on him.'

'Yes, but that's because—'

'He's on their side?' he asked.

'No, he isn't,' I said, thinking I had never considered Gabriel my enemy.

'Do you really trust him?' my grandfather asked.

'Yes. Envy likes him, too. I hope she's okay.'

'Why wouldn't she be okay?'

'She ran off. I told her to go. A soldier kicked her,' I said, thinking how much I wanted to hug her right now, not just for her comfort, but for mine.

'She'll have gone home,' my grandfather said. 'She can look after herself. You, on the other hand …'

'Why would our own authorities release the gas?' I asked. 'It would be a waste of a weapon. They would need it to use on the northern region. Even if it only disarms people temporarily. We need all our resources for the war.'

A man's laughter came from the cell next to my grandfather. He either laughed at me or to himself.

'Andromeda,' my grandfather said, sighing. 'I love you, but sometimes …'

'The war is costly as it is,' I concluded.

'Andromeda …' my grandfather sounded almost exasperated suddenly. Angry even. 'There is no war!'

Chapter 11

Lie upon lie upon lie. My life. My town. Everything a lie. Even the war was a lie. But this wasn't Eden's biggest secret. It couldn't be. The *war* had been going on for six years. Eden had kept other secrets for far longer.

'Why would they lie about a war?' I asked.

'So that you remain living in fear of what's out there,' said the man watching from the darkness.

'Who are you?' I asked.

'A friend.'

'I don't know you,' I said, wondering how I had managed to accumulate another friend in such a short space of time.

'We met before. Briefly,' the man said.

I squinted at the small barred opening in his black cell door, but in the darkness I couldn't make out any details. Why did this man think he was my friend? I wondered if he was another oddity like Gabriel. Perhaps he was the man I had seen by the ancestral stones in the forest?

'This is Silas,' my grandfather said. 'He was the man in square shouting about a flood, and knowledge lost, before the soldiers removed him. It was the day we went to the Grand Tea Room.'

I recalled the shabby bearded man with bright blue eyes. That incident had been about a week ago. I even recalled the taste of the hot chocolate on my tongue.

'You accused me of knowing what you know, when the soldiers dragged you through the crowd,' I said.

'Was I wrong?' Silas asked.

'Silas is an unusual name,' I said.

'Andromeda is an unusual name, too.'

'My dad chose it.'

'And my father chose mine,' Silas said. 'Therefore, we have something in common. Do you know who and what Andromeda is?'

'A Greek princess and a galaxy,' I said.

Silas laughed.

'You've learned well,' he said.

'But my dad shouldn't have known those things.'

'We shouldn't know anything,' Silas said.

'Where does the name Silas come from?' I asked.

'It's biblical. My father shouldn't have known about the Bible either.'

Silas was the second man I had met with a biblical name. I wondered if all my future friends would have names mentioned in the Bible?

'Are we going to rot away in here?' I asked.

'I expect so, poppet,' my grandfather said. 'All the men of Eden are in here, rotting away it seems.'

'All the men of Eden?' I said with trepidation, as my mind began to whirl.

'Yes,' Silas said. 'Think about all the people who have disappeared down the years. Think about all the men they've sent off to a non-existent war. Where are they? They're all in here. As are all the men from other nearby towns too. Towns we had never heard of, out there surrounded by forest. Just like Eden.'

'My dad is in here?' I shrieked. I thought I was going to be sick. My heart thundered away so vigorously I thought my grandfather and Silas would hear it, too.

'Your father will be somewhere in this stronghold,' Silas said.

'But it's been six years,' I exclaimed. 'My dad's been in *here* for six years?'

I had to lean on the door to stay upright. I now thought I would faint. The lies in Eden ran even deeper than I knew. I couldn't stand to think that my father had been in this despicable place for six years. How many more lies would I uncover? Everything appeared to be a lie. My father must have been crazy to name me after forbidden knowledge. Why hadn't he thought it would get him into trouble?

'I knew the moment I set foot in this place,' my grandfather said. 'I could hear all the men. Then I saw them behind every door. They're all in here. I should have known there was no war. That arrogant, lying, conceited, you-know-what of a mayor. His cronies all stayed in the town. They're all of fighting age.'

'They wouldn't have gone if there was a real war,' Silas concluded. 'They'd have dictated from the sidelines.'

'True, true,' my grandfather said.

'You said they want to keep us living in fear?' I asked Silas.

'It's the only way they can control you,' Silas said. 'You have everything you need according to them. You don't need anything else. Plus, the town is rationing. It has the very basics required in order for the townsfolk to survive. That is all.'

'We've never been free,' my grandfather said. 'Because we have never known the truth. I could cry if I wasn't so angry. All my years. I'm almost ninety. Now I'm about to pass on, I begin to learn what I've always suspected is true.'

'But if you've always suspected something wasn't right with Eden, why didn't you tell your friends, and they would've told their friends, and so on and so on, and before you know it you would've had a whole gathering of townsfolk to confront the authorities,' I said. 'You mentioned some things down the years, but I didn't realise you thought there was something wrong with everything.'

'I suppose I've been a coward,' my grandfather said. 'Most of the time I was fearful of speaking what I believed to be true. Your grandmother used to tell me off for saying things when I did, even in the house. You probably don't remember. I think she was frightened I would be taken away. So I stopped saying things, even at home. I suppose I was also frightened about where I'd end up. But I've ended up here anyway.'

'Why have they put us together?' I asked. 'Is it to torment us?'

'Either they've got no more cells below, or they want us to talk,' my grandfather said. 'They want to know what we know. They're listening in.'

'But the guard left,' I said. 'Unless he's listening behind the door?'

'There could even be someone else in the corridor,' my grandfather said. 'I can't see a thing.'

'Well, we know of one other person listening to us,' I said, no longer knowing who to trust.

Silas laughed again.

'I like your way of thinking,' he said. 'If I wanted to know what someone else knew, I would put myself in the cell next door. However, I was here before both of you. How do I know you're not being retained in here to get more information out of me? Having said that, when I saw you in the square the day I was arrested, you appeared terrified on my behalf.'

'But you were shouting about flooding in front of the soldiers,' I said. 'What happened to you? I mean, what's your story?'

'I was a child, when both my father and uncle disappeared one day. I never saw my uncle again. It wasn't until I got a little older that I began to suspect he'd been taken away. You see, quite often he would tell me stories about Eden. I was young.

I didn't think anything of it. I enjoyed the stories. I thought they were made up. I didn't learn anything like those stories in school. He told me the Earth had shook in anger at some point in the past. People had annoyed her. She sent the previous townsfolk of Eden endless rain. She had the people washed away. Some tried to escape by sitting on the roofs of their homes, but the torrent rose and they too were swept away. But the older I got, the more unsettled I felt in the town. Why did the buildings look ancient? Supposedly they had been built only a few hundred years earlier by the descendants of the First Ancestors. But they were already crumbling away. Surely such buildings would be designed to last? Why were some buildings and places forbidden? Why were we walled in, never to leave? Why do we have curfew? Why were there monsters in the forest? Long story short, I became something of a troublemaker. I have a tendency to talk too much ... I'm doing it now. I obviously discussed my thoughts with the wrong person one night. Men came looking for me when I wasn't home. A neighbour tipped me off. I realised I had put my life in danger, and I made myself disappear. But I didn't go far. I stayed central to everything. It was a fluke really that I chose the building I did. It was as though the ancestors had willed me to go there. I broke into one of the abandoned buildings in the old citadel. Abandoned but still authority owned. I discovered—'

'The House of Books?' I asked, dismissing my earlier concern about who Silas might be.

'Good name. The House of Books became my new home.'

'My friend found your sleeping area,' I said. 'That explains why no one came back. You were in here.'

'Yes. I don't know how long I lived like that. I lived off water from the drinking fountain, which I collected after curfew. Also stale bread and cake thrown out by the bakeries, along with food waste from the cafes ... whatever I could get my hands on. They would throw out good stuff sometimes.'

My heart sunk as I thought of Gabriel, knowing that was how he was surviving, too.

'My world died,' Silas continued. 'A new one was born. A house full of history. I learned many things. One of the abandoned buildings was a library, which I found myself in. The temple was a cathedral. The weird column in the square was a war memorial, dedicated to the fallen soldiers who fought and shed blood in an actual war from centuries long before. Their bodies never came home. They remain within the soil of a foreign land. That's why the war memorial was erected. It gave the families of the war dead somewhere to go to pay respect. That war was called the Great War, at the time. Later it became known as the First World War, because another global war came after it. I learned that two out of every three soldiers died during battle in the Great War. That equated to over sixteen million deaths. Two out of every three men were slaughtered in bloody battle. Let that sink in for a moment.'

I did. It was horrifying. I tried to imagine sixteen million dead men. Their mangled bodies piled up in my mind. Layer upon layer of bloody, broken men lay strewn across each other. They formed a giant tower of death. I felt a terrible pang of guilt for not knowing it had ever happened.

'What a waste of life,' Silas said. 'Around three quarters of a million British men were killed in the Great War. Some of them had come from Stonburh. Most of them never returned. The only thing the townsfolk of Stonburh could do was pay for and erect a memorial, just like all the other towns, citadels, and villages. But what did those men fight for? Because they certainly didn't fight for future generations to forget about them. Or to become ungrateful. Or to be completely ignorant to the fact these men ever existed. A memorial stands in the square, and the townsfolk of Eden have no *memory* of what the object means. Two out of three men died fighting in that bloody war, and Eden can't show respect because the townsfolk were never informed. If Eden were truly fighting a war, it would be because humans don't learn from the mistakes of the past. Or rather the authorities don't learn, since they would be the only people who know. The authorities are the people who have no problem sending thousands of men off to slaughter. Although, from what I read of war in general, it wasn't just the authorities; the richest people in society had no problem with the poorer people in society dying in their thousands either. To lie about Eden being at war, when they know what happens in real war, dishonours those who died years ago even further. To create the lie that Eden is at war is shameful.'

I had to agree. It was truly heartbreaking to hear about a real war. We did dishonour the men who had died. Although it wasn't the townsfolk of Eden's fault that we didn't know about this war. In the past, I was sure I had even seen some of the townsfolk sitting on the steps of the war memorial eating lunch or a snack when the benches were all occupied. I don't think they would have sat upon it had they known it was a memorial to honour the dead.

Silas released a long sigh before continuing.

'Anyway, during my time in the House of Books, I also discovered one of Eden's bridges had collapsed into the river after years of water erosion. That shows you how old the bridge was, and how old the citadel actually is.'

'You said something once about water erosion on the citadel hill, Grandad,' I said, as I tried to glimpse my grandfather's face behind the tiny bars.

'Yes, I did,' he said.

'I think quite a few of the townsfolk have noticed the telltale signs of water corrosion around the hill of the citadel,' Silas confirmed. 'I also found documents stating the town had been flooded many times in the distant past. Your House of Books is a house full of history. Not just of the town, but of the world. A whole wonderous world exists out there.'

'I know,' I said. 'Not one giant piece of land. But numerous lands. Numerous oceans and seas. Numerous people and cultures.'

'Yes, it made sense,' Silas said. 'But then it didn't make sense. They'd lied. I just couldn't work out *why*?'

'Perhaps we'll never know why,' I said, wondering if knowing the reason behind the lies would even make any difference. Although it wouldn't now, for sure, since we were all in prison. I wondered if that meant that both Silas and I had been close to uncovering the reason behind the lies? Prison was our punishment?

'You said you never saw your uncle again,' my grandfather began. 'But presumably you saw your father again?'

Silas huffed.

'Unfortunately, I did see my father again. I say *unfortunately* because he was a changed man when I saw him.'

'Where is he now?' my grandfather asked.

'He's dead.'

'I'm sorry to hear that,' my grandfather said.

No one spoke for a few moments. I think the very real prospect of spending our remaining days and nights in a cramped and damp cell brought death that bit closer. At least for me, I no longer expected to get to a ripe old age.

'Why did they keep all the old buildings?' I finally asked.

'You're not meant to notice what's right in front of you,' Silas said. 'You're not meant to question what you can see.'

'So anyone who uncovers the truth, or even starts to question, disappears?' I said.

'It seems they wish to keep the townsfolk in the dark. We've been fed a dish of lies to keep us from exploring anywhere beyond the outer wall. There *is* something in the forest. But it isn't monsters. Unfortunately, my first journey into the forest was coming here. I can tell you the earthquakes are a lot worse out here, too. It can't be monsters causing earthquakes.'

'And now we'll never know what the monsters really are,' my grandfather said. 'Or why they lied. All three of us, stuck in here. Fat lot of good we are.'

'Why were you shouting in the square on that day when we saw you.' I asked Silas. 'You must've known the soldiers would arrest you?'

'Good question. I was drunk.'

'What's drunk?' I asked, thinking this was another word I had never come across before. 'Is drunk another word for drink? Drinking what?'

Silas laughed.

'I was drunk on a drink, yes,' he said. 'I'd discovered how to brew mead from a book in the library. Very rudimentary stuff, considering I had little equipment, and I had to sneak past the nightwatchmen to get the extra things I required. I made it in the kitchen area of the House of Books. I can't say the mead tasted great. I don't think I managed to get the exact measurements of the ingredients I needed to brew it correctly. I expect you don't know what alcohol is either?'

'No,' I said.

'It's a drink which goes to your head. It appears to dull the senses when you drink enough,' Silas said. 'But you can drink too much of it. It exacerbated my rage and loosened my tongue.'

This notion of alcohol puzzled me. I had never heard of a drink which went to your head. All my drinks went to my stomach. I was sure of it.

'Perhaps on that day you saw me I no longer cared about myself,' Silas said. 'I cared about the townsfolk. I wanted them to know. To start asking questions. I'd spent days and nights reading and occasionally looking out of a window down at the square, annoyed at how everyone appeared to just accept their lives the way they were. Someone had to be like me. I saw you some nights with your dog. But one night turned out a little different from the others.'

‘When the storm came?’ I asked.

‘Yes. That storm brought forth something else. Of which I can’t explain.’

Angels, I thought. I could have told him about Gabriel being an archangel, but I chose not to. If Gabriel had any power, he would find us, and rescue us all from the dark fortress.

We spent the night talking about democracy after Silas mentioned how our rights had been taken away from us, the people. Democracy was born in ancient Athens: Demokratia. The word could be translated as people power. Dēmos meant people. Kratos meant power, or strength, and a similar word to kratos – kratein – meant to rule. Democracy meant the people of ancient Athens had a right to debate and vote. The people held the power. Later, governments were created around the world by the people for the people. The people were sovereign, meaning self-governing. At least that was how it was supposed to be. Governments were created because it was deemed easier to have a smaller group of politicians representing the entire populace. The people could vote for the politicians they preferred, and these politicians formed a government. Politicians were supposed to speak on behalf of the people. The people had a voice through their elected politician and government.

But Silas pointed out that this had not been happening for quite some time, if not centuries, even before our history was rewritten and Stonburh was renamed Eden. Politicians across the land had used and abused the system. They lied about what they would do if they were given the opportunity to form a government. They had no intention of doing what the people wanted. Instead of listening to the people, and speaking out on their behalf, the politicians ignored the people and did what they wanted. The people held no power. The politicians in government held it all. But the government were not supposed to be in *power*, they were supposed to be in *office*. The people gave their authority to create a government to serve the people. Members of the government had taken an oath to serve the people. But the government chose to disregard their oath. The politicians were only interested in themselves. They chose to ignore who they were supposed to represent. They chose to forget who paid their salary. The people paid taxes, and these taxes paid the politicians. The taxes were also supposed to be spent on things the populace required. But sometimes taxes were spent on things the people hadn't voted for.

I thought about how paying taxes that went towards the salaries of the politicians was an interesting concept, as it meant that not only were the people clients of the politicians, the people were also the employers of the politicians. Silas pointed out that this made the politicians beholden to the people, and not the other way around. The politicians should have been accountable to the people, but they blatantly disregarded the wants and needs of the people, which meant the nation and its people didn't concern them. Which meant they were corrupt. This made the democratic vote invalid. The sovereign people and the sovereign nation had been destroyed. The democratic vote was an illusion. There was no democracy.

The people's money didn't just go to main government, it went to local government and civil servants, mayors, the police, basically all jobs under something called the public sector. The public sector were public servants paid by the people to do the job for the people. The public servants were also supposed to provide services that helped the people of the nation, and put the people of the nation at front and centre of everything they did. Therefore, I considered that aside from services, taxes were akin to protection money. The people paid the politicians and other public sector workers through taxes to carry out their interests on their behalf. But it sounded like the politicians had done everything but carry out the wishes of the people of the nation. There really was no democracy.

We talked and talked until I couldn't keep my eyes open any longer. I wouldn't have been able to read my new book, even if I wasn't tired, as I had no lantern to do so. Should a guard come into my cell during the night, I didn't want him to find the book, so I placed *The Truth* under the most deflated pillow I had ever seen.

Once that was done, I wrapped the only bedsheet provided around me, as though I were a caterpillar cocooning myself. I dreamt that I was pursued by monsters in the forest. Some skulked nearby, while others trailed me. But I could never catch sight of them. Then the river rose and swallowed the grass and wild flowers. It rose further and swallowed the trees. Somehow I witnessed all of this and still ended up in my fortress chamber. Water lapped over the dirty mattress. Buoyed by the water, I floated towards the ceiling, my nose pressed against the cold dark stone above me. I must have drowned before I woke up.

A slither of sunlight blazed through the narrow window above my mattress. It shone across the off-white sheet, leaving the rest of the cell in shadow. The way the light only fell upon the bed gave me the impression that the light wanted to transport me away from the desolate place. Unfortunately, the light was incapable of doing such a thing, and I lay there, disheartened.

I watched a spider spin their web in the far corner of the room. He or she had no idea it had set up home inside a prison. It busied itself, spinning a trap to catch an unsuspecting fly. I found myself mesmerised by the web building, instead of repelled by the fact I had spent the night with a spider in the cell. I hoped it hadn't crawled across my face in the early hours. Spiders are curious creatures, but I still thought them hideous. You never see a family of spiders. And with good reason. If you placed a number of spiders in a box and returned to the box the following day, you would find one lone fat spider, floating on its web, surrounded by remnants of partially eaten and silk-encased brethren. But that's what you get for being a cannibalistic insect: self-inflicted solitude. How some people thought spiders charming I will never know. Aside from all those eyes and legs, they devoured their own kind. A bit like the authorities of Eden.

I arose and glanced out the window onto a bright sky. I regarded the other towers of the fortress. They sat a little below the tower I was held in. I strained my eyes and neck to explore the sky either side of my tower. But I couldn't perceive any other towers at the same height, and assumed I was in the tallest one.

I slid away from the window and peered through the tiny opening at the top of my cell door. I found my grandfather staring through his, looking right back at me.

'Morning, poppet,' he said.

He appeared to have aged since he had been held captive. I felt disgust towards the mayor and his cronies, as my grandfather called them. I couldn't understand how they could do this to an old man. I considered his thin skin clinging to his skull, and the prominent veins like rivers on the backs of his hands, while he entwined them around the tiny bars. He wasn't living through his final years. He was living through his final months and days it seemed.

Sometime later, I heard footsteps beyond the wide door which sat between our small corridor of cells and the stone staircase. Then I heard the clanking of metal as the wide door was unbolted. Two guards appeared with trays of food, while another guard stood watch.

'Stand back,' one of the guards said to me.

He unlocked my cell door and placed the tray on the floor. Once the guards had supplied my grandfather and Silas with their breakfast, they swiftly fled and bolted the main door behind them.

The contents of the tray consisted of a small bread roll, a bowl with what looked like tiny pieces of cardboard, which passed as cereal, a small glass of water, and a small mug of some brown liquid.

I raised the lukewarm mug to my nose but couldn't discern the scent.

'Is this tea or coffee?' I asked.

'Neither,' my grandfather said. 'It's watered-down shoe polish.'

I had a thirst, so I downed the brown liquid regardless. My grandfather was correct. A chemical aftertaste defiled my tongue.

I lapped up the water, hoping to wash down the taste of the brown liquid. But this was also tepid for some reason, and had a similarly unpleasant aftertaste.

During the latter part of the morning, another guard approached my cell with a set of jangling keys and unlocked my door.

'You have to come with me, miss,' he said.

'Where are you taking her?' my grandfather hollered.

'I don't want to go to another part of the prison. Can't I stay here with my grandad?' I pleaded.

'She doesn't belong here,' my grandfather said. 'You people are mad with cruelty.'

I ran to my grandfather's cell door and held his hands through the bars. My grandfather began to cry. I forced back my own tears, which brought on an uncomfortable burning sensation around my eyes.

'Just come with me, miss. We don't want any trouble, do we,' the guard said.

It wasn't a question. And no, I didn't want any trouble. I certainly didn't want to get my grandfather into any more trouble. I had already tucked *The Truth* into the band of my trousers. When I exited the cell, I held my hands over my lower abdomen to hold it in place, which must have given the appearance of a dutiful prisoner, rather than a thief of forbidden knowledge.

I went through the same scenario as the night before. Several different guards supervised my descent through the labyrinth-like floors of the prison. But this time it was the man with half a face who became my final guard.

He wore a mask over the deformed part of his face. However, either he or another soldier had painted the mask in what they must have considered a flesh colour. But it didn't quite achieve this. The mask appeared more light orange than the actual peachy paleness of his skin. The painter of the mask had even drawn an eye. I think it was this which gave me the overall feeling of unease. The wide eye didn't blink or move. It stared at me, and I couldn't escape it. The eye knew I had a book on my person. It knew I wasn't to be trusted. But the eye couldn't speak. Therefore, the man with half a face was none the wiser. I wanted to ask him how he had come to lose half his face, since there was no war. But I thought better of it.

We emerged in the courtyard.

Grey clouds had stolen the morning sunshine, sending the place into a gloom. He hobbled over to a black carriage. I hesitated. I pondered whether there could be another prison further out. Especially since this prison was full of men from other towns, not just Eden, according to Silas. Perhaps my father wasted away in a secondary prison. Or a third. There could be numerous prisons across the land. All lurking in the dense forest.

I considered that I might be about to find out where another prison lay.

I glanced up at the immense mass of dark stone, and the tallest tower, which detained my dying grandfather. The fortress had an air of menace even without the rainstorm. The tormented cries from cell windows added to the macabre atmosphere. This was a place for bleak skies and storms in the darker hours.

'Please get in, miss,' said the man with half a face, as his tongue lolled about in his mouth. 'And, miss, please don't do anything stupid.'

I almost laughed. Doing something stupid was all I had done of late. Or rather, doing something stupid because the laws of Eden were stupid. It shouldn't be a crime to read old books from a library. It shouldn't be a crime to know about the universe, the world, and my own real history.

The man with half a face opened the carriage door, and I shuffled inside.

The horses sped us away from the hideous fortress. And my grandfather.

The driver must have considered my transportation a matter of urgency, because we flew through the forest at such speed I was convinced the wheels didn't even touch the ground. The horses' hooves pounded the earth as they grunted with exertion. They sounded strong and feisty. I wanted to be a horse in that moment. I wanted to be a bird. Although I would have settled for any forest creature, as they were all free.

The river surged through the valley and crashed over rocks as we followed it again. The torrential downpour in the evening had caused it to swell.

The aroma of the forest rose to meet my senses once more. I embraced the invigorating scent. I would enjoy the forest one last time, as the sun found gaps in the canopy of leaves. The grey clouds dissipated the further we sped away from the fortress.

On the other side of the swollen river, a mass of large stones rose high. But the trees had grown through them. The large stones were the foundations of buildings, and some smaller stones poked through the ground around a larger decaying structure. Thinking back to the map of the parish, and the front cover of the Stonburh Cathedral guidebook, I realised it resembled a crumbling churchyard. Nature fought back against wonky headstones, crosses, and angel statues. Here, the statues had retained their wings. They marked the final resting places of the ancestors. I considered that the foundations must be part of the village of Solstice. The honey-coloured stonework had collapsed around thick tree trunks and the vines of creeping plants.

After some time had passed, we slowed. I caught a glimpse of a wall through the treeline.

The driver mumbled something to someone, and we dashed off again. The horses' hooves hit stone rather than earth. We approached the little gatehouse set within the wall and sped over the little bridge on the other side. I realised I had completed the reverse journey of the night before. The mayor really was playing with me. If only I could become a giant rat instead of a timid mouse.

The carriage raced through the town and winding roads before hitting the main street and charging towards the old citadel. The carriage rattled across my favourite bridge and then climbed up past all the delightful shops and cafes.

My relief to be back in Eden was juxtaposed by the feeling that I might vomit as we juddered and jolted over the cobblestones, and twisted violently around every corner. The omnibuses were a much smoother ride. But the omnibus drivers had never been on such a vital mission.

We came to a grinding halt outside the Guildhall.

I remained inside the carriage, not knowing if someone would approach.

'Are you getting out or what?' the driver asked.

I fumbled for the little door handle and stepped down as a soldier wearing a gas mask appeared.

I glanced up at the driver as I closed the carriage door. He, too, now wore a gas mask.

The soldier nodded towards the Guildhall and escorted me into the foyer.

I still felt groggy from the ride. But I also felt weak from hunger. Plus my mouth felt dry. The breakfast had been insufficient, and I had consumed it hours ago.

I stumbled on the checkerboard tile floor of the Guildhall's foyer. I had always found the tiles to have a striking but simple elegance. But on that morning they made me want to eject the morsels floating within my stomach. My faintness caused my eyes to glaze over. I was convinced I could smell sweet violet and delicate rose, and it reminded me of a perfume my mother wore. Or rather had worn. She hadn't bothered since my father had been sent to the fictitious town of Frontline.

A beautiful angel floated across the floor towards me. She opened her arms and spread her wings as she turned into a flame.

'Come on, Andromeda, let's go home.'

Chapter 12

We embraced for an eternity, me sobbing and my mother stroking my hair. Then my mother drew back and held my face in her hands.

'Let's go,' she said.

'Envy,' I blurted. 'I left her. Did she—'

'She's okay. She's the reason I'm here.'

'I saw Grandad in the prison,' I said. 'I don't know how to get him out of there.'

The amount of guilt I felt for leaving my grandfather behind overwhelmed me, even though I hadn't chosen to leave him behind. Why was the mayor toying with me in this way?

'We'll talk at home,' my mother said.

She wiped the tears from my cheeks and kissed me upon my forehead.

'You're just like your father,' she said.

'I thought I was just like you?'

'A little perhaps.' My mother smiled. 'We need to put these on,' she said, as she removed a gas mask from one of the two canvas bags she wore over her shoulder.

My mother wore red lipstick as well as her perfume. Plus I

noted her stockings. She had obviously dug out a pair from her drawer. They had a black seam down the back. I wondered if she had dressed like that to impress someone.

My mother caught me taking in her striking appearance.

'Should I bake a cake when we get home?' she asked. 'Would you like that? I think I have enough sugar.'

She wrapped her arm in mine and we sauntered to the doorway.

'Yes, a nice sponge cake,' she said. 'With cream and jam.'

My stomach rumbled. Despite my concern for my grandfather, my stomach thought it was more important in that moment.

We helped each other with the masks and strolled out into the sunshine and a scene of horror.

The old citadel remained the same. But the townsfolk all looked as though they belonged somewhere else. Even on another planet. They had giant bug eyes and round snouts for noses. The gas masks meant everyone had lost their humanity. Although I wondered if the townsfolk had already lost some of their humanity. The rationing had given everyone a gaunt appearance. The masks now hid this. But I knew most were almost skin and bone under their attire and large insect-like facial features.

Wearing the mask gave me the impression that I was listening to someone else breathing. I had never heard myself breathe before. Or I had never noticed or thought about it. With the claustrophobic mask, my breathing became more defined. It was as though another person, or spirit, had jumped inside me and had taken over my body.

Six years of lies decorated the square. War posters clung to lampposts, community noticeboards and the sides of buildings. Most of the posters were weather-worn, while some were newer replacements. The posters lied about doing our bit for Eden, and supporting our men in the town of Frontline. They lied about rationing; we had to do with less so our men had everything they needed to stay strong and fight. Only they didn't fight in a war. They fought for life inside a prison. The posters lied about everything.

I squinted up at the top windows of the House of Books. One of the shutters behind a window had a slither of an opening. No one else would have noticed. I wondered if Gabriel surveyed the square again. Gabriel the archangel. The angel who I considered my light through the dark age.

'Mum—'

'We'll talk when we get home,' my mother said.

We caught the next omnibus and sat downstairs. No one spoke to their friends or neighbouring passengers. I think it was more because the masks made dialogue unclear, rather than they had nothing to say. Two children appeared to find wearing their masks quite comical.

Once we had crossed the gatehouse bridge and began descending into the suburbs the townsfolk removed their masks, as did my mother and I. The masks had left vicious red imprints on all the women's faces. The children refused to remove theirs, preferring to resemble strange creatures from another world.

As my mother sat with her hands upon her mask, I noticed her fingers appeared raw. Inflamed pink lesions bloomed around her fingertips.

She smiled at me.

The shadows inside the omnibus fell across her sunken cheeks and eye sockets, and revealed how exhausted she was. She had possibly stayed up all night sewing, and worrying about my grandfather and me.

I felt guilty again. Guilty for not being there to help, and guilty for becoming so engrossed in the House of Books, that I hadn't noticed my mother had been working alone.

I knew what awaited me when we reached the door of our cottage: love.

My best friend lunged for my mouth, but she headbutted me instead when she attempted to land a kiss. I laughed for the first time in days. I only ever laughed with Envy. She was the only one who could make me chortle with joy.

Envy wriggled within my arms as I tried to hug her. Her wagging tail smacked off the sofa chairs and off the little tables. She was impossible to console. Her nose crashed into mine, and I thought her love would leave me covered in bruises.

I allowed the book, which had remained concealed in my trousers, to fall from my waistband.

My mother made tea and toasted some crumpets, which we drizzled with honey. I guzzled it all down, despite a pang of remorse for my grandfather.

'How did you know?' I asked, as I pushed my empty plate away.

'How did I know where you were? I didn't,' my mother said. 'But neither you nor your grandfather had come home in over twenty-four hours. I thought you were staying over in the citadel somewhere. I know *something* has piqued your interest in the citadel of late. But when Envy appeared, barking and scratching at the door, and alone, I knew something terrible must have happened. But it was after curfew, so I couldn't do anything until this morning. I telephoned the Guildhall and announced you as a missing person. Then I called Doctor Hartnell—'

'What? Why? I think she told the mayor about me,' I said.

'Why would she do that?' my mother asked.

'Because I noticed she had some new books in her office. I said I knew where she'd got them from because I knew about the library. Which is like a giant house for books. I shouldn't have said it. I was angry. Because of that, she knew that I knew about the House of Books. I gave away the fact I'd been in a forbidden building. And that it was the one with the books. Therefore, I'm obviously reading things which are forbidden knowledge. I'm sorry I didn't tell you sooner about the House of Books. I didn't want to worry you.'

My mother glared at me.

'Speaking of books,' she said, as she rose from the table and collected an item from the sideboard. 'Doctor Hartnell gave me this to give to you. It feels like a book.'

She placed the package wrapped in brown paper and string before me. Now I had two new books.

'I don't want it,' I said defiantly. I didn't want a stolen book from the woman who steals almost an entire bookcase worth of books. Even if it had come from my favourite place.

'She means well,' my mother said.

'She told the mayor I'd broken the law by going into the House of Books,' I said.

'Doctor Hartnell hasn't told the mayor you've broken the law. She did have to tell him something else, though.'

My mother shifted in the chair.

'What did she have to tell him?' I asked.

'We concocted a plan,' my mother said. 'Doctor Hartnell was to go to the Guildhall and state her concern about you, because of your health.'

'You mean my—'

'She told them you're mad,' my mother said.

'Mad!' I exclaimed. 'First, she tells me I have a condition. Then she says it's a stress disorder. Then she tells me it's another type of disorder. Now she's telling everyone I'm mad. I think I should have seen a different doctor. Perhaps Doctor Troughton would have—'

'She doesn't actually think you're mad,' my mother said.

'You just said—'

'A *ruse*,' my mother said, as she clasped a hand over mine. 'And what's this about a disorder?'

‘I’m not seeing Doctor Hartnell again,’ I said, removing my hand from my mother’s clasp and folding my arms across my chest. ‘I’m not seeing anyone. I’d like to be left alone. For good.’

‘It was the only way we could get you out,’ my mother said. ‘I had to go and meet with the mayor and beg him to allow you to come home for your health. He’s a tough, sly individual.’

My mother hung her head.

‘I thought I’d better make the effort,’ she said, as she ran her hand over a stockinged shin. ‘Anyway, what’s this disorder?’

‘Autism something disorder,’ I mumbled.

What’s that?’

‘Doctor Hartnell didn’t tell you?’ I asked, wondering why she hadn’t when she blabbed about everything else.

‘No,’ my mother said. ‘So, what is it?’

I sighed. I was fed up talking about Doctor Hartnell. She was one of the mayor’s cronies, that’s all I needed to know.

‘Well, that’s how I knew she’d been reading stolen books,’ I said. ‘Because she didn’t know about autism before. Then suddenly her bookcase is full of stolen books, and she knows all about this new thing.’

‘That doesn’t tell me anything,’ my mother said.

‘I’m weird,’ I said, raising my voice. ‘My head’s not right. I see the world differently. I’m no good at socialising. I’m no good with conversation. I’m no good at anything.’

‘We’re having a conversation now,’ my mother said calmly.

‘Yes, but you’re my mum.’

‘You speak with the neighbours. You speak with the shopkeepers.’

‘Yes, but sometimes it’s uncomfortable,’ I said. ‘I don’t always know what to say.’

‘You’re good at things,’ my mother continued. ‘You’re good at drawing. You’re good at looking after Envy and the hens. You care about nature. You know all there is to know about the planets and the moons.’

'I know even more now,' I said, thinking how much my mind had expanded since reading the *Space Encyclopaedia*. In fact, I thought my brain would explode from all the new knowledge I had accumulated in such a short space of time.

'You're quick to take in new information,' my mother said.

'When it's interesting,' I said, thinking how much more exciting the books in the House of Books were compared to the books I had read in school.

My mother laughed. Then she stopped suddenly, as though she felt guilty for laughing.

'Plus it makes a difference having a good teacher,' I said, thinking about Gabriel.

'Someone's teaching you?' my mother asked.

'Sort of,' I said, squirming in my chair. 'But the books I read in the House of Books are my main teacher,' I concluded, hoping that would prevent my mother from asking another probing question about a mystery teacher. I shouldn't have mentioned having a teacher, but Gabriel popped into my head and the words fell out of my mouth.

My mother smiled at me.

'On top of all those things you're good at, you're also the bravest girl I know,' she said. 'Since, as you say, you've broken the law and gone inside a forbidden building. And you've survived a night in prison. You must have realised the mayor would want you out of the way? How did you end up seeing the mayor?'

'I didn't want to see him,' I said. 'The soldiers took me into his house. I didn't know what to do. Then he mentioned Grandad and offered me a chance to see him.'

'But you must have known what that meant? And you were taken to the prison—'

'I thought I'd never see anyone again.'

'How did your grandad look?'

'Frail,' I said, mournfully. 'I don't think he'll live much longer.

I can't bear to think that he'll die in there. Not in a cold damp cell. When the time comes, he should die in his favourite armchair by the log burner. That's what he would want. I know it.'

I upset myself. My mother squeezed my trembling hands.

'Am I just like Dad?' I asked.

'In so many ways. I see it more now,' my mother said.

'Do you think Dad has autism something disorder?' I asked, suddenly wondering that if I was like him in so many ways, perhaps we had the same thing. Perhaps that was why we had both gotten into trouble?

'I don't think so,' my mother said. 'But clearly you both like pushing the boundaries. They'll be watching you.'

'Did they watch Dad?'

'They watch many people,' she said.

'Mum ... there's no war.'

My mother leaned back in the chair and sipped her tea.

'I never thought there was,' she said.

I stared at my mother in utter shock.

'You never thought there was?' I said, stunned. 'Even though we received letters from Dad?'

My own mother had hidden her beliefs from me. She too had been lying for six years. A horrible thought struck me.

'The letters *are* from Dad, aren't they?' I asked.

'Yes, they're his handwriting.'

'And the photographs are real?'

'They're real,' my mother confirmed, as she stared at pictures of my father on the mantelpiece.

Although my mother had also been lying for six years, unlike the authorities, I expected she hadn't been lying out of malice. She'd lied out of kindness. She had wanted to protect me.

'Then the authorities must have forced all the men to pose for those photographs while in prison,' I said.

'It would appear that way,' she said, nodding.

'But you always suspected he'd been taken somewhere?

Possibly even prison?' I asked, wondering how she could keep her thoughts hidden for six years. She was either mad, or much stronger than I thought. 'Did you tell Grandad?' I asked.

'Your grandad has a big mouth.'

'You thought Dad might be suffering somewhere awful,' I said. 'But not in the town of Frontline?'

My mother gazed into her teacup.

'All of us have always known,' she said. 'You're just like your grandmother and me in that regard. You're intuitive. You've always known something was amiss in Eden. When the townsfolk stop to think about it, they all realise something is wrong with this place.'

'We have to get Grandad out of prison,' I said. 'We also have to assume that Dad is in there, too.'

My mother smiled at me lovingly.

'It doesn't change my life,' I said.

'What doesn't?'

'The autism disorder. Whether there's a name for what I have or not, I don't care. We've all been lied to about everything. That's my main concern. I don't want autism to define me. The most important things in my life are getting Dad and Grandad out of prison, exposing the lies, and gaining knowledge from the House of Books. Those things mean everything to me now. It's not enough that I know the truth, I want everyone to know the truth. I don't want the townsfolk to die in ignorance. If I don't expose the lies, we'll all be trapped in the lie of Eden forever. We'll all have to continue living the lie, because I failed.'

I caught the next omnibus into the old citadel. Envy sat in my lap. I had a shopping basket with me. Not with the intention of taking books home, but bringing things into the House of Books. I brought food and other items for Gabriel.

I let my red hair flow, just like the women in the paintings at the mayor's house. I wouldn't wear the scarf anymore. I no longer cared. If the soldiers and the authorities thought I was mad, then so be it. I would utilise this. I would come and go as I pleased. Now I had discovered the House of Books, they knew I wouldn't leave the place alone. But I wondered if they knew someone was living inside the House of Books. I wondered if the mayor really did know about Gabriel. Or whether, as I had previously thought, it had just been coincidence that he had mentioned the name. It had to be a fluke that the mayor had a painting by Gabriel whatshisname.

Some of the townsfolk mingled on the main street piling up logs, ready for the evening's bonfires.

As we approached the gatehouse bridge, everyone on the omnibus placed a gas mask over their face. Including me. I had to keep up some pretence after all.

Envy and I entered the House of Books via the terrace.

Gabriel rushed forward from the shadows.

'Are you okay?' he asked. 'What happened? I wondered where you'd gone?'

'I spent the night in prison,' I said, matter-of-factly.

'Prison!' he exclaimed. 'Why? How did you get out?'

'The mayor let me out. And you know why they sent me to prison,' I said, waving an arm in the direction of the nearest bookcase. 'Because— Hold on. Where are the books?'

The bookcase nearest me stood empty. As did the bookcase next to it. As did most of the bookcases on the first floor. I leaned over the balcony. All the bookcases on the ground floor stood proud but were void of books. My heart began to pound. I glanced up towards the second floor, but I was relieved to see row upon row of glorious books upon those shelves.

'Have you moved all the books to the top floors?' I asked. 'The authorities will notice. They'll realise it wasn't me because I spent the night in prison.'

'Not me,' Gabriel said. 'Soldiers came in here last night and took the books away. They were in here for hours. I assume they'll come back for more tonight.'

My heart ceased pounding. I think it stopped altogether, for I had died. The mayor was destroying the place I loved. He was ripping out its very soul.

'They must be taking them to one of the other abandoned buildings,' I said. 'Where else could they keep them?'

'The Guildhall? If there's room,' Gabriel said.

In that moment, I felt as though I could punch the mayor square in the face. He was ruining my life. And why? Because he didn't want me to know my own history. I don't know if I would've actually hit him, had he stood before me with his usual self-satisfied grin across his arrogant face. But at least I could imagine thumping him. I have to say, that alone felt good. *I* removed books from the House of Books. Not *them*. I took books with the intention of bringing them back. Unlike the authorities, I planned to return the books to their correct home. They belonged upon those dusty wooden shelves. I knew the books the authorities had stolen would never be returned.

'The mayor … I hate him,' I said. 'Have they taken all the books in the Health section?'

'They might have done,' Gabriel said. 'Why?'

'No reason,' I said, as I pictured Doctor Hartnell surrounded by piles of books and laughing manically as she became the font of all knowledge on conditions and disorders.

'We can search the other abandoned buildings tonight if you like? See if we can find them,' Gabriel said.

'Maybe we can do that. But another night. I have a different plan for this evening. But first, I've brought you some aspirin. Luckily, we had some at home. I hope the tablets are still okay,' I said, as I examined the crumpled packet.

'What's that for?'

'Because you're sick,' I said. 'Although you look a little better this afternoon. You haven't coughed or sneezed yet.'

'Then I'm not sick,' Gabriel said.

'But you might still have a temperature?'

'I don't think I do,' he said. 'I don't think I did the other day.'

'But you might get sick again, so you should just take the tablets.'

'You're being very bossy this afternoon. Did you get this attitude from prison?'

'Well next time I'll just let you get sick,' I said, rolling my eyes at him.

'I'm only teasing. I'll take the ... aspirin, was it?'

Gabriel scrutinised the packet. He did it in such a way I had to assume he had never seen a packet of aspirin before.

'You don't have aspirin where you come from?' I asked.

'What plan anyway?' he asked, avoiding the question, as per usual. 'You said you have a plan for this evening?'

'I saw my grandad in prison.'

'How is he?' Gabriel asked.

'He's dying,' I said. 'He was confined to the cell opposite me. We were kept at the very top of the tallest tower. They put me in a cell facing him on purpose.'

'Sorry,' Gabriel said, as he lowered his eyes, and his shoulders appeared to sag.

'We have to get my grandad out of there,' I said, 'and my dad, too. Well, all the men. None of them should be in prison.'

'Great. How do we get them out?'

'You can get them out,' I said.

Gabriel's eyes narrowed.

'How can I get them all out on my own?' he asked.

'You have power.'

'*Power*?'

'You're an archangel,' I said, thinking how shocked Gabriel must be that I had worked out his secret all by myself.

At first Gabriel just gawped at me. Then he began to chuckle. His chuckle was a sound I had missed. Yet annoyingly, his laugh was once again brought on by something I had said.

'Whatever gave you that idea?' he said.

'Because ... you're not an archangel?' I said, deflated. 'Then what are you?'

'I'm a man.'

'Oh. I thought you were special.'

'Sorry to be a disappointment to you,' Gabriel said. 'But I'm not that privileged to be an archangel, or any other type of angel.'

'But the gas didn't affect you?'

'I covered my nose and mouth, like this,' he said, wrapping his shawl tight around the lower half of his face.

'But you can't just be a man,' I said, bitterly frustrated.

'Why not?'

'You're too weird.'

'Thank you,' Gabriel said, proudly.

I believe Gabriel smirked at me. However, I scowled at him. In fact, I gave him my best scowl. One reserved for those who become highly irritating. I folded my arms across my chest to protect myself from a barrage of smugness.

Gabriel placed the packet of aspirin on the nearest small table.

'I don't understand how you thought I was ill but you also thought I was an archangel,' he said. 'How would an angel get sick?'

'Well, I must've supposed that they could,' I said a little sulkily.

'You are funny,' Gabriel chuckled.

'I am not funny,' I protested. 'I don't see what you always find so amusing about me.'

'But you're the funniest person I've ever met,' he said.

I failed to see how that could be true. Perhaps I was unintentionally funny. But if Gabriel found me more unintentionally funny, I deemed it might be cruel to laugh at me.

'Anyway, I've brought some food for you,' I said. 'Plus,

I've brought my grandfather's gas mask for you wear, so we could leave the citadel together. I also brought you some of my father's clothes, as you're tall like him, so his trousers will fit you better. I thought we could go into the forest.'

'And do what?' Gabriel asked.

'Get my grandad. Well, at least that had been my plan.'

'That simple, is it? No guards? No keys required?'

'I thought you were an archangel,' I said. 'I thought you had power. I didn't think I would need keys. Anyway, last time I was here, you said you'd think of something. You'd *find a way*. But you obviously haven't thought of anything.'

Gabriel appeared to shrink as he hung his head.

'Sorry,' I said, a little ashamed of myself. 'I'm just …'

'Upset and angry?' he said. 'I can understand that. However, I'm waiting on some others. We probably could get your grandfather out. I suppose you could show me where the prison is. But I need help from others.'

'Who?' I asked.

'It's a complicated story.'

'Yes, I expect it is,' I said. 'It'll be whatever big thing it is you're hiding from me. You can tell me all about it when we're in the forest. We've got a long way to go. But you should eat something first.'

Before we set off for the evening, Gabriel gobbled down the bread, the small chunk of cheese, and the little tomatoes I had brought him. I had also packed a small flask of tea for him, which he slurped away at. He shared some of the cheese with Envy, despite his obvious hunger. It melted my heart to see how kind and affectionate he was with her, especially since she couldn't have possibly been hungry. I had given her a little something to eat before we left for the citadel. But cheese had always been a particular favourite of the greedy little madam.

I checked the shelves in the Health section. I couldn't locate a single book on autism. I couldn't locate a single book on conditions or disorders. Those shelves were vacant.

We left the House of Books, both masked up and dressed for troublemaking, me in my grandfather's clothes, and Gabriel wearing my father's clothes. I had considered that Gabriel's usual attire would have suited our upcoming adventure better, but since his clothes were light, almost white, they wouldn't do. He was too conspicuous. And don't get me started on the weird robe, shawl thing.

The clock above the Guildhall struck six as we boarded an omnibus. Gabriel found the whole thing quite novel, as though he had stepped back in time. He ran a hand over the seat and the varnished wood interior.

His eyes brimmed with wonder. They appeared even larger through the mask.

If I thought he found the omnibus quaint, he found the cottages more so when we alighted close to my home.

He had refused to take his mask off, even though I said he looked ridiculous wearing it now we had left the old citadel.

He wandered around the lanes peering into people's windows and doorways, examining their plants and flowers. Anyone would have thought he had never seen a cottage or a garden. If Gabriel wasn't an archangel, and was actually from the forest, I wondered what type of accommodation the forest people lived in?

I urged him on towards the outer wall, where the river flowed through the broken grate.

The sheep scurried for the trees, bleating their usual objection as we approached. I don't know how frightening I would have appeared to them. But I expected a charging dog and a tall man wearing a weird contraption over his face would have been terrifying.

I hoped no one had watched us from a window nearby as we advanced upon the outer wall.

Envy slid under the grate first, seemingly knowing what I was up to.

'Do you have a lamp in that basket?' Gabriel asked.

'I have a lantern, yes.'

'Lamp, lantern, what's the difference?' he asked with a shrug, as though he really didn't care to know the answer.

'To me, a lantern is more portable, more for outside,' I said. 'A lamp sits permanently on a table, or lights a street.'

'I see. That's very specific of you,' he said. 'Anyway, it'll be dark soon I expect.'

'Will you take the mask off then?' I asked.

'I might do.'

I think I rolled my eyes at him. *I might do* he said. I couldn't fathom how he thought I was the funny one out of the two of us.

Gabriel took my basket from me and followed Envy's example, easing himself through the broken grate. I was glad he had gone first. I wouldn't have wanted him watching my legs flailing away while I attempted to scramble my body through. It was bad enough that he watched my front end emerge through the grate.

Gabriel grabbed my outstretched arms and raised me to my feet.

We entered the Forest of Beautiful Lies.

'We need to follow the river, as I had done in the carriage,' I said. 'I don't know if there's a more direct way. But we'll get lost if we don't follow the river.'

'Where was the stone circle?' Gabriel asked.

'Up on the plateau ahead,' I said.

As we rambled through the forest, once again I had an overwhelming sense of belonging to the most beautiful place I had ever seen. As though I was born into a world of invigorating green foliage and clear flowing water.

We climbed the hillside to the plateau. Gabriel approached the first stone we came across.

He ran a pale hand over the dark grey surface. Then he moved towards the next stone and spread his arms out wide as he stood between the two. He continued to weave around the stones and measure the distance between them with his arm span.

'Impeccable,' he muttered to himself.

He tapped on some of the stones and leaned all his weight upon others. He caressed the stones which had fallen, as though he consoled them.

We remained within the stone circle as the sun set behind the trees.

Gabriel finally removed his mask. I lit the lantern as we sat amongst the stones.

'This place is beautiful,' he said.

'I know. I feel I belong here. I feel connected somehow.'

'I feel that too,' he said, looking around in a manner that implied he had never been in a forest before. Which surprised me. It also meant that he might not be from the forest. He was perhaps just a person from another town, somewhere beyond the trees.

'It's so calming,' I said, feeling how wonderful it was to be under the canopy of lush green leaves.

'It makes sense that it would feel calming,' Gabriel said. 'This is all the true First Ancestors of this land knew. Thousands and thousands of years have passed, but to live amongst the trees and long grass remains our home. Because somewhere deep down inside of us, within our subconscious, we recognise that being enveloped in green is home. That's why you feel connected.'

'Can you tell me anymore about the true First Ancestors? You said they were pagan, and that means worshipping many gods. Plus, they respected nature. What else did they do?' I asked, as I drew my knees up to chest, ready to be enraptured by Gabriel's response.

'They respected nature because they were aware that nature

could kill them, as much as it also gave them life. Nature is not evil, but it can be cruel. They had short, hard lives. Children died of things which can be easily treated today. If they made it to adulthood, it was a miracle. Before they became farmers and settled on an area of land, they were hunter-gatherers and constantly on the move. They had to be, as their food source constantly travelled around the land. When they went off to hunt, they were aware they might not all make it back.'

'Why?' I asked.

'They weren't hunting cows and pigs, which have been domesticated down millennia. They hunted the ancestors of cows and pigs. Those animals were huge. The ancestors had to deal with large horned aurochs and tusked boars. Nature gave these prehistoric animals horns and tusks as defensive weapons. Those weapons were perfect. A horn or a tusk could cause serious injury which could result in death. It was a risk they had to take. They wouldn't survive otherwise. Plus, they also had woolly mammoth to contend with. The woolly mammoth was a huge hairy elephant with tusks. The ancestors had more respect for animals because they knew how hard it was to kill one. Because sometimes it was the men who died, and not the animal. The first art in the world was cave paintings. These cave paintings depicted animals and hunting scenes. That says something. I think this shows their reverence for animals, alongside the toughness of their everyday lives. If it were not for these strong-willed ancestors, who fought every day for life, we would not be here. We wouldn't have survived as a species.'

I felt in awe of what Gabriel had just told me about the true ancestors.

'Now I know about the first true ancestors, I won't forget them,' I said. 'We should never forget the ancestors.'

'Yes, it's fitting that we thank the ancestors tonight in one of their sacred places.'

I liked the idea that Gabriel and I honoured the ancestors

as we spoke of them, and sat amongst their sacred stones. Although it baffled me how Gabriel wasn't an archangel. How could he know so much about everything and not be something special?

We stayed amongst the stones for a while, until I decided we should press on. We had a prison to locate, and darkness had already consumed the forest.

'What's that?' Gabriel asked, as we clambered down from the plateau.

'What's what?'

'Can't you hear that?'

I strained my earholes but couldn't detect anything. Envy didn't even appear perturbed, and therefore she'd heard nothing either.

'It's coming from over there,' he said, pointing ahead of us. 'I think I see a little light.'

I couldn't see or hear anything. But Envy began to glower at the same spot Gabriel had pointed to.

'Probably best to blow out the lamp,' he said.

I did so.

We approached a golden light as we slunk further forward.

The dense forest dropped away, and we peered down into a huge illuminated valley.

Within the light-filled gorge, I discovered monsters were real. The monsters were ginormous metal dragons.

Great heaving mechanised brutes reached for the stars, while others slept in the shadows beyond the large clearing. A team of men scurried around below them.

A thunderous roar caused me to inspect the sky, but no storm appeared. It was the menacing dragons and their guttural bellow. The monstrous machines appeared to sink further into the earth. Their groaning grew louder and louder. The ground shook and I clung to the nearest tree. I knew the rumbling would surge across the entire north-west side of Eden.

For the monsters to cause such a disturbance, I assumed most of the body of each metal dragon lay underground. Each must have torn away at the soil, which had lain still for thousands of years.

I realised the wide valley was man-made. Men had used these monsters to create the deep clearing. Now they dug further.

The hulking machines had unearthed something, and this something broke free of the surface. Once this something had breached the soil, the earthquake ceased.

The men brought forth more atrocious pieces of apparatus to help grip the large object.

Giant teeth emerged first, all in a large circle. It reminded me of the stone circle. But these teeth were black and jagged, as though shattered underground. The base of the large beast began to emerge on one side. This was a new colossal creature. The metal creature belonged to another world than the one I believed I knew.

The body of the black beast cracked at one end, and the men rushed forward. It snapped completely and the machines struggled against the weight. The mysterious mass slid back into the ground and one of the monstrous apparatuses tumbled in after it.

Another quake followed the swallowing of the behemoth. I wondered then if the earthquakes came more from the movement of the gargantuan object rather than the digging monsters.

The remaining machines only held a fragment of what they had unearthed. Although the spiky fragment looked substantial.

One of the metal dragons swung the piece around at a steady pace, towards the men below.

The giant splinter hit the ground with a thud. All the men swooped. They appeared to consider the dark surface of this new-found wonder for a while. Then two of the men procured some implements, which made a constant din while in use. It seemed to me they intended to cut a doorway into the body of the fragment.

A light-coloured entity fell from the opening and landed at the feet of the men.

Gabriel edged forward.

The entity was the same length as the men. It resembled a human wrapped in bandages. Or rather, a suit so tight it resembled a second skin. It reminded me of Gabriel.

The men all lurched forward as one removed what looked like a greyish gas mask minus the round snout.

Even from the distance where Gabriel and I stood, I realised the removal of the mask revealed a bulbous skull.

Gabriel slunk back into the dense forest.

'I don't understand. I don't understand,' he muttered.

'What don't you understand?' I asked.

'I thought we could leave. They said we could be free. They didn't say we'd be imprisoned underground. We've been betrayed.'

Those were the last words I heard him utter before he disappeared into the complete darkness of the forest.

Chapter 13

Envy and I stumbled about in the dark. Tree roots took my feet from under me several times. Even after relighting the lantern, I couldn't keep my footing. I became frantic. Gabriel had gone.

I couldn't stay in the forest all night. Because of the stress of losing Gabriel, I had almost forgotten why we had ventured into the dark canopy in the first place. Then I reminded myself about my grandfather. I could no longer attempt to locate the prison, not in my state. I could no longer do anything for my grandfather this night.

Envy whined and grumbled. My lower limbs throbbed and my upper limbs bled from scratches.

I headed back to the river and followed it all the way to the grate at the wall.

The sheep had hunkered down for the night under the trees.

Smoke wafted in the air.

It appeared the townsfolk had relit the bonfires in their gardens and in the streets. If any spark from the flames got too close to a thatched roof, that would be the end of the respective cottage, and possibly all the nearby cottages. I supposed the fear of spirits rising from the dead was somehow more terrifying than losing a roof, or losing your whole home if buckets of river water couldn't quench the blaze, or if the fire carts, each equipped with a steam-powered water pump, didn't arrive fast enough. Perhaps the entire town would go up in flames. Given the orange hue gravitating towards the heavens, I considered there were enough blazing bonfires to begin the destruction.

I fell onto my bed in exhaustion. My eyes stung when I closed them. I managed to doze off after a while, although I woke numerous times and thought of my grandfather dying in his cell. I thought of Gabriel alone in the forest. Not an archangel. Just a man, according to him. With no power. And lost. Not privileged. God hadn't made him an angel. Had Gabriel implied he was cursed?

I would have to go to the Guildhall in the morning. I would have to demand they release my grandfather. I had nothing to lose anymore. What could they do to me? Put me back in prison? Perhaps I could see Doctor Hartnell and ask her to intervene regarding my grandfather's health.

I didn't know how I felt about Doctor Hartnell anymore. My mother said she had helped to get me out of prison. But I didn't know how much Doctor Hartnell really knew about Eden. But before I would go to the Guildhall, I planned to do some breaking and entering. I had to find the place where they hid the books from me.

It was a beautiful clear day as Envy and I set out to catch an omnibus the following morning. At least one person got on at every stop. They all reeked of bonfires. Smoky residue remained in their hair and garments. I had to deduce that even I too must have carried a vestige of bonfire, since I had darted past quite a few to reach my cottage the previous evening.

As we approached the gatehouse bridge, the townsfolk removed their gas masks from the little canvas bags and placed them over their heads. As before, all the townsfolk resembled giant bug creatures.

I alighted at the stop before the square and meandered up towards Prendergast Books. I feigned an interest in browsing the window display, which featured all the usual basic tomes to keep the townsfolk in ignorance. Tomes which provided just enough for us to feel we knew our world, but in truth, told us nothing but lies. Instead of browsing, I watched the townsfolk amble about behind me in the reflection of the glass. No one paid any attention to me. Even my red hair hadn't drawn a curious glance. I was just another person with giant eyes and a snout for a nose.

I passed along the shop and café fronts, then slipped down a narrow passage.

I turned back to check no one spied on me. I removed my mask and placed it in the little canvas bag.

Envy and I hurried along the labyrinth of narrow passages which led onto the courtyard I required. I entered the alleyway which ran behind the back of the Grand Tea Room, and found the back of what I understood to be the Assembly Rooms. Judging by the size of the building, and since the Assembly Rooms were created for dancing and socialising, I presumed the rooms would be enormous. Big enough for row upon row of books, I hoped.

No windows lined the ground floor at the back of the Assembly Rooms, only a wide door. A faded sign peeled away from the wood. I believe the first word may have read FIRE. The second word was illegible. The door frame had begun to rot away, but the door appeared sturdy. I yanked on the handle and heard a click from inside. The door opened outwards with ease and then fell from the decaying frame.

Envy and I leapt back as the door landed with a crash. I

glared at the dejected door and ceased breathing for a moment. I listened out for footsteps as I half expected a soldier to appear. I heard nothing. No one came. But I felt terrible. I had damaged a building created by the real First Ancestors.

I had no time to grieve for a door. I had a mission. I had to stay focussed. I stepped inside and shuffled along a carpeted corridor. The red carpet was spoiled by chunks of plaster which had descended from the ceiling. Wallpaper peeled from the walls and hung despondently. But the claustrophobic corridor led to a magnificent foyer. Wide carpeted steps ran down towards a set of three double doors, which was the true entrance to the building. Paper lined the glass panes at the top of the doors to prevent prying eyes from finding this beauty. A frosted skylight above the grand entrance allowed enough golden illumination to filter through.

Alongside fragments of plaster, space dust had also burrowed into the carpet and settled on every surface. But the foyer's faded beauty still offered an air of charm. The doors and bannisters were made of a dark wood, which complemented the red carpet and gilded light fixtures. Mirrors smothered most of the walls, giving the impression that the foyer went on and on forever. I observed multiple visions of myself everywhere I turned. If the red, gold, and dark wood of the foyer was a precursor of things to come, I expected the rooms to be lavish.

I entered a humongous room through a glass-panelled double door. Great pillars lined the walls. Light exploded from the long windows high above and glinted off one of two large chandeliers. One of the chandeliers had crashed to the floor at some point in time, taking some of the frescoed ceiling with it. What remained of the giant fresco depicted people from the long-distant past. They stared down upon me as they floated within the heavens. Some were not looking at me at all, they seemed to be going about their lives, albeit flying or reclining upon white fluffy clouds. Coloured robes billowed about the physique of each flying ancestor. Angels, and small babies with wings, soared across the ceiling amidst the ancients. As did some large birds I didn't recognise. Even the horses had wings in the painting. Their silvery white coats gleamed as they galloped across the sky. I wished I could have flown up to the ceiling to join the ancestors in a closer inspection of their world. They were at least ten metres above me, and I couldn't appreciate all the finer detail. They resembled a dream, whereupon waking, the detail is hard to recollect. But what the painted ceiling did convey was how the ancestors resided in the sky with the angels.

I thought again about how Gabriel told me he wasn't an angel, even though he fell to Earth from the sky. But now he appeared to be trapped here, unlike the others who came with him. The other being like him, who fell from the weird object in the forest, was dead. I wondered if he had been condemned. The being found himself imprisoned underground, and died. I had to assume the imprisonment was what Gabriel had meant by betrayal. Although I had seen one very much alive by the stone circle on my first venture into the forest. Perhaps they were angels but Gabriel was just a man?

The stunning beauty of the room distracted me. I got so lost in admiration for it that once again I had forgotten why I had gone somewhere. No one had set foot in the room for years, judging by the dirt and space dust which Envy and I transported across the floorboards. I assumed that in the past the floorboards would have shone like those in the Grand Tea Room. But in my time the dirt had dulled the wood.

I could imagine the ancestors dancing around me. I wanted the past to come to life, as it had done in the House of Books, and the square, and cathedral. Then the ancestral shadow figures would come along with the angels.

I recalled the music of the angels and pirouetted around the dirty floorboards, which creaked with every step. Envy leapt at my legs, and gave my grandfather's trousers a good dusting in space particles.

I ceased twirling about and considered the room. It was a perfect replacement for the House of Books. Mountainous volumes could stretch towards the ceiling. But no books inhabited the space. But then I recalled it was Assembly *Rooms*, not Assembly Room. There had to be at least one other large room in existence.

Envy and I left the grandeur of one room and located its twin next door. Unfortunately, both chandeliers had plummeted to the floor in this room. Plus, both had taken a considerable amount of the ceiling with them when they had dropped, although I could still enjoy the beauty of the damaged fresco regardless. The ancestors interacted with the angels, while more animals lingered amongst them. I believe I even perceived a green dragon, but some of its scaly body had fallen away with one of the chandeliers.

Alas the room was also void of books. Just like the previous room, the dust upon the floor proved not a soul had entered in years.

Envy and I left the Assembly Rooms the way we came in and then wandered through the alleyway and narrow passage. I placed my mask over my head before we headed out on to the street which led up to the square.

I contemplated what I would say to the mayor as I stomped across the cobblestones.

Envy ceased trotting alongside me. I turned to scrutinise why.

She glared upwards, as the eastern sky darkened to a slate grey.

A storm blew in with sudden vengeance. Thunder followed the shock of light, which struck another tower on the temple … or rather, cathedral. I really had no idea which word to use anymore. The word cathedral was the truth. But the other word – temple – was only half a lie. And I had used that word my whole life.

The floating spectres arrived with the downpour. As did the shadow figures who skulked amongst the screaming townsfolk. Their indifference to our existence struck me again. The way they strode through the square was as though we had entered their world, rather than they had entered ours.

Even through the gas masks, I couldn't misinterpret the high-pitched wails of the townsfolk.

Tiny orbs of light fell from the darkness, along with a song of remorse. The huge dark shapes hovered in the clouds. I couldn't smell the bitter acrid scent spliced with sulphur which I usually did. But as I wore the mask, I presumed this obstructed all odours in the same way it was supposed to prevent gas from reaching the lungs.

Envy entwined herself around my legs, but drenched as I was, I couldn't move. The old citadel shone, as it bathed in mystifying bright sunshine through the deluge.

For a brief moment, I wondered if I could dash back to the Assembly Rooms, to witness their revival. I imagined the shadow figures loitering in the foyer, while other shadow figures danced through the rooms where the ancestors watched.

As I considered the angels, one changed trajectory above me, and descended.

I thought it was Gabriel at first, and he had wrapped the feather-light shawl around his head. But as the angel lowered the shawl and revealed his face, I noticed he had a more mature appearance.

Like Gabriel, he wore a whitish grey suit. The exposed flesh on the face and hands appeared sallow and thick. His wide forehead dominated his face, causing the nose and mouth to appear small in comparison, and as though they were no longer of much use. His eyes transfixed me. They were an intense black like Gabriel's, as though the pupil had overpowered the iris.

Droplets of melody formed within the rainstorm. I realised

the man was addressing me, but I didn't recognise the verse. Until the words changed.

'Apologies,' he said. 'I forgot myself. You speak an old language.'

'Do I?' I said.

'To me you do. One almost lost through space and time.'

'Sorry?' I said, wondering how language could be lost, especially through space and time.

'You require breathing apparatus?' the man asked.

I removed my mask. The bitter acrid and sulphurous scent assaulted my nasal passage once more.

'It's a precaution,' I said. 'In case our authorities attack us again.'

'The authorities here attack their own people?' the man said. 'This is indeed a strange place.'

'It's gotten a lot stranger of late,' I said.

I couldn't fathom why I was discussing this with a man I didn't know. But just like Gabriel, the man had an air of calm. I felt at ease.

'We are looking for Gabriel,' the man said. 'He belongs with us. Where is he?'

'He belongs with you? You want to take him away?'

'Gabriel belongs with his own,' the man said, sombrely. 'We've let him run free for long enough. He's had his fun. It would appear you've been quite a distraction. But now he needs to take things more seriously.'

It was true, Gabriel didn't belong to me. He was his own free man, or angel-type thing. I wondered if this man was a relative, Gabriel's father even. I have to say, Gabriel had certainly been having fun, up to a point. I remember the first night when we met properly, and how much he wanted me to go on an adventure with him. The adventure was Eden ... or rather, Stonburh hidden in plain sight.

'Do you know where he is?' the man asked.

'I lost him in the forest,' I said. 'That was the last time I saw him.'

'How did you become separated in the forest?'

'He got upset. He ran away,' I said, as I brushed some of my rain-soaked hair from my face.

'What caused his upset?' the man asked.

'He saw something,' I said. 'We both did. There were monstrous machines. They found a huge object. There was a dead body. It looked like you.'

I winced at my own insensitivity.

'Sorry,' I said. 'But it did look like you. Its clothing was like yours. Only … the body must have been there for some time. As, really, it was a skeleton.'

'I see.'

The man's face crumpled, as though the news crushed him. Just like the vision had crushed Gabriel.

'Thank you for telling me,' he said.

'Gabriel had mentioned something about it not being what you were promised,' I said.

'No. We haven't succeeded as yet.'

'Succeeded in what?' I asked.

'Gabriel hasn't told you where he comes from?'

'No, Gabriel hasn't told me anything,' I said. 'Not about that anyway, or about you.'

The man gave me a warm smile.

'I'm sure you will see Gabriel again,' he said, 'and he can tell you our story when you do. Once more, I thank you for your honesty. Goodbye for now, Andromeda.'

'How do you know my name?' I asked.

The man didn't respond. He ascended and disappeared into the dark cloud, along with all the floating spectres. Floating spectres which I now realised couldn't possibly be spirits of any kind, let alone ancestral forest spirits. They were people. But for some reason they appeared as ghosts in the sky.

As the cloud rumbled and rolled away in the direction of the forest, I thought about Gabriel. Even when he wasn't around, he was still annoying. It transpired he didn't just have a personal story to disclose. His people had an entire story. But the rascal hadn't told me anything.

With the darkest cloud gone, the rain abated from the old citadel. Only light grey clouds remained, and they too began to disperse.

All the giant bug creatures remerged from doorways and side passages. But they slipped through the square in trepidation. They all stared in my direction.

Envy barked as one of the soldiers sprang upon me.

I recognised him from the day when he had collared me down the alleyway to the House of Books.

He tore the mask from his face.

'What do you think you're doing conversing with the enemy?' he roared.

'He isn't the enemy. You're the enemy,' I shouted back.

'Whose side are you on?'

'There's no war,' I said. 'The mayor's a liar. You're all liars.'

The townsfolk standing closest to me began to mutter amongst themselves.

'You really are mad,' the soldier said. 'They're trying to destroy our way of life.'

'What life? We don't have a life. We're confined to this town. It's all lies. I know what you're doing in the forest. I have eyes and ears everywhere. Don't think I don't know. Don't think I don't know we've been lied to about everything.'

I hadn't really understood what they had been doing in the forest the night I lost Gabriel, but my words appeared to rattle the soldier. At least, I thought he had an expression of concern. Also, the murmuring coming from the townsfolk had intensified.

A woman screamed somewhere behind us.

This sent the already nervous townsfolk into another panic, as everyone followed her stare.

In the distance, through the dissipating grey clouds, came a fiery comet. As it drew closer, I recognised it as a black dragon with wings.

Some of the townsfolk removed their masks for a better look, while others cowered under their giant bug faces.

The dragon made a strange choking sound which grew louder as it approached the square.

Then all went silent as the winged creature loomed above.

I realised it was no dragon. It was a manufactured monster. It plummeted at an angle and found the House of Books.

Rocks burst from the citadel, while flames threatened to consume me.

I slipped into absolute darkness as my lungs filled with smoke.

Chapter 14

The world turned black.

Someone was stroking my hair. *Wake up, poppet*, a soft female voice said.

Through the darkness came a bright light. My grandmother's face appeared. Her white hair shone like a halo as the light illuminated her from somewhere beyond my vision.

Go back now, Andromeda. It's not your time.

A blackened cloud surrounded me. Smoke and dust smothered the air and stole the oxygen.

A sharp pain shot across my back and neck when I tried to move. My ears rang. My eyes burned. The townsfolk coughed and spluttered around me. My body felt heavy. An arm lay across my face. It wasn't mine.

The soldier suffocated me. I shuffled around as I attempted to slide his body from my torso, but his weight was too great in my weakened state. Smaller objects dropped from me as I wriggled. I reached out and touched the ground either side of me. I couldn't find my friend.

'Envy,' I called, with a rasp.

A whine came from nearby.

Jingling bells grew into an ear-shattering roar as the fire carts approached.

Horses' hooves, heavy footsteps, and shouting sounded through the smoke and dust.

The air turned damp.

The blackened cloud had begun to clear when I finally manged to detach the soldier from me.

I swivelled around and found Envy's soft fur. She raised her face to mine and I kissed her nose. She appeared as dazed as me. She had some grazes but no obvious wounds.

Unlike the soldier.

Blood had congealed around a vicious cut on his head. I knew he wouldn't rise again. He was dead.

The old citadel had transformed into a rocky landscape. Only the rocks weren't rocks. They were pieces of broken masonry.

I surveyed the square. Bodies lay strewn across the cobblestones and among the now desecrated stonework.

The townsfolk sobbed and wailed.

Pieces of paper fluttered downwards like giant snowflakes.

Soldiers on the fire carts hollered for more water. My thoughts turned to some of the real firemen, who had been sent away to fight in a non-existent war, but in truth they now languished within the horrendous fortress in the forest.

Nurses sprinted back and forth from the hospital. Two by two they carried stretchers of the injured townsfolk.

A bronze plaque coated in a green fuzz caught my eye as it lay amongst the damaged stonework. I believed it to be the plaque which I had observed high up on the façade of the House of Books. I reached across to liberate it from the stones.

I hadn't dared to face the House of Books, but I couldn't hold it off any longer.

I glanced round and discovered a gaping wound in the citadel's skyline.

The columns and entire front of the building had gone,

exposing the innards. The balconies hung precariously like a broken ribcage. Adding to all this, the House of Books was now receiving a soaking from the soldiers on the fire cart. The steam-powered pump on the cart forced water through two snaking hoses. The soldiers appeared to be struggling to keep the hoses under control. Several times, I thought the force of the water surging through each hose would send the soldiers flying into the air. But the Edenshire horses – who were attached to the fire carts – stood stock still, and this steadied the steam-powered load.

The House of Books wasn't the only structure with a violent wound; the closest flank of the Guildhall to the House of Books had also suffered an amputation.

Despite the destruction, the clock began its genteel chime in advance of striking the hour as though it were indifferent to the devastation. The clock was oblivious to the fact that the building it resided within was now naked on one side.

The gongs began, as I scrambled to my feet still clutching the plaque.

The clock struck eleven as I left Envy behind and hobbled towards the shell of the building which had become my favourite place.

The main doors had evaporated.

'Miss, I wouldn't go in there,' one of the soldiers shouted, as he doused the House of Books with water.

Small fires continued to burn in separate areas.

I stumbled over the rubble which carpeted the foyer. The internal doors lay in vicious shards.

'Miss,' the soldier screamed, 'it's not safe.'

I wasn't interested.

The ground floor was a mound of damaged books and debris. I slipped over the soggy wreckage of broken glass from the skylight and windows, giant wooden splinters from the bookcases, and shattered books and loose pages.

I came across a dry book which appeared unharmed. But as I rescued the volume from its rocky grave, the spine disintegrated and the pages tumbled from my fingers.

Towards the back of the deceased House of Books, I caught sight of the telescope. It seemed intact, but it lay in a forlorn manner upon its side.

I collapsed amongst the saturated rubble. I had never been happier than when I studied in the House of Books. I had had my own renaissance. I was reborn. I had no longer cared I was considered different whenever I immersed myself in those long-forgotten dusty tomes, nor when I spent time with Gabriel. But now my world was over. My grandfather was fading away in prison. As was my father. Gabriel had vanished. The authorities had begun to remove *my* books to another location. And the House of Books had been destroyed.

The winged black dragon had exploded into my favourite place, and thus stolen it from my grasp. I wondered if scrap metal from another town had been used to create the dragon. Scrap metal remained in demand to use for explosives according to the posters in the citadel. Yet there was no war.

Could this all be my fault? Was this the mayor's idea of revenge? I had found the House of Books and I shouldn't have done. The authorities didn't want me to know. But I did, hence why they had taken it from me. Just like they had taken everything else. The mayor was willing to end the existence of the House of Books to prevent the townsfolk from having any knowledge of the past.

An horrendous thought struck me: what if Gabriel had come back to the House of Books? What if he had been snooping about the local history archives when the dragon hit?

I dropped the plaque and got to my feet. I searched through the rubble for his corpse. Through tears I tore at the debris and flung it behind me. But I was relieved to find no haunted pale face staring at me from under the violated bookcases and stonework. Therefore, I had to assume Gabriel remained in the forest. Perhaps he had gone back to the forest to stay for good? But then, why didn't the man who I presumed to be Gabriel's father know where Gabriel was?

I hunted for books which may have survived intact.

To my surprise other townsfolk struggled over the debris and began to rummage. The few remaining soldiers, who weren't dispersing water over the House of Books or the Guildhall, couldn't keep them back. Like me, the townsfolk were not interested in what the soldiers had to say. Some of the women and elderly sifted through paper and defiled volumes.

'What is this place?' one of them asked.

One young woman, who looked about my age, took a seat upon a dry spot of rubble and began reading from a book she had unearthed. She appeared to forget about the horror all around and lost herself in a fictional story. Or perhaps she became engrossed in the truth, historical truth, geographical truth, or scientific truth. The book could have covered one aspect of the truth, or the whole truth of our world.

I returned to the corroded bronze plaque, which had become a little damp. I wiped away some of the fuzzy green layer from the surface with my sleeve.

This revealed the lettering. And there was no mistaking the words.

It read: Andromeda House.

The name of my favourite place was Andromeda House. In that moment I could have laughed at the irony of it all. My father hadn't named me after the nearest galaxy. He hadn't named me after a princess from Greek mythology. He had named me after the abandoned building which I ended up falling in love with.

I'm not ashamed to say I burst into tears.

Envy emerged through the damp mist and rubble. I found comfort in my best friend.

The minutes passed like hours as I sat hugging Envy. I didn't want to let go. Time had slowed. I could appreciate her.

A commotion came from the square as the clock chimed for half past the hour. Soldiers covered the dead in sheets as the mayor walked through the traumatised throng. More townsfolk had arrived in the old citadel. Having heard a blast, I presumed they had come to investigate.

From the corner of my eye, I caught a glimpse of a cobalt-blue robed figure from a biblical painting. The robed figure approached at speed.

'Andromeda,' a female voice cried.

It was my mother in a deep blue coat. She flung her arms around me.

'Thank the First Ancestors you're alive,' she sobbed.

'I saw Grandma,' I said.

'Did you?'

'She looked happy. She was surrounded by light.'

My mother nodded and stroked my face.

'This place is called Andromeda House,' I said, holding up the fuzzy green plaque.

My mother wiped her eyes.

'There's your answer then,' she said. 'How you came to be named Andromeda. This was your dad's favourite building in the citadel. Of all the beautiful buildings, he said this one conveyed an elegance which couldn't be matched. He'd be broken-hearted to see it looking like this.'

I pondered my father's words. I had always considered the building to be the most elegant. I don't recall ever having had that discussion with my father. I must have simply inherited his thoughts.

'Did he know it housed books?' I asked.

'I don't think so,' my mother said. 'I don't believe he ever went inside a forbidden building. Your dad is brave in many ways, but when it comes to breaking the law, he's not as fearless as you.'

A darkness ascended over the ruins of the House of Books.

The dark shadow came courtesy of the mayor. He stood on the spot which had once been the grand entrance. He glared at me. I detected a sneer as his lips rose and his eyes blazed.

I had always been nervous of authority. Afraid of the mayor in a way. I had always considered he must be a highly important and highly intelligent person as he had been made mayor. But as I had discovered, believing you're a person of significance does not make you a person of significance, or intelligence. He had taken the power all for himself. But in reality he was no one special; he had nothing but contempt for the townsfolk. I don't know how the townsfolk felt about him, but I had nothing but contempt for the mayor in return. He was just a man full of his own self-importance. And I knew from his malicious sneer that my instinct on who had ordered the destruction of the House of Books had been correct.

Heat seared through me as I teetered to my feet. It wasn't the usual intense warmth I felt from embarrassment. I didn't burn with shame. I burned with anger. The heat grew so fierce I knew it needed venting. I had found my fire, and I allowed the fire to explode from my body.

'You did this,' I yelled, as I stormed forward. 'You destroyed my world.'

'No. You did this,' the mayor said. 'You never should have stepped inside this building. Had you not, this building would remain. It is now for the good of Eden that this place is gone. Everything we have done, we have done for the good of Eden.'

'You had no right to take my history away from me. You took our history from all of us. You told us lies. You said there were monsters. You told us to hate people we'd never met. You said they were deformed. You said there was a war.'

My roaring at the mayor attracted more of the townsfolk, and they gathered behind him.

'We've kept you safe,' he bellowed, as his eyes darted about wildly.

The mayor seemed to sense the unified glare of the townsfolk as they encroached closer.

'Kept us safe from what?' I asked.

'Monsters do exist out there,' he said. 'We've shielded you from them. The world is a terrifying place. You were safe here. But you couldn't leave things alone. You destroyed your world.'

My mother launched herself over the rubble towards him.

'How dare you speak to my daughter like that,' she said. 'My daughter speaks the truth. You have told nothing but lies. You've imprisoned us all. You think this is some kind of perfect idyll? No one in Eden has a say in anything, and we're confined to our own town. Supposedly because of the spirits and the monsters, and now the war. But we've never been fighting anyone. You've told lie after lie about spirits, and monsters, and war, in order to create fear amongst the townsfolk. You haven't kept us safe from anything. You just wanted to restrict our lives.'

The mayor baulked.

'Who was it who made you mayor all those years ago?' my mother continued. 'Was it a position you assumed you had a right to have? Perhaps the townsfolk should be asked who they would like to run Eden. Or we could just run Eden ourselves. Wouldn't that be an interesting way of doing things,' she said matter-of-factly.

'Do you dare to suggest that I hand over authority to simple townsfolk?' the mayor asked.

'I do dare,' my mother said, 'and who says the townsfolk are simple? Is that what you think of us all? I believe that proves you shouldn't be in charge of Eden, or anywhere.'

The townsfolk who had gathered around us began to talk amongst themselves, some were even nodding enthusiastically.

The mayor's eyes changed. At the time I couldn't discern the transformation. Thinking on those eyes again, I realise they darkened in dread.

When I got home, I cleaned the bronze plaque as best I could. I gave it pride of place on top of my writing bureau, amongst small vases of dried flowers and my drawing of the House of Books.

My mother had placed the gift from Doctor Hartnell on my writing bureau. I had left it on the dining table the day before, and I still hadn't unwrapped the brown paper. I wasn't about to now. Instead, I consoled myself with some of the books I had taken previously. I was glad I hadn't finished a single book. I would never be able to return what I had borrowed. But at least I had something solid to cherish. My memory of the House of Books would live on within the pages of those special volumes.

I flicked through some art and architecture books, trying to locate something similar to what I had seen on the ceiling in the Assembly Rooms. Then I encountered the perfect sibling. Within the book on architecture by Sir Christopher Wren, I came across a few pages discussing a place he had designed called the Old Royal Naval College. This college resided in a place named Greenwich. Situated inside the college was a Baroque room named the Painted Hall. The stunning art in the hall had been created by a man named Sir James Thornhill.

None of this meant anything to me. It didn't matter. I had discovered the art which inspired the ceiling art in the Assembly Rooms. At least, I assumed it had been that way around and not the other. The only difference was the colour palette of the Painted Hall. It was a little darker than the colour palette in those rooms in the old citadel. But I loved the dark opulence of the Painted Hall.

I flicked through the other architecture books and discovered buildings designed by Inigo Jones, Nicholas Hawksmoor and John Vanbrugh. Like Christopher Wren, they had been active in or around the seventeenth and eighteenth centuries respectively. I also came across John Nash, who was active during the nineteenth century. Although, since I currently lived in the thirteenth century – or thought I did because of the lies – I couldn't comprehend how long ago the real seventeenth century had taken place. But I recalled Gabriel had said I could add around one thousand years onto my year. Therefore, I supposed I was really living in the late twenty-third century.

Studying these architects, I was able to compare the style of architecture with all my drawings of my favourite buildings in the old citadel. I couldn't say for definite that these architects had designed any of the buildings in the citadel, but I could recognise their influence.

Due to the huge columns, the House of Books, along with what had once been the Theatre Royal, Stonburh Museum, and Stonburh Art Gallery, all had an air of Hawksmoor, Jones, Vanbrugh, and Wren. The Assembly Rooms, the Grand Tea Room, the Guildhall, and the university buildings, which were now the school and hospital, were more in the style of Nash.

Most of the buildings in Eden weren't influenced by any of these architects at all. For example, the fire station was something altogether different. Plus, all the tall, crooked structures in the citadel were from another time entirely. It made me realise how centuries of history had been captured in the architecture.

I decided, since I now knew the names of the abandoned buildings, I would add those names to my drawings. All except *Library*. The House of Books would remain the House of Books.

Envy leapt from my bed and charged for the stairs. Someone tapped or scratched upon the front door.

My mother screamed from the sitting room.

I sprang from my bedroom to investigate.

I slipped on the final step of the stairs and landed in an undignified heap on the sitting room floor.

I glanced up to find my grandfather swaying in the doorway.

If he had not been standing upright, I would have said he was dead. His face had taken on an ashen hue, and his eyes seemed lost in their dark recesses.

My mother guided him to his favourite armchair, while poor Envy attempted to gain his attention by jumping and pawing at his legs. But he appeared not to notice her at all.

'Your hands are freezing,' my mother said.

She rekindled the log burner once my grandfather was seated.

I don't think my grandfather even blinked for several minutes while he sat staring at the far wall.

Envy had found a comfortable position in his lap and nudged her nose in his face. But once again, he didn't acknowledge her existence.

'Would you like some tea, Dad?' my mother asked.

My grandfather didn't respond.

I took his hand in mine. It felt as though I touched the frozen ground in winter.

'Grandad?' I said.

I wasn't at all convinced he was truly with us. I wondered if he had passed away in that terrible place, and we were receiving his spirit. But as I considered his hollow face, I noticed his eyes glistened in the flame from the log burner. Surely if he were dead there wouldn't be any life in his eyes?

'How did you get out, Grandad?' I asked, as I waved my hands back and forth in front of his eyes.

My grandfather raised his eyebrows.

'Tea?' he said.

'What?'

'Did your mother say she's making tea?'

'Yes.'

'Good. Haven't had a decent cup of tea in days,' he said.

'But you always complain about the tea we have.'

'Do I?' he said, seemingly forgetting how often he complained about all beverages.

'Yes, you do,' I said. 'Since rationing anyway.'

My grandfather gazed upon Envy, who had snuggled herself into his jumper.

'What do you want then, aye?' he said, wrapping his arms around her. 'It's nice to be home. Always a warm welcome from this one. Where's my pipe?'

'It's in the drawer, where it always is,' I said, as I left his side to obtain his pipe and tobacco from the dresser.

His face beamed as he lit his pipe and took a few puffs. Then his faced changed to one of disappointment.

'Uh, better than nothing I suppose,' he said.

He smacked his lips as though attempting to dispel a displeasing aftertaste. One of shoe polish, I expected.

My mother reappeared with a tray laden down with our teapot and three teacups, along with a piece of the sponge cake with jam and cream filling she had made.

My grandfather's eyes widened in delight.

'Would you like something hot to eat?' my mother asked. 'I can reheat the stew.'

'Cake is good,' he said, as he set his pipe down, 'and it's my favourite.'

Envy settled in my grandfather's lap, and I poured him some tea.

'I should go away and come back more often,' he said.

'How did you get back?' my mother asked.

'I don't know,' my grandfather said, as he cut into the sponge with the little cake fork. Then he shoved a piece of sugary goodness into his mouth.

'You don't know how you left the prison?' I asked.

'Is that where I was?'

'But you saw me in there, too. Don't you remember?' I asked, wondering if the guards had perhaps hit him over the head with something before he managed to escape.

'Oh, yes, yes. I did see you,' he said. 'That was prison, was it?'

'Where did you think you were?' my mother asked.

'Somewhere with terrible food.'

'How can you not recall how you got out?' I asked, thinking how his memory had never been this bad.

'I must've fallen asleep,' my grandfather said. 'When I awoke, I found myself outside. I was wandering around and around in the heat. Oh, and the *wind*. The wind was awful. Cut you in half it would.'

'But the prison was cold. When were you anywhere hot?' I asked.

'When I found myself outside under the red sky,' he said, as he gobbled down another piece of cake.

'Perhaps I should call Doctor Hartnell,' my mother said, 'and tell her it's an emergency?'

'I don't need a doctor,' my grandfather said. 'I'm an old man. My mind's not what it used to be. When you're on the verge of death, you see and hear all sorts of things. I think you become more open to what's on the other side.'

'Other side of what?' I asked.

'The other side beyond what we know and can see,' he said. 'I suppose sometimes our world and their world must collide. It's in these moments, when the veil slips, that we see the shadows of the other menfolk.'

'What are you talking about?' my mother asked.

'I'm telling you what I saw,' my grandfather said.

'Shadows?' I said, thinking about the shadow figures who appeared every time the people who resembled angels arrived.

'Shadows, shapes, giant beings. They're watching us,' he said.

'Who's watching us?' I asked.

'The other menfolk. Magnificent, they are. Tall and graceful. With beautiful large wings. They came through the light. After the red sky and the storm. They showed me all the stars and said that's where I belong. Can you believe it? I belong to the stars. The stars are where I ought to reside. Out there I can be at peace and float free. This town is nothing but a restriction. This entire town is a prison. My place is out there guided by starlight. I have found my true purpose. We're meant to ascend out there. This is what they have shown me.'

'I think you're delirious,' my mother said. 'Drink your tea, you'll feel better.'

'I won't feel better,' my grandfather said. 'I can't just fade away in death. Part of us stays behind. Did I ever tell you I still see your mother?' he said, as he glanced over at my grandmother's urn on the sideboard.

'She's dead,' my mother said.

'Her body's gone, but her spirit remains. She's in the light, with the menfolk who watch.'

'Okay, perhaps you should go to bed,' my mother said. 'I think you're frightening Andromeda.'

'But I'm not frightened,' I said. 'I even saw Grandma today.'

'See,' my grandfather said, triumphantly. 'She hasn't really left us.'

'Why are the other menfolk watching us?' I asked.

'I don't know,' he said. 'But they must have watched me, because they knew my whereabouts. They knew I shouldn't have been there. I remember now. A door opened and they came through. Three of the menfolk hovered before me. Darkness became light. They obliterated the night. Then they each transformed into a giant golden bird.'

I turned to my mother.

'I think the prison has made Grandad very unwell. The damp must have gotten into his brain.'

The book entitled *The Truth* called to me that evening. The gold lettering of the title shimmered in the lamplight. I sat at my writing bureau and read until the candles and lamp began to fade. I thought about lighting another candle, but I turned to find Envy sleeping on my bed, curled up head to tail, and I changed my mind. She always had the right idea. I went and snuggled up next to her. I couldn't sleep though. My mind raced, contemplating all the words I had devoured.

According to the book, there was an unknown world out there: Planet Nine, sometimes known as Planet X. This planet is somehow hidden within our solar system. But it's enormous. Yet no one has seen it. Some astronomers and scientists believe in the likelihood of an ice or gas giant at the boundary of our solar system. The hypothesisers say it has to exist because something huge is having an influence on our local planets in terms of climate. Planet Nine has an elliptical orbit. Meaning sometimes it veers in close toward the known eight planets, but most of the time its trajectory throws it out into the farthest darkness. The scientists believe Planet Nine could influence weather patterns here on Earth. They already acknowledge that the gravitational tug of the gas giant Jupiter, and our closest neighbour Venus, cause changes in our weather cycles. Therefore, why not a super-giant planet at the edge of our solar system.

I found this all intriguing. But the book was about to enter a whole new realm of weirdness.

Planet Nine was also referred to as Nibiru, where a race of gods known as the Anunnaki hail from. Anunnaki means *those who from heaven to Earth came*. Tales of these gods originate from ancient Sumerian culture.

The book appeared to believe the Anunnaki are real, and came to Earth thousands of years ago. These giant alien gods decided to create a new slave race on Earth by passing on their DNA to monkeys, and from which the first humans sprang. This is how humans can account for our sudden appearance on the world stage. This implied our existence was the result of an experimental abomination.

According to the book, this passing on of Anunnaki DNA also explains how the Sumerians had such vast knowledge in relation to our place in the solar system. The book questioned how it was possible the Sumerians could know the exact size of the planets in comparison with each other.

For a moment, I wondered if this could all be true. Did the Sumerians generally believe an alien race came to Earth and created humans to work as labourers for the alien gods? But wasn't this their mythological origin story? Wasn't this the tale they told their children? Gabriel had told me all about fiction, folktales, and mythology. In Eden, we had tales of the First Ancestors. I had learned all about them as a child. They were tales which had been passed down. Which had now turned out to be fictitious.

The book put forward the argument that the Anunnaki gave humans the wheel, the plough, agriculture, and irrigation. The first language spoken, and the first writing – cuneiform – were also given to us. The book was saying our ancient ancestors invented nothing. They discovered nothing. They didn't explore their land. Or study the night sky. They didn't want to learn. They had no aspirations. They had no questions. They couldn't ponder upon their lives. They couldn't recognise patterns. They couldn't work out a damn thing. They lacked curiosity about their world. Our ancestors never would have progressed on their own, so devoid were they of any thought processes. The tools were bestowed, not invented. Our ancestors were not even able to communicate before the aliens gave them the gift of language and writing.

This narrative infuriated me. The story made some of our true ancestors incompetent. The reason provided as to why the alien race wanted labourers, and we were created, was to mine gold for the gods. They required this precious metal to support the atmosphere on their home planet, as gold shields radiation. If the Anunnaki were real, could they not have obtained gold from somewhere else? Why would they have to create a race of humans to collect gold? As with any theory, it raised more questions than answers. I couldn't fathom how, despite a myriad of animal species evolving on Earth, according to this book, humans did not. Humans are the children of invading aliens and monkeys. Apparently we didn't learn through process.

But if people believed the Sumerian stories – that humans didn't evolve and were created by aliens – could something else have created the aliens? Could it be that they didn't evolve on their current planet but sprang from somewhere else? Did *another* alien race give the Anunnaki life and tools? If the answer is no, they evolved, why say humans couldn't have evolved, but an alien race could? All the questions posed around how mystifying it is that humans appeared on the scene would have to be asked of this alien race, too. But if the answer is yes, the alien race was also created, who or what created the Anunnaki? Also, do all alien races across time and space require other beings for making gold?

I had already learned from the *Space Encyclopaedia* that gold is a rarity in the universe. The metal is formed when two neutron stars collide. Billions of years ago, two neutron stars collided in our galaxy, and the explosion created gold in the Milky Way.

The book *The Truth* also mentioned the watchers. They are angels. It stated that the watchers are discussed in The Book of Daniel and The Book of Enoch. But I didn't know those books. Gabriel had said he wasn't an archangel. He had said he was just a man and not privileged. But I supposed he would say that if he didn't want me to know he was a watching angel.

Disappointment crushed me. My mind was a muddle. I felt I was none the wiser for having read *The Truth*. After all the trouble I had gone through to conceal the book, I concluded it might be, as my grandfather would say, a load of balderdash. People could, and would, say anything was true. But perhaps even the ancestors had been lied to? What if an element of Sumerian mythology was true? Could their mythology have been based around a small truth? That was quite a scary thought. I didn't know what to think anymore. I thought I was getting to grips with everything, but sometimes learning new things became overwhelming. I wondered if the references to the books of Daniel and Enoch meant those sections could be more relied upon. Whoever Daniel and Enoch were, my heart sank to know I would never come across either of their names in the future. I wouldn't have the opportunity to read their books, since the House of Books had gone the way of a neutron star collision. I may never find out why Stonburh had to become Eden either.

And I wondered if I would ever see Gabriel again.

Chapter 15

My grandfather had certainly appeared delirious that night. Neither my mother nor I had ever known him to speak such gibberish. Or balderdash.

I came downstairs in the early hours of the morning and sat with my grandfather by the log burner. We were going to carry him to his bed, but it would have been so awkward getting him up the stairs we decided against it. Plus we thought he needed to stay by the log burner, as he felt so cold.

Envy snored at my feet while I read some more from the *Space Encyclopaedia*.

I read that humans will one day colonise space. We will have to if we want to survive the death of our sun.

The Earth is our home, but so is the solar system, our galaxy, and therefore the entire universe. We can start the process of saving ourselves by going to the moons of Jupiter and Saturn. The eventual aim is to spread ourselves out amongst the stars. That way we have a better chance of surviving. We might be the only intelligent life in our galaxy. We just don't know. If we leave, we have an opportunity to explore and give intelligent life to all the millions of star systems over the next million years, if intelligent life isn't already out there, of course.

We would have to colonise Mars first. But this will only be a temporary base, since Mars is too close to Earth, at an average distance of about one hundred and forty million miles, which seemed like a great distance to me. But my real ancestors were thinking much farther into the future. They took into consideration the expansion of the sun. When that happens, Mars will be in the firing line too. Therefore, Mars will act as a giant space station for whatever type of fuel and resources we need to continue on to Saturn's and Jupiter's moons.

The surface of Mars is home to deep valleys, canyons, and vast desert plains. Plus numerous giant extinct volcanoes, including the tallest volcano in our solar system: Olympus Mons, which stands at seventy-two thousand feet. I didn't know what volcanoes were at the time, and I couldn't imagine seventy-two thousand feet.

Mars is a frozen, rocky planet, but it hasn't always been this way. Billions of years ago, Mars was the water world with potential, while Earth was as toxic as Venus. This all changed due to something called the Late Heavy Bombardment. Asteroids pelted down upon all the planets in our solar system for tens of millions of years. After this cataclysmic event, Earth had transformed into Mars' twin sister. Both planets were perfect for life. But something catastrophic began to unfold inside Mars. Its molten core began to cool. Then Mars' protective magnetic field failed. This meant solar winds could penetrate the skies of Mars. The winds tore away the atmosphere, and temperatures plummeted as a result.

Once again, I was learning how precarious life was. Mars had been the Earth of its day, long before Earth was hospitable. Mars could have been the planet that life evolved on in our solar system. Now the water on Mars remained locked in ice.

The encyclopaedia stated that water is key to our survival. This is why we should head for the moons of the gas giants. I noted that Jupiter's Ganymede, the large moon which Gabriel appeared obsessed with, has a saltwater ocean. It's even larger than Earth's, but it lies under ice sheets about one hundred miles thick. The scientists think another of Jupiter's moons, Europa, has a saltwater ocean. But again, this is under thick ice sheets. Another moon, Callisto, has water too. Callisto could be a good place to go, but she often gets overlooked.

Saturn's Enceladus also has ice water. The Cassini probe found water vapour sprouting like geysers at the moon's south pole, meaning there is a liquid ocean beneath Enceladus's surface. This is also salt water. It bleeds salt water into the atmosphere from hydrothermal vents, meaning there's extreme heat coming from the core. One of Saturn's other moons, Titan, has an Earthlike surface, as it has great lakes. However, they are lakes of methane. But Ganymede, Europa, Callisto and Enceladus all have potential.

All those strange words: geysers, hydrothermal, methane. My mind was a muddle. I was still concerned that if I wasn't careful, my brain might really burst from all the new knowledge I had been cramming into it. But I had to devour all the knowledge I held in my hands. The mayor, the soldiers, and the nightwatchman, all knew I had taken books. What if the authorities came to my home to take me and, or, the books away? I had to at least try and retain as much information as I could. Therefore, I continued with the *Space Encyclopaedia*.

It stated that with Mars having acted as a giant stepping stone, we would then head off to the moons of Jupiter and Saturn, where we would then set up new permanent homes. Those moons will be the safest moons in our solar system once the sun begins to expand. However, even the solar system won't last forever. Humans will have to keep moving on. Future humans could end up anywhere in the universe where there's water. We will need to locate another moon or planet like Earth, which sits within a Goldilocks zone.

I didn't understand what Goldilocks zone meant. It had something to do with liquid water rather than ice water. But the additional explanation of *not too hot, not too cold, just right* seemed odd. I wondered why the encyclopaedia didn't just say perfect conditions. The ancestors had some weird sayings.

However, the ancestors were also incredible. They had discovered such a planet in another solar system. They had named the planet Proxima B. It was bigger than Earth and closer to its star, Proxima Centauri. But the star was a red dwarf, which meant the star was smaller than our sun, and therefore not as hot. Because of this, the planet sat in its solar system's Goldilocks zone. There was one problem though. The planet was four point two light years away. Which is twenty-five million, million miles.

Even if humans could get to Proxima B, we wouldn't be able to stay there forever. Future humans will continue to move further out into the galaxy and the universe because it's changing. Stars die, and new ones are born every day. When we're out there, we will have to constantly look for other suitable planets and moons. The universe is alive. It hasn't finished evolving. We could go on until the end if we're smart. But luck will play its part too. This terrified me.

'What are you reading?' my grandfather asked, as he stirred in his armchair.

'The book about space,' I said.

'You haven't got any more books, then?'

'I have some, but I won't be able to get any more,' I said forlornly, picturing the House of Books in its prime.

'Why not?' he asked.

'The House of Books has gone, Grandad. Something fell out of the sky and destroyed it.'

'Fell from the sky?' he said, as he leaned closer to the log burner and rubbed his hands. 'Why would they want to destroy it?'

'The authorities? We know why,' I said, a little agitated. It appeared my grandfather had definitely received a bump on the head before leaving prison.

'No, I mean the other menfolk,' he said.

‘The other menfolk? If what you said was true last night, you said they were watchers? If all they’re doing is watching, why would they destroy a building? Anyway, the mayor already confirmed it was destroyed on his authority.’

‘Perhaps you’re right. They didn’t strike me as a destructive species. But they have been watching us, and they are like menfolk. Only … I don’t think they’re from here.’

My grandfather repositioned himself in his armchair, closed his eyes, and fell right back into a deep slumber.

My grandfather’s words got me thinking again about Gabriel’s apparent obsession with Ganymede. Plus, the fact that his people came from the sky got me wondering. Was Gabriel a visitor from another planet? Perhaps his people were trying to find a new home?

After breakfast I ventured into the old citadel, along with Envy. We had the omnibus to ourselves for the entire journey.

I wanted to inspect the damage to the House of Books. I wanted to verify if it was as bad as I could recollect. It was. The building also suffered the indignity of being cordoned off within a threatening-looking barricade. The barricade was made of giant spiked crosses, with what looked like chicken wire wrapped around them, which created a pen. The spiky barricade wouldn’t have looked out of place outside the prison fortress. But in the citadel, it added to the menace in the air. Soldiers swarmed within the pen, preventing anyone from getting too close. Some collected damaged books and placed them in boxes.

The few townsfolk who had gone into the citadel still wore their gas masks. The rubble had been cleared from the cobblestones and sat piled up in a corner of the square. The Guildhall stood half proud, half deformed. I actually felt sorry for the building. I had no animosity for the structure, only for the liars who remained inside. I wondered if anyone had been working in that part of the building when it was torn away. I didn't linger on this thought for too long though.

I continued on, past the Guildhall and around to the temple.

Some of the temple gardens had suffered from the blast. A section of the wall behind the House of Books and Guildhall lay strewn across the flowers. A trench had formed where the wall had once stood.

The Temple of the First Ancestors remained intact. Or should that be Temple of the Ancestors Before the First Ancestors? Or perhaps people had even gone before them?

I meandered through the nave with Envy by my side. I recalled the day when the cathedral had come to life. I could still hear the choir. I envisioned the angels. I imagined the shadow figures surrounding me. I wanted the stained-glass windows returned. I wanted the colours to dance across the stone floor once more. I wanted the robed statues standing proud upon their plinths returned. I wanted Jesus upon the cross, even though he suffered. I wanted the cathedral restored. I wanted to see it once more in its prime. I no longer wanted this empty shell. A shell whose meaning had been lost.

As I sauntered closer to what had once been the section for the choir, I discerned whispering coming from one of the alcoves to my left. I poked my head around the wall and peered into what would have been a chapel.

I discovered the mayor, along with a soldier, kneeling on the stone floor, the mayor's head hung low. His hands were clasped together and pressed to his chest.

He conversed with the air before him. Muttering under his breath. I felt embarrassed to have found him so vulnerable. Some of my hatred for the man evaporated while he grovelled before something much greater.

I slunk a little closer, but indicated for Envy to stay behind me.

Within the muttering, I caught the words: 'God forgive me.'

The soldier didn't utter a word. He hung his head. I believe his hands were clasped in his lap. I couldn't observe him as clearly. From my viewpoint, they were both in profile, and he was behind the mayor.

The soldier glanced up. He must have sensed an intruder, for he turned to face me.

At first, I didn't recognise his face without the beard. Nor did I recognise him without his shabby clothes and long hair. But I recognised his piercing blue eyes.

It was the shabby man who had been arrested in the square for speaking about a flood and knowledge lost. The man who ended up in the cell next to my grandfather. The man who, through our prison cell doors, had told me all about real wars, and even explained democracy to me. The man I came to know as Silas.

He shook his head at me, as though I shouldn't be there. I shouldn't have caught him in such a compromising position.

The mayor was oblivious. He continued muttering. This time I think I caught: 'God, forgive him.'

Silas began mouthing something to me. I think a look of pure anger blazed from his sapphire eyes.

I couldn't understand what he was attempting to say. I couldn't lip-read him. I just knew he was vexed.

I sped from the temple.

Silas was one of *them*.

Silas was a soldier. It was all a lie. His antics in the square and his subsequent arrest had been a performance. He *had* been in prison as a spy. I tried to recall everything we had spoken about behind our cell doors. Had my grandfather divulged family information before I arrived? My mind exploded in fury and I couldn't think straight.

It was bad enough to discover that Silas was a traitor, but

also witnessing the mayor prostrate like that unnerved me. He wanted God to forgive him. A god which no one in our time had any idea existed. This was a religion from the past civilisation. This was an old forgotten god. We didn't have religion. We had nothing in comparison. We didn't believe we were created. We appeared. But thanks to the House of Books, I knew this to be the story of evolution. We evolved from tiny single-celled organisms. It sounded crazy. It was all crazy, whatever way you looked at it. I understood why people in the past wanted to believe they had been created by some higher being. Creation was more of a comfort. I understood why they needed their faith. It gave them reason in all the chaos.

But to me it seemed we were here because we were here. We are part of nature. Life is what we make of it. Sometimes it will be good, and sometimes it will be bad. All in one lifetime. Life was all about chance.

With everything I had learned since Gabriel introduced me to the House of Books, it appeared the universe didn't care about us. The universe had unintentionally created living breathing creatures. It wasn't interested in our lives. It wasn't interested that we had family and friends, and communities we cared about. The universe appeared hostile to life in a way. Life could thrive on a planet. But life could also be wiped out by an array of natural disasters on the very same planet. Or even something destructive from within that planet's solar system. But I supposed not out of malevolence. Just indifference to any living creature's existence. Humans are just beings who live on one of the countless rocky planets in the vast cosmos. Our rocky planet is the life-giving ocean world, nestled between a world of iron and another of sulphur.

Nature gave birth to us. Nature is beautiful. But it's also cruel. We see this every day. But that's the other thing we forget. Nature brings death. It gave us life, and it can take it away at any time. Nature has killed off numerous animal species down the millennia. They never got a chance to establish themselves. Humans are lucky to be one of the animals who survived this far. But one day the thing we were born of will kill us too. Because it all has to end. One day even the Earth will die. It's a terrifying truth to know that none of this will be here, and no one will exist. But even more terrifyingly, if we don't save ourselves, perhaps no future alien species will have ever known we had existed. They may believe they are the first example of intelligent life.

This idea got me pondering: was there a chance this had already happened before, billions of years ago, to a previous alien race?

That evening in my bedroom, I decided to unwrap the gift from Doctor Hartnell. As I sat at my writing bureau and unravelled the brown paper, a notecard tumbled from the wrapping and landed in my lap.

> *Dear Andromeda,*
> *I believe you should have this. I hope it helps you in some way.*
> *Your friend, Agnes*

I never knew Doctor Hartnell's first name was Agnes. I never knew she considered herself my friend. But if she hadn't informed the mayor that I had admitted to being in the House of Books, then I concluded she wasn't my enemy.

The gift was a book entitled *Living with Autism Spectrum Disorder*. I knew immediately it had come from the House of Books. There was the telltale six-digit numbered label at the bottom of the spine. I presumed this was one of the books she had accumulated recently, as none of the books in her office prior to the big haul from the House of Books had had the little white label on them. The labels must have been removed on the few books Doctor Hartnell already owned. However, the first few pages of *Living with Autism Spectrum Disorder* had been torn from the book. There was no page with the label glued inside with the words 'Stonburh Council Library Service'. Neither was there a page with the first date of being published.

At first, I thought perhaps Doctor Hartnell had ripped those pages from the book, but it didn't make sense, as she knew I knew about the House of Books. So then I presumed that the mayor must have ordered for the first pages to be torn out. That made more sense. It would explain why Doctor Hartnell hadn't known about this autism thing before. She had never known the truth about Eden. She was as much in the dark as I had been. She must have known there was a place where the authorities could obtain information. But I expect she probably didn't know there was such a place as a library right under her nose.

I stared at the words on the cover: *Living with Autism Spectrum Disorder*. Well, I was living with it. I had no choice. But like I had said to my mother, I didn't want it to define me. I had more important things to deal with. I hadn't considered it at the time when I had said those words, but I realised as I held the book that I had been trying to disregard my diagnosis. I viewed autism as an imposition in my life. But really, it was part of me. My mother was right. Doctor Hartnell meant me no harm. I could see that now.

I leafed through the book, scanning through pages in no particular order. Some of the things I read I could relate to. For example, I had never been comfortable with change. I struggled to adapt to new things. Even the smallest things. Once, when I was a child, my mother had decided to swap the dresser and the sideboard around. This threw me completely. On several occasions I managed to bump into the sideboard as it poked out further than the dresser had. Overnight, I had lost awareness on distance and scale. The sitting room didn't look or feel right. My mother ended up moving both items of furniture back to their original positions. She never moved anything else again.

Also, I considered how the House of Books had been a huge change for me. I had always hated change. The House of Books was something which should have been new and daunting, but was actually new and exciting. It was a change I fell in love with, and therefore I embraced that change to my world. Other traits I didn't recognise in myself at all. I read with interest how some autistic people may talk incessantly about their own interests all the time, and other people may not be able to get a word in. But on the other hand, another autistic person will find it difficult to express themselves or their interests, and may not say much at all in a group conversation. I found myself in the latter category. I was more quiet mouse than chattering crow. Although I think I had gotten better at these things. What I had come across so far in the book made me realise that autism truly was a spectrum. Traits could differ greatly.

I considered that the book would help me. I understood myself better than I had ever understood myself. The book could offer more guidance if I chose to delve further into the world of autism. I couldn't ignore it, hoping it would go away. It would never go away. I wasn't weird. Perhaps I was to others. This was annoying, but I wasn't trying to be weird. I was uncomfortable sometimes. I still hated large crowds. I still hated having a myriad of eyes upon me. Acknowledging the autism would make it easier, because now I knew why I felt awkward. I closed the book and accepted my diagnosis. I had autism.

I placed the gift amongst my new favourite tomes and glanced out of my window. To my surprise I caught sight of Gabriel lurking beyond my garden.

He smiled at me, before he turned to face the outer wall. Then he disappeared into the darkness.

I darted down the stairs, while Envy advanced upon me.

I grabbed a lantern and we dashed from the back door through the garden and the back gate, which led onto the field and outer wall.

The poor sheep were as perturbed as ever by the intrusion. They bleated and scarpered across the field, heading for the trees.

I could no longer detect Gabriel, but Envy barked and began charging along the wall.

I presumed Gabriel must have leapt over the wall near my cottage, whereas Envy and I headed for the river so we could utilise the damaged grate.

Once through, Envy belted away from the river up towards a rocky outcrop.

I lagged behind holding the lantern aloft.

Gabriel stood at the top of the outcrop, with the dark forest as his backdrop.

Envy was busy smothering Gabriel with kisses when I reached him.

I realised the outcrop provided a fantastic vantage point for viewing the old citadel.

'I'm glad you're okay,' I said, once I caught my breath. 'I was worried when I lost you. You gave me a fright.'

'Sorry,' he said. 'But I'd had a fright myself after seeing that body, and I just wanted to leave.'

'But you came back,' I said, joyous to see him again. Although Gabriel looked sad, as though his appearance back in Eden might not be permanent. 'Did you free my grandad?' I asked.

'Yes, we did. But I feel we have brought you risk.'

'You think they'll come to take him away again?'

'No, they'll leave him, he's frail,' Gabriel said. 'But you aren't, and you've been seen conversing with one of us.'

'The man I spoke with was looking for you.'

'He found me,' he said. 'The man you spoke with is my father.'

'I wondered if he was. He said I speak an old language.'

'It is an old language for us,' Gabriel confirmed.

'He said it had been lost through space and time.'

Gabriel nodded.

'It's a dead language,' he said. 'But we still know it.'

'A dead language? You don't speak this language where you come from?'

'No. But we know most of the old languages,' he said.

'It's not an old language, it's current. Are you saying that aside from the authorities hiding our true history, everyone in Eden is speaking a dead language?' I asked, wondering what else I was yet to still uncover.

'I'm just saying it's an old language to me,' Gabriel said with a shrug.

I supposed that it would make sense that people from another planet might speak a different language. I just didn't understand why my language would be considered dead to these people.

'What happened after your dad found you?' I asked.

'He wanted me to go with them. But I'm not ready yet. I asked them to help me instead. That's how we got your grandfather out.'

'You all went to the prison?'

'Only to the top of the tallest tower,' Gabriel said. 'As that was where you said you'd been held.'

'Did you get Silas out, too?' I asked, wondering if Gabriel and his father had accidently let out a traitor.

'Who's Silas?'

'He was in the cell next to my grandad. But he's out, and he's one of them,' I said, feeling a bitterness towards a man I'd trusted. Plus anger at myself for dismissing my initial gut reaction.

'One of whom?' Gabriel asked.

'The liars,' I said.

'I don't think there was anyone else in a cell at the top of the tallest tower,' he said.

‘Silas must have been already set free,’ I said. ‘But then he’s always been free. He was never really imprisoned.’

‘This man lied to you?’

I hung my head in shame for believing Silas’s lies. My poor grandfather had believed him too.

‘I want to find my dad,’ I said.

‘I know. Perhaps we should have released all the men from prison.’

‘Could you have done that?’ I asked. ‘They shouldn’t be in there. They should all be released. There’s no war.’

‘But your town *is* at war.’

‘Are we?’ I said, thinking Gabriel must be mistaken.

‘Yes, in two ways. I believe some people outside of this land have attempted to take control from your authorities and alert you to the reality.’

‘Have they? What’s the second way?’ I asked.

‘Your authorities are at war with monsters.’

‘The mayor said something about shielding us from real monsters,’ I said. ‘What monsters are they hiding us from?’

‘People like me,’ Gabriel stated.

‘But you’re not a monster,’ I said. I could never consider Gabriel a monster. He could be odd, but he was kind, caring, he had a good heart, and he wanted me to know the truth.

‘I could be considered an abomination,’ he said. ‘That’s enough.’

I thought about the how the Anunnaki had supposedly created humans from passing on their DNA to monkeys, and how I viewed that as an actual abomination.

‘Well, I don’t think you’re an abomination.’

‘I have to go,’ Gabriel said. ‘You have to forget about me. My people can’t stay here if we want to live.’

‘Are you all sick?’ I asked.

I thought Gabriel was about to reply, when lightning shot through the darkness and the god of thunder roared.

Tiny golden orbs fell within the warm rain. The bitter acrid scent entered my nostrils and burned once more. The sulphur appeared stronger this time, making me want to retch.

The lightning came again and lit up the valley and hills in an explosion of white, which revealed the large dark shapes in the clouds.

From our vantage point at the edge of the forest, I perceived water lapping at the wall surrounding the old citadel. As though the river had risen at least a hundred metres, although the torrential downpour must have interfered with the glow from the lamps around the citadel, so I could have been mistaken. Plus we found ourselves plunged into darkness once more.

'I'd like to show you something,' Gabriel said.

He wrapped his arms around me, and I became weightless. We rose in the air as though gravity had dissipated from the forest.

Gabriel placed a hand over one of my ears and I heard a terrible storm. Not the one which continued to explode around Eden, but a distant gale where the wind raged.

I closed my eyes as Gabriel guided his forehead towards mine.

The dark crimson sky stormed aflame. The heat suffocated my skin. I noted that I wore a suit like Gabriel, but I had the addition of a mask. Not a gas mask, but some other kind of mask, with a wide visor. I also wore the robe, or shawl. It was wrapped like a scarf around the bottom of the mask. Even through this my lungs burned. Dust billowed in the vicious wind. The dirt spattered across my visor and the incessant hum caused my ear canal to throb. I had never experienced weather like it. The windstorm screamed as it blasted across the open expanse.

Gabriel appeared to have gone. Or at least I couldn't observe him through the billowing dust. The atmosphere appeared to be attacking my suit, my epidermis, my very being.

My movement became disjointed as I stumbled across hot rocks which seared through the soles of my light grey footwear and warmed my feet. Wherever I was, I was not meant to exist there. My body was not designed for those conditions.

I realised Envy was no longer with me either. She was always by my side, no matter where I went. But not this time. Although I felt relieved at that. She would be dead if she stepped one paw into this environment.

Clouds moved with rapid speed. Some appeared dark and ominous, but none threatened to bring any rain. In the bleak landscape, it seemed rain had not quenched the land for centuries.

The rocks under my burning feet dissipated into hot cracked mud. Something danced upon the near horizon. An ocean or huge lake lapped at a shoreline.

Aside from the rocks, mud, and water, nature had abandoned the place. No creatures flew across the sky. No creatures roamed across the open land. No trees or plants of any kind rose in pride to touch the dark red atmosphere. If anything had ever lived or existed upon the land, it was long gone. Stripped down to nothing, ripped to shreds, as if it never was. The storming winds had shaped this land into a wide-open barren panorama.

I journeyed alone in the vastness of the burning land. Gabriel had once said there is a logical explanation for everything. But I couldn't see anything logical here. I couldn't recall how I got to the barren landscape. I had simply arrived. I turned back to pinpoint where I had come from, but it appeared I came from nothing. And I couldn't comprehend how long I had ambled across the nothingness.

I pushed a grey shoe into a heat-cracked void in the mud. It wasn't like any mud I had encountered before. Not like the life-giving soil at the temple gardens, and not like the soft earth after a rain shower, where the birds collect worms. It was not like the dark muddy sand at the river's edge, either. This mud had a fierce menacing appearance, to match the fierce atmosphere.

This mud had smothered and suffocated. Hidden histories lay beneath its surface.

The clouds which ripped across the flaming red sky had concealed something from me. When the sky broke through a little, it became apparent that an oncoming night did not bear down upon the land. It was a dark day with an obscured sun. The nuclear star blazed high behind the blanketed cloud cover.

As I approached the shoreline, I realised the light clouds rolling atop of the water were clouds of steam. A presence willed me to continue forward as ethereal music rose from the water's edge. It was their song. Gabriel's people lived down there. They moved within the darkness of the body of boiling water. And they were crying. Their choral song was one of sorrow and loss.

Gabriel appeared. He wasn't wearing a mask, but he carried one. Instead, he wore the shawl around his face. A pair of goggles covered his eyes.

He reached across to examine my mask. I presumed he was checking whether it was properly attached to my suit.

He removed his goggles and placed his mask over his head, lowering his shawl as he did so.

Having fixed his own mask, he stepped into the water and offered his hand to me.

I accepted it, just as I had done on the first night we met.

The mud became gloppy. My feet sunk into the heat of the goo which threatened to swallow me. Sharp objects lay within the mire: white fragments broke the surface along the shoreline. They resembled broken pieces of bone.

Water lapped at my ankles. I could sense its sweltering temperature through the suit as I waded further. The sharp objects poked out from the lake bed and attacked the soles of my shoes.

Gabriel allowed the lake, or sea, to consume our lower limbs.

Once my head went under, my feet became free of the tormenting bone-like fragments. I floated down. Deep into the darkness. Too deep. But even here I couldn't escape the heat. I had wandered to the edge of this world to delve into a scorching ocean. A never-ending darkness stretched out below, while above me the ocean surface screamed a blood red.

Still clutching Gabriel's hand, I landed feet first upon something unexpected, yet smooth and comforting. My footwear slipped and squeaked across a strong material rather than the ocean floor. Then my feet hit something more textured, like raised bumps, or rivets. My footwear slipped between the protrusions until I found the slippery smooth surface once more. A current dragged me along, and I leaned forward, allowing my hands to glide across the smooth exterior.

I lost Gabriel in the darkness.

The song of lamentation grew louder as I slipped around the outside of what I assumed to be a wide tunnel. Gabriel's people had created burrows under water. I wondered where these burrows led. As I crawled and floated forward along the outside of the tunnel, a faint light appeared underneath me. It provided the only illumination amongst the gloom. I now had a window onto the inner world of the tunnel. However, my eyes struggled within the murk, despite the welcoming light.

A hand from within the illuminated tunnel reached out towards mine. The thick translucent material caused the shadow of the hand to mutate into an elongated palm with five long thin fingers. I flattened my palms upon the clear tunnel wall and placed one hand directly above the imprint below.

Light began to glow from all around. Section by section a vast network of transparent tunnels, which appeared to spiral outwards from a central hub, became a beacon of golden illumination. Each tunnel appeared to stretch out for miles across the ocean floor. Some tunnels looked as though they led to huge dark objects in the distance.

Gabriel's people all appeared to press their palms upon the translucent ceiling of all the tunnels closest to me, in greeting.

I felt an overwhelming sense of sorrow. Of hopelessness.

I was amongst the people who my grandfather referred to as the other menfolk. Gabriel brought me to them to witness their existence for myself. But not just to observe. To understand. To have my eyes opened. What did I see?

I awoke with a jolt. Sunlight had begun to filter through my thin curtains.

Envy lay at the end of my bed, snuggled up head to tail.

I couldn't decide if I had actually gone somewhere with Gabriel in the night, or whether I had had a nightmare.

If it had been a dream, I could recollect all of it. Recalling every detailed element of a dream is unusual.

The barren land. The blood-red sky. My grandfather had said he had seen those things. This meant I was in possession of the truth. And the truth was a story of horror. Of late, I had spent the best part of my time learning about the destructive power of nature in the universe. The stories and the truth I had devoured proved nothing lasts forever. Suns die and asteroids collide with planets. External forces threaten every single celestial globe across the cosmos.

Gabriel and his people come from somewhere beyond our skies. But this somewhere is coming to the end of its life cycle.

Everything dies. They know what is coming for them. They have paid heed to the pattern. Because they have watched the cosmos for some time.

Chapter 16

My grandfather remained asleep in his armchair when I came downstairs to get breakfast. He appeared comfortable and I didn't want to wake him.

I consumed my breakfast in the kitchen sitting on the stool by the sink. I watched my mother tidy the overgrown parts of the garden.

I thought about my father. I wanted to know for sure whether he was in the prison. I had made that assumption, but what if he wasn't? What if some of the men had been sent somewhere else? What if there actually was some distant town called Frontline? I decided I would confront the mayor. I was no longer afraid of him. It felt good to no longer be afraid. I gulped down my tea and rammed the final piece of honey-drizzled crusty bread in my mouth.

When I got to the citadel, most of the townsfolk continued to wear their gas masks. I wondered why they hadn't opened their eyes to what was really happening in Eden.

One young child ran away from her elder brother, who

chased her around a bench. She squealed in delight at the game. Or perhaps she squealed in terror at the monster.

I told Envy to wait by the Guildhall steps.

I marched through the open double door and stomped across the checkerboard flooring as though I had no regard for its striking but simple elegance anymore.

I startled the white-haired man behind the reception desk.

'I demand to see the mayor,' I said.

'He's not here.'

'I know he's here. He's always here,' I said. 'And I demand to see him. Don't you need to telephone him or something?'

'I told you ... he isn't here.'

'Are you saying he's at home? I know where he lives. I can just go there,' I said, thinking how I had no qualms about turning up at his house. The mayor had, after all, demanded I met with him there before, when his soldiers dragged me in from the street. Surely now I could invite myself to his home whenever I liked?

'You can't just go to his house,' the white-haired man said.

'Why not? If he isn't here, then he must be there. Are you going to telephone him? Or perhaps you need to send someone to tell him that I'm here?'

'I am not telephoning him. I'm not sending someone to tell him. You don't have an appointment.'

'You're being very rude,' I said. 'Surely a mayor must expect that the townsfolk might wish to speak to him about things at short notice? We can't all book appointments in advance. Should I book an appointment for Monday next week? Just in case something else pops into my head sometime between today and Sunday?'

The receptionist had such an odd look on his face. But I really couldn't tell you what he might have been thinking.

'You again,' a soldier said, as he appeared at my side. 'I'll deal with this one,' he said to the white-haired man.

The receptionist nodded his gratitude, and pretended to carry on with some paperwork.

'I demand to see the mayor,' I told the soldier.

'Been working in the allotments have we?' he asked, eyeing my trousers.

'You know where I've been.'

He knew I had spent my days frequenting the House of Books when the night option was taken away from me. They all knew. He also knew I had even spent a night in prison. He knew everything.

'What are you up to this time?' he asked.

'I want to speak to the mayor. Is that a crime now, too? Like how reading old books is a crime?'

'We've told you to be careful.'

'I am being careful,' I said. 'But maybe I shouldn't. Maybe I should explore the Guildhall and attempt to find the mayor's office for myself.'

'I can only assume you're looking for more trouble. You should be grateful you're free.'

'We're not free. If you think you're free, you're an idiot,' I said.

The soldier chortled.

'Is that so? I admire your spirit. Your doctor said you're mad. You're not mad, are you?'

'No,' I said, defiantly.

'Didn't think so.'

The soldier leaned across the desk to face the white-haired man.

'Call Tim. Let him know I'm bringing an uninvited guest up to see the mayor.'

Everything about the Guildhall was a lesson in opulence. Well, in the parts of the building which remained.

I wondered if the building was safe with almost half the structure gone. But it appeared to be made of stronger stuff than my little cottage.

We climbed the wide carpeted staircase, past faded portrait paintings of important-looking men and women. I surmised these were the true First Ancestors from when Eden was called Stonburh. One painting which caught my eye as we turned on the staircase was of a woman with a mound of grey hair piled up high upon her head. But when I examined her face, I realised she wasn't an old woman with grey hair, she was young and vibrant, with rosy cheeks. It must have been a wig. The wig was laden with jewels. She wore a huge pale blue dress with frilly sleeves. I assumed the dress would have reached the floor, but I would never know, as the painting ended just below her waist. She would never have gotten through the front door of my cottage in that dress. I considered she would have been restricted by a lot of doorways.

As we arrived at the top of the staircase on the third floor, we came to a tall window which provided an excellent view onto the square.

A draught came from under a large double door at the end of the corridor to my left. I knew then that behind that door the room had fallen away, and the door was exposed to the elements.

Another soldier appeared.

'I'll take it from here,' he said to the soldier who had brought me up the stairs.

I presumed this new soldier was Tim.

Tim ushered me along the opposite corridor, away from the draught.

I wanted to see the mayor, but all the things I had planned to say slipped from my mind. Although I was no longer afraid of him, he was still the man in charge of Eden. Plus, Eden was slow to wake up to the reality of our world. If the mayor wanted to keep me in prison until I died, he could arrange it. If he wanted me dead today, he could arrange it. My mouth grew dry as Tim tapped upon a double door.

'Come in,' the mayor said.

Tim pushed open the door and gestured I go in. He then closed the door behind me.

The mayor sat behind a large wooden desk. The room was a complete match for the luxurious office in his house. Even the Grand Tea Room wasn't as impressive as the mayor's accommodation. More beautiful paintings lined the walls. He had a plush carpet and rugs. The furniture had been lovingly crafted. The contents of the room consisted of nothing plain, nothing simple, nothing made just for function. Nothing like the furniture and paintings in my humble cottage.

For example, we had a table and chairs, but that was because we required a table and chairs. Our table and chairs functioned without beauty. They had no curves. They had no soft seats. They had no ornate details. What they had were sharp lines, hard edges, and uncomfortable seats. But you were supposed to be up and about doing things once you had finished eating. The dining table and chairs in our sitting room were nothing more than a necessity. Everyone else in Eden lived like my family.

But the mayor lived and worked in extravagant surroundings. I also noticed a sofa covered in cushions. Perhaps he lay upon the sofa during his afternoons, when the stress of dictating what he wanted done in Eden became too great and he needed a lie down.

The mayor smiled a sweet welcome. But like him it was a lie. Behind the smile lay his true face, one bestowed with a harshness and temperament to match.

'You're a meddlesome little thing,' he said. 'I regret my forebears didn't remove everything from Stonburh. I suppose you know that name? I regret we didn't tear down every building and start again. That way, you never would have had any questions. The complete eradication of the past would have meant you never would have known. That's what they did in other towns and citadels across the land. They tore it all down so the people had no idea anyone went before them.'

'How do you know they've torn buildings down in other places?' I asked.

'Because we trade with them. I have seen them.'

'You've been to other towns?'

'Yes, and sometimes the mayors of those towns come to Eden for meetings.'

That sounded about right. The mayors could do whatever they wanted. They lived in luxury and travelled wherever they wanted, while we lived frugally and couldn't go anywhere.

'Do you conduct these meetings late at night?' I asked, thinking on how I had had to sneak down passages and alleyways on the night Gabriel introduced me to the House of Books.

'Sometimes the meetings run late,' the mayor confirmed. 'Because they have to begin after curfew. Not that curfew has ever stopped you.'

I couldn't really argue with his comment. So I didn't.

'You have meetings because we trade?' I said. 'What are we trading, other than wool? Why do you need meetings?'

'Your mother makes clothes?'

'Yes.'

'As do many women here,' the mayor said. 'Most of those clothes, and everything else, are sent to other towns and citadels.'

'Everything we make you send away?'

'We need things in Eden that we can't make here,' he said, 'and foodwise we need more than fruit and vegetables.'

'You have meetings about clothes?' I asked, thinking how these mayors really had nothing better to do. They have ruined our lives, and all they do is sit around talking about skirts and trousers.

'We discuss all trade. But mostly we have meetings about joint concerns. We face the same threat.'

'The threat of the townsfolk discovering they've been lied to?' I asked.

'If that's what you want to think,' the mayor said.

'You say everywhere else has ruined their towns and citadels? Ripped out the history?'

'Yes, it's a shame in a way,' he said. 'Although some destruction had already begun in the past. Some religious houses had been torn down to make way for new religious houses. But then, those too were torn down, when we wanted to ... change things. I think the forebears of Eden couldn't bear to tear down Stonburh. I can understand it. It's too beautiful. But that beauty is my downfall. They should have changed the names of everything. They should have destroyed everything.'

'You destroyed enough,' I said, 'and what you didn't destroy you hid. You said these things were forbidden. You said there were monsters in the forest. You said there were deformed humans beyond the forest. You made us petrified about the world beyond Eden's outer wall. My mother was right, you have done nothing but create fear.'

'Our forebears did that. I simply maintained the deception,' the mayor said. 'You have it better than most. The vast majority of people across this land have no access to green space in their towns and citadels. Their gardens have been destroyed. They don't have access to any allotments in order to grow their own vegetables. There are no fields. They live in towns of concrete upon concrete, and all the concrete leads to their outer wall. Most outer walls are much higher than ours. They can only view the very tip of the forest. They too have been told the forest is not a place for them. They don't know about the natural environment. Not even a blade of grass breaks through the grey of their towns or citadels. They wouldn't know how to care for the land even if they had access to a field. The knowledge was removed when their authorities removed the farmers. No one knows how to grow crops. Only one town grows crops in a clearing within the forest. That town's authorities deal with those crops, and keeps the food distribution to a minimum for the whole country. Although you don't know too much about caring for the land, or animals, even in Eden. We have allowed you the basics. Our farmers know how to shear sheep for their wool, and how to milk cows. No more, no less.'

'Is that supposed to make it better?' I said. 'You just carried on as your predecessors had done? All you mayors across this land, and most didn't allow the townsfolk to have gardens? Or any green space? You've all kept knowledge from us. You've all lied to your townsfolk. Pretending these people hadn't gone before us. And in Eden, pretending they hadn't built our town.'

'Does it matter who built it?' the mayor asked.

'It does to me,' I said. 'It matters because I can't stand the lie. Lying is unjust. Your lies have eradicated an entire people. They have disappeared from the face of the Earth.'

'They're dead. Of course they have disappeared.'

'But they achieved everything,' I said, 'and you stole it from them. Their memory should live on in their art and architecture. But you are trying to say we did that. The angel statues in the water fountain were broken so we wouldn't ask why the people had wings. The statue of a king was removed so we wouldn't ask who that historical figure had been. The statues were removed from the cathedral so we wouldn't ask who the robed figures were. Yet you believe in what some of the true ancestors believed. I saw you in the temple, praying. I know what that means. You've taken what you wanted from them and destroyed the rest.'

'They're gone. They died hundreds of ago. Theirs is a long-dead era. We are the new era,' the mayor said, with pride.

'And to you that means eradicating their history, bones and all? Because history is old? All history is from a previous era. That's why it's called history. It doesn't mean you have the right to destroy it. You removed their headstones. Then you removed their bones. You have done nothing but dishonour them.'

Something suddenly occurred to me. If the authorities could remove the skeletons of our ancestors with no shame or regret, they could do anything.

'You burned the buildings,' I said. 'What was once the Theatre Royal, and one part of the university, were destroyed on purpose. It wasn't an accident. It wasn't an historical fire from the time of the descendants of the First Ancestors.'

'If by me, you mean my predecessors, then yes,' he said. 'They did try to burn the citadel initially. But they couldn't bring themselves to finish the job. I mean it when I say you don't know what the other towns did. They built homes next to fallen graveyards. They even built homes on top of graveyards. The headstones were smashed, the bodies dug up, and the graveyards flattened. In those towns people live above what was once a place for the dead. Life literally replaced death, and wiped out our true forebears with bricks and mortar.'

'That's horrible,' I said, thinking it was atrocious that the authorities had done that, and it was atrocious that the mayor had said it so matter-of-factly.

'There are too many people in some towns and citadels, it would seem,' he said. 'There's not enough room for the living, let alone the long since departed.'

'What happened to the skeletons when they were removed from outside the cathedral?' I asked. 'That was the townsfolk of Stonburh's final resting place.'

The mayor shrugged.

I felt sick to my core. He didn't know what had happened to the bones of our ancestors. And he didn't care. I wondered how he would feel if the people of the future would have no care or respect for his bones, let alone the buildings. If bones, buildings, art, and our life stories were all we could leave behind, destroying them was despicable.

'The reverence for our ancestors is lost when you take away their achievements and remove their remains,' I said.

'It's disrespectful to the people who lived here before us. We shouldn't ever forget them. They are why we're here. They gave us life. They left us this place. Even you yourself said it's beautiful. We should honour them by looking after what they created.'

'I told you before, we changed history because we thought that was best for you. We thought we were keeping you safe, in a way. A fresh start.'

'You rewrote our history because you thought you were keeping us safe? I don't call a life of ignorance protection.'

The mayor laughed.

'Ignorance is bliss,' he said. Have you never heard that saying?'

'That may be so, but the truth always comes out eventually,' I said. 'The longer the truth has been hidden, the worse the lie appears when the truth does materialise. You must realise that? You've lied for decades, if not centuries. When all the townsfolk find out, you're finished. No one likes being lied to. No one likes a cover-up. But the damage has already been done. You cannot bring back what you have destroyed. It has gone forever. I would have thought a mayor is a custodian of a town or citadel. Not a destroyer. When you eradicate history, you have nothing to learn from. We are set to make the same mistakes as the ancestors. If we don't know what wrongs they did, we will repeat those past wrongs through ignorance. Can't you see that?'

I was fuming at the ignorance of this man before me. I may have been ignorant of many things prior to discovering the House of Books. But it wasn't by choice. The decision to keep me ignorant was made for me. And long ago, since my parents and grandparents didn't know the true history.

'How long has this been going on for?' I asked.

The mayor sighed.

'At least two hundred to two hundred and fifty years, give or take,' he said.

'That long? How did you do it?' I asked. 'How did you get everyone to lie initially? Were the townsfolk forced to lie? Or did they become willing participants? Did they simply accept they had to lie from then on in?'

'I don't know, I wasn't there.'

'But … everyone would have just had to go along with the lie. Until you got to the generation who were born into the lie. Then that generation never knew any different,' I said, thinking about how my grandparents, my parents, and me, were all born into this lie. 'How did you become mayor?'

'My father was the mayor, and his father before him.'

'It must be more than that,' I said. 'It must be that you were willing to do what someone above you demanded. Still, now, there is someone out there who is above you, and you follow orders. Everyone just does what they're told: you, the townsfolk, the townsfolk from when the lie began, everyone. They were cowards,' I snapped, as I could feel the anger rising within me.

'Who were cowards?' the mayor asked.

'The townsfolk from over two hundred years ago,' I said. 'They were cowards as they went along with the lie. They accepted it and didn't think about us, the future generations.'

'We thought what we were doing was for your own good. We didn't want you to know your past went back that far. Most of the ancestors met a terrible fate. The forebears of Eden didn't want you to know that humanity can easily disappear from the face of the Earth. Of late, I realise we have protected you from more than that. I never knew what they were at first. I was loathe to admit what they might be. But now I know. They are the true destruction of us.'

'Who are you talking about?'

'The ones visiting from the sky during the storms,' the mayor said. 'Those who existed before us. Those who exist out there. Those who live in darkness. They wish to take our light, and everything we have. They are the end of us. They've been waiting for centuries, and now it's their time.'

The mayor spoke of Gabriel and the other menfolk as though they were something to fear and despise.

'How do you know they live in darkness?' I asked. 'How do you know they want to take what we have?'

'Why else would they be coming here?' he asked. 'They have taken advantage of human weakness. They are the new gods. They just appeared on the horizon one day, and now they won't leave. We haven't got the capacity to stop them. We'll all expire. There will be no one left. Like humans never existed. Has Earth always been ours? Had we ever considered something would want to take our planet from us? Mankind needed purpose. What we have discovered is, we got lucky. Perhaps sheer luck was always the more terrifying outcome. All those stars. All those suns. Life must exist somewhere else. But what does it mean? It can only mean all I have ever known is a lie.'

'I know that feeling,' I said, folding my arms across my chest.

The mayor sniggered.

'Then you appreciate how the forebears also lied to me. They never explained these beings. Even for me, ignorance was bliss. Knowledge is power. But not in this instance. This knowledge brings fear. Fear is the result when you know the truth. But what has appeared here terrifies me even more. What they are has consequences for what I believe. We can no longer consider ourselves exceptional. Humans separated themselves from other animals, and animals remained below us. But that's the problem. Here on Earth, we are superior. We are the intelligent higher being. But what about elsewhere? We're not even special within our own galaxy. Our solar system doesn't lie within the centre of our galaxy. Our solar system spins within a spiral arm. The Orion–Cygnus Arm to be precise. An arm. Not the heart. The Milky Way galaxy alone has around two hundred billion stars. How many planets harbour some kind of life? We are no longer extraordinary. Perhaps we're just lost in the vastness of space. Fumbling around in the darkness attempting to make sense of our existence when nothing can make sense. Not anymore.'

'Life does make sense,' I said. 'We're part of nature. Like everything else.'

The mayor appeared to ignore me. In fact, when he continued speaking, he no longer regarded me. His eyes glazed over while he found something of more importance beyond my frame.

'When I was a boy, I thought I saw a ghost. But it was one of them. Eventually the ghost disappeared from my memory. All the truth in the world became false from the moment I forgot. I became blind to the shadows. Blind to the movement in my peripheral vision. My father had told me all about God when I was a child. I knew what the cathedral meant. I found God again when I became a man. But now my faith has been tested. At first, I couldn't admit to myself what I had seen. Then I thought back to when I had seen them before as a boy. I realised why I thought it was a ghost. Because it couldn't be real. But it was. I had subconsciously lied to myself my whole life, rather than acknowledge the truth. I had seen His other children, who live just beyond us. But our worlds were becoming entwined, and now we'll all collide. They are stronger than us. His other creation of men.'

I felt bewildered by what the mayor had said.

'I know one of them. You've got him wrong,' I said.

'Him? Your friend?'

'You've got them all wrong. He and his people are nothing like how you're describing them.'

'You should be careful who you make friends with,' he said.

'You're an idiot. You're all idiots. I thought the authorities were supposed to be more intelligent than the common townsfolk, and that's why you're in charge. I assume you think you're more intelligent? But for people in office, you're all morons. I suppose that's the problem. The people who have given themselves total control over how things are run believe they are entitled to that amount of power. They don't ever consider whether or not they can actually do the job. You haven't completed an aptitude test. You think you're smart, but you've got no common sense.'

'I beg your pardon?' the mayor said.

'You can beg my pardon all you like,' I said. 'You're still an idiot.'

The mayor had a most peculiar expression upon his face.

'My friend doesn't mean anyone harm. Far from it. He's always been kind to me. He showed me the truth. You've done nothing but lie.'

'For your own good,' the mayor said.

'And you threw the men in prison,' I said, finally remembering why I had gone to see the mayor in the first place.

'Part of the deception, and a distraction,' he said.

'Then you put me in prison.'

'To frighten you. I can't say it worked. Since here you are. Again.'

'Is my father in that prison?' I asked. 'Are all the men of Eden in the prison? You haven't sent them anywhere else?'

'Like where?'

'The town of Frontline?' I said.

The mayor chortled.

'There is no town called Frontline,' he said.

'But I wouldn't know that, would I? Thanks to your lies, I don't know the names of places, or what else exists out there. I don't know who or what to believe.'

'Not much does exist out there between the towns and citadels. Not anymore.'

'The forest exists out there,' I said. 'The forest is beautiful. Other things must exist out there. Otherwise, what are you so afraid of?'

'Your *friends* have taken what was left, and now they will take us.'

I rose from my seat. I had had enough.

'You lie,' I said, as I headed for the door.

As I stormed from the mayor's office, two soldiers were in conversation down the far end of the opposite corridor, where the draught whistled under the double door.

I recognised one of the men as the newly shaven Silas.

I fled down the stairs before Silas could register my presence. I didn't wish to hear his excuses.

But he must have caught sight of me as I heard him call my name. His tone was more that of a question, as though he wasn't sure whether he had spotted a glimpse of flaming red hair or not. I could have been an escaped forest spirit for all he knew. One who liked to play with fire.

Envy sprung up to greet me as I descended the steps.

A bonfire blazed away in the square. I wondered why it was already lit.

Although, as the mayor appeared paranoid about Gabriel and his people, I presumed it was to prevent a repeat of them arriving during daylight hours. How anyone thought a bonfire would prevent them from taking over the sky, I had no idea.

As I stomped closer, I realised that what I had thought to be logs were not logs.

'They're burning books,' I yelled.

Envy whined at me while I kicked my feet into the flames to free some volumes.

A small crowd gathered around me.

'Help me,' I begged. 'They're burning the books. They're trying to hide the truth.'

'She's right,' an elderly man said. 'We've got to help her.'

Some of the townsfolk began to kick and poke about in the flames.

The elderly man flung his gas mask into the fire and stuck his walking stick into the flames. This dislodged several tomes, which landed with a hiss upon the cobblestones.

'What do you think you're doing now?' a soldier asked.

'Leave me alone,' I said.

Envy pounced upon him and barked.

'Why are you burning books?' the elderly man asked. 'This young lady is right, you've hidden things from us.'

'This is none of your business,' the soldier said, shoving Envy to the ground. 'Everyone, move away.'

Envy hurled herself at the soldier again, and continued to bark.

Alerted to the commotion, other soldiers from across the square began to approach. I didn't have time to think about what I was going to do. I just did it.

'They've taken history from us. It was all in the House of Books,' I said, waving an arm towards the shell of the building. 'They don't want you to know the truth. No spirits reside in the forest, evil or otherwise. No dog-headed humans loiter amongst the trees. And neither is the forest home to giant dogs which can tear you apart. The forest is beautiful. The forest is the truth.'

'I believe you,' the elderly man said. 'This young lady speaks the truth.' He turned to the rest of the townsfolk. 'We all believe her, don't we?'

'Yes, I believe her,' a woman said.

Then the entire crowd, which had grown in size, all confirmed they believed me, as they kicked out more sizzling books from the fire.

I launched myself upon the nearest community message board, which still displayed some war posters.

I tore at them with a fury.

'There is no war,' I screamed. 'It's all a lie.'

'There's no war either?' I heard a woman say.

‘They’ve lied about that too?’ said another.

As I continued to tear at the posters, I could feel the anger rising from the townsfolk as they vented their confusion and fury. But I heard the soldiers threaten the townsfolk with arrest, as they pushed everyone away from the fire.

Two strong arms grabbed me around the waist and dragged me away from the board.

I had assumed it was the soldier who had berated me for kicking books free of the flames, until he spoke:

‘Please come with me,’ Silas whispered in my ear.

I attempted to dig my heels into the cobblestones, as Envy now leapt at Silas’s side.

‘No, no, you lied,’ I shrieked. ‘Let me go.’

The townsfolk seemed to watch me with a combination of horror and pity, I think, but the soldiers held them back.

‘Let me go. The townsfolk should know the truth. They deserve to know.’

‘I agree,’ Silas whispered, as he hauled me back in the direction of the temple gardens.

Chapter 17

Silas lit some candles while I sat upon a stone seat. Beyond the candles, the darkness extended on and on past two huge pillars.

I thought whispers came from the darkness and echoed around the vaulted ceiling, but I considered it must have been a breeze. A draught came from somewhere. It blew across the back of my neck as though someone stood behind me and exhaled every last drop of breath.

'I need to get back to the square,' I said.

'You can't go back to the square,' Silas said. 'It's not safe at the moment.'

'But they're burning the books.'

'It's too late for the books. I'm sorry. But you can save yourself.'

Silas knelt to scratch Envy's ears.

'She's a beautiful dog,' he said, 'and friendly. Once she realises you're not a threat.'

'She is beautiful. She's my best friend.'

'How did you come by her?' Silas asked.

'She was a stray,' I said. 'We don't know where she came

from. My grandad and I found her wandering the lanes by our cottage. We could see she was very young. We took her in because I said we should. I couldn't leave her outside all alone. Not after I had found her.'

'You have a heart of gold,' Silas said.

'Then my heart must have come from a neutron star collision.'

'A what?'

'Gold and other precious metals are created when neutron stars collide,' I said. 'A neutron star is what's left of a giant star when it collapses.'

'Is that so?' Silas said.

I nodded.

I thought about the *Space Encyclopaedia*, which sat upon my writing bureau alongside other tomes. Every single volume had a smattering of space dust trapped between the pages. Every glorious book held the scent of ages. A scent not unlike where I sat with Silas.

'Where are we?' I asked.

'The cathedral crypt.'

'Crypt. I think I know the word,' I said, recalling the Stonburh Cathedral guide book. 'It's creepy down here.'

'It could be haunted,' Silas said.

'Haunted?'

'There are a lot of bodies down here.'

'Are there?' I asked, horrified. I respected the ancestors, but I didn't want to be surrounded by their bodies.

'Yes, there are,' Silas said. 'You're sitting on one.'

I leapt from the stone seat.

Silas laughed.

'The dead can't hurt you,' he said. 'Only the living.'

'The ancestors kept their dead down here, too? I thought they buried them in the ground outside the cathedral? I know some are under the nave floor.'

'They did bury most outside,' Silas said. 'But some were also entombed down here. Probably the earliest of the real First Ancestors, and the ones with some money I expect. Would you like to see their tombs?'

I shook my head.

'They're sealed,' he said. 'They're just skeletons within the tombs. You don't have to look at the skeletons. Just the tombs. Come on, there are numerous ones to see. It's quite beautiful down here.'

'It's cold down here,' I said.

'Yes, that too.'

'And there's a draught. You can feel a draught, can't you?' I asked.

'Yes, right down the back of my neck.'

'Don't say that,' I said, rubbing my own neck, and thinking how I felt even colder now I had acknowledged the draught.

'It's just the ancestors,' Silas said.

'Don't say that either.'

'I'm just teasing.'

Silas, it appeared, was as annoying as Gabriel.

'Are you living down here now?' I asked.

'I slept here last night.'

I think I may have shuddered. I couldn't think of anything worse. Sleeping amongst the dead when you were alive.

'The soldiers saw you drag me away. They'll be looking for us,' I said.

'Not down here. No one comes down here. Even though the cathedral was one of few places not forbidden.'

'Yes, I suppose so. No one knows there's anything underneath the temple. No one knows anything about anything,' I said.

'But we do,' Silas said. 'Come on. Let me show you the vastness of this place.'

'But that means heading into the darkness.'

'With a couple of these,' he said, as he collected two large pillar candles from nearby. 'I'll keep the other candles lit here so you can easily find your way back to this spot. Like I said, the dead can't hurt you, and I won't hurt you. If I meant you harm ...'

'You'd have done it by now,' I said.

'Exactly,' Silas said, as he handed me one of the large candles.

Envy followed while Silas guided me through the archways and past what he called sarcophagi. They appeared sealed, and they looked heavy. Too heavy for a lid to be moved with ease. That gave me comfort. But the draught seemed to follow. I glanced back several times thinking I would catch a wandering spirit, but I only found the candles flickering away in the distance.

'How's your grandfather?' Silas asked.

'I think he's gone mad,' I said.

Silas laughed.

'He's doing well then. But seriously, is he okay?'

'He's sleeping a lot. His appetite is back though,' I said, thinking how I had discovered an empty cake plate that morning, as it had appeared my grandfather had finished off my mother's sponge cake in the night.

'Good, good. I'm glad he's comfortable at home,' Silas said.

'How did you get out of prison?' I asked. 'Why are you wearing a soldier's uniform? And why were you with the mayor in the temple?'

'You saw my previous clothes. They'd seen better days. When I got out of prison, I was provided with a clean uniform. I had a bath and a shave.'

'Did the mayor allow you to leave prison?' I asked.

'He couldn't keep me in there forever. Not like the others.'

'Why not?'

'I'm ashamed,' Silas said, regretfully.

'Of what?'

'I'm ashamed to be his son. Well, one of his sons.'

'But you said your dad was dead,' I said, recalling the conversation in prison.

'He is dead. That man in the Guildhall is not the man I knew as a boy. He's just a mayor now, and not a good one.'

'But you were praying together.'

'He was,' Silas said. 'I wasn't. I just went along. He was praying for my soul.'

'Do you love your dad?' I asked, thinking how I didn't know if I would have said my father was dead when he was very much alive, even if he wasn't the same man I knew as a child.

'If I ever did love him, I don't anymore. How can I love someone I don't respect?'

'He told me he's just continuing on with what the previous mayors have all done before him,' I said.

'Yes. He's a puppet really,' Silas said. 'Just doing what someone of higher authority told him and the previous mayors to do. That needs to change. It was inevitable that people would wake up eventually.'

'He also told me he wished they had destroyed the citadel. If they had gotten rid of all the beautiful architecture, we would have remained ignorant.'

'But they couldn't do it, could they? They couldn't quite destroy this place.'

'He said all the buildings had been destroyed in other towns and citadels though,' I said, thinking how sad it was that buildings were destroyed to hide the history.

'Then I suppose *Eden* is lucky that Stonburh wasn't demolished,' Silas said.

'He also said he enjoyed the beauty of the old citadel.'

Silas snorted.

'He's a mass of contradictions,' he said.

'He should be removed from the Guildhall,' I said. 'You should dump him in the forest and leave him there. Then he can fend for himself. Or you could put him in the prison. Then we can all live in peace, and knowledge of the truth.'

'You've really thought this through.'

I think I blushed. Not that Silas would have noticed in the candlelight. It wasn't like me at all to suggest such a thing. But the mayor had left me seething, and I couldn't restrain my thoughts. And my thoughts were unusually dark. I had been pushed too far.

'They also eliminated surnames linked to professions,' Silas said. 'Do you know about some of our ancestral surnames?'

'No. I don't understand. What do you mean surnames about professions?'

'They indicate your ancestral heritage,' Silas said. 'Some surnames represent an area where our ancestors came from. We still use some of those names. Authorities kept those, because no one knows these places ever existed. The meaning has been lost. No one knows what their surname signifies if it's linked to an unknown area. But the surnames linked to professions of our ancestors from centuries ago would be things like thatcher, baker, smith. You could be Andromeda Smith, as a long-dead ancestor of yours could have been a blacksmith. But of course, Eden has smiths, bakers and thatchers. Surnames like that had to be erased because we know what those words mean. The townsfolk would question why they had a surname linked to a profession no one in their family had previously been involved with. Therefore, the authorities had to eliminate those names. No one was allowed an ancestral heritage. Too dangerous, obviously.'

'I didn't realise they also took the names,' I said. 'My family name is Woburn. Do you know what that means?'

'It could be a place name, and therefore one your family was allowed to keep. Or perhaps it was a name given to you to replace a forbidden name.'

'Do you believe I might have had a different family name?'

'Entirely possible,' Silas said. 'When I was in the library, I came across numerous volumes in the local history archives listing all the residents who had ever lived in Stonburh. Their full names, when they were born, who they married, what they did for a living, and when they died. They're our real ancestors. But we will never be able to link ourselves to them because the authorities changed most of the townsfolks' surnames. They've done everything they can to—'

'Enable our ignorance about where and who we come from,' I said.

'Yes.'

'You said you agree that everyone should know the truth,' I said. 'How do we go about telling everyone?'

'Well, shouting about it in the square in front of all the soldiers is probably not the solution,' Silas said.

'Excuse me, but isn't that what you were doing the first time I saw you?'

Silas laughed.

'Yes. With a little help from home-brewed mead,' he said. 'Or rather, House of Books brewed mead.'

Glorious memories of the House of Books came flooding into my mind. I recalled the beauty and history of the building which had once been my favourite place, and which now lay in ruins.

Silas smiled at me, as though he could see me exploring those dusty shelves too.

'I have to say, I'm proud of you,' he said.

'Really?' I said.

'Yes, you don't need the help of alcohol to speak your mind.'

This was true, I thought. I felt stronger. I didn't require assistance from a drink which goes to your head instead of your stomach.

'But lying to the townsfolk for years is unjust,' I said. 'All the lying is wrong. I can't stand it.'

'Again, I agree with you. Also, I have a feeling that before nightfall everyone in Eden will know the truth. Those townsfolk who were helping you remove books from the fire, and were listening to what you said, will be telling all their family, friends, and neighbours. Your work is done. You've told everyone the truth. Plus, your favourite place was blown apart. That exposed a building full of books, which they're currently burning. You can't tell me the people of Eden aren't pondering on what lies within all the forbidden buildings now.'

'Yes, I suppose so.'

We paused by a large sarcophagus, and Envy decided to lie at my feet. I felt some unease knowing a skeleton rested behind the intricate carvings. The lid reminded me of the roof of a house, albeit made of stone.

'What happened to the real First Ancestors?' I asked. 'Do you know?'

'I believe a great flood took most of the true ancestors of this land,' Silas said.

'But the town has flooded many times before, hasn't it?'

'Yes. But I'm talking about a great flood,' he said. 'One which almost swallowed the citadel. As the waters rose, the people of Stonburh read up on the flooding myths, and read up on the historical floods of the area in general. Flooding is a natural occurrence of course. But the flood which took most of our ancestors was on another magnitude.'

'There are flood myths?' I asked.

'Yes. The Sumerians—'

'I've read some things on the Sumerians,' I said.

'But not the flood myth?'

'I obviously didn't get that far.'

'The Sumerians had a great mythology, like all civilisations,' Silas said. 'They created a tale our ancestors knew as the Epic of Gilgamesh. This was already centuries old by the time of Stonburh's ancestors. The epic tale had been carved on clay tablets. This was the first known writing. Our ancestors knew this writing as cuneiform.'

‘I’ve heard of that,’ I nodded.

‘In the Epic of Gilgamesh, a man informs Gilgamesh that he and his wife survived a great flood in the past. The gods planned to send a flood because they were angry with mankind and his arrogance. The man and his wife survived because one of the gods told him of the plan. The god said he should demolish his home and build a boat big enough to house all other living beings. The flood came, and the waters swallowed the earth and took everything but the boat. There’s a flood story in the Bible. God warns Noah he will send a flood to cleanse the Earth of mankind, as mankind has become too arrogant. Noah is instructed to build an ark, and save two of every living creature, plus save as many of his kind who believe in God. Noah’s friends fail to recognise God, and therefore they don’t earn a place on the ark. Only Noah, his wife, and children survive the great flood. There are other great flood myths and stories across the civilisations of the past. Every religion had one, including the Hindus, from a land called India, and the Zoroastrians, from a land which became known as Iran. Both religions also state a man survived, because he was pre-warned to build a giant boat. In most flood stories, the chosen few survived because their boat came to rest atop a mountain. This also happens in the Greek mythology flood myth.’

‘I’ve read some Greek mythology,’ I said, glad that I could at least confirm that I knew something about a place, and its stories. Like how I already knew about the Sumerians and cuneiform. All my learning in the House of Books meant I could begin to piece some of the historical world together.

‘The ancient Greek tale also features a god angered by man, Zeus in this case,’ Silas said. ‘But a Titan intervenes. The Titans were deities who preceded the Gods of Olympia.’

‘So the stories are true? And the gods are either angry or intervene?’ I asked.

‘Yes and no,’ Silas said. ‘I would argue there are truths and exaggerations. You see, the real ancient civilisations had to make sense of their world somehow. Creating angry gods, who wanted to destroy mankind, was their way of explaining natural disasters. They probably couldn't perceive that nature is as destructive as she is beautiful. Flooding is part of the Earth's cycle. The Earth heats up, the Earth cools down, naturally. Cycles of severe flooding happen every century. The Earth had already gone through at least five major ice ages over a period of millions of years by the time our ancestors appeared on the scene. Now, as I'm sure you can guess, when an ice age period comes to an end, and the Earth begins to heat again—'

'All the ice melts,' I said.

'Yes.'

'Like Doggerland?'

'You read about Doggerland?' Silas said.

'Yes, a massive piece of land which people once roamed across, and which now resides under a sea.'

'Yes,' Silas said, nodding, 'ice melts during Earth's greenhouse period, or interglacial period, and the oceans and seas rise. During the height of a greenhouse period, the Earth heats so much there won't even be snow or ice atop any mountains. The flooding can be catastrophic of course, as what was once land is under water. What the real ancestors viewed as the world during their time would have been just their known land. They didn't know about the other lands across the oceans. But they all had the same stories because every land has experienced catastrophic flooding. The flood had happened and wiped out much of a previous advancing civilisation. Not a super advanced civilisation, but a progressing civilisation all the same. The people here before us had mostly been destroyed. Our real ancestors were the survivors. There are also tales of humans living underground or inside the Earth. Those stories may have come from survivors of floods. Humans could have emerged from inside Earth after one of the major floods. Within the ground or inside Earth could simply be caves. Then a mythology sprung up around that.'

'I don't know if I'd like to live in a cave,' I said. 'It would be too dark for a start.'

'But where would you go if the waters began to rise?' Silas asked. 'A cave in a hillside or mountain, I expect. Our true ancestors were not entirely destroyed, otherwise we would not be here. But they almost were. It has happened before. It will happen again. Civilisations have disappeared and been replaced. Civilisations can fall for other reasons. But natural disasters have played a huge part.'

'I have a book on the old civilisations. *Ancient to Med*—something.'

'Medieval,' Silas said. 'You'll see a pattern emerges. They all collapse and disappear. No civilisation lasts forever.'

'This is as terrifying as the *Space Encyclopaedia* I'm reading,' I said.

'It can be terrifying. Or it can be comforting. It depends which way you look at it.'

'I've come to understand that the world is hostile. Do you find it terrifying or comforting that no civilisation seems to last?' I asked.

'Perhaps it depends on what mood I'm in on the day. Today it's comforting. It happened to them. It will happen to us. And it will happen to everyone who comes after us. Some things are out of our control.'

'But, if all civilisations collapse, surely there's no point in fighting? Is that what you're saying?'

'Oh, I didn't say I wouldn't fight for what I believe in,' Silas said. 'You and I can fight together. I've already infiltrated a small group of soldiers.'

'You've befriended the soldiers?'

'Some of them are okay. They're really just doing their jobs. Keeping their heads down.'

'Not the ones I've met. They've always been horrible,' I said.

'Those ones are too far gone.'

'You mean persuaded to think a certain way?'

Silas nodded.

'Like someone else I know,' he said to himself.

'You've got some weird friends then, if you're spending time with soldiers whose minds aren't their own.'

'Ha, you're a fine one to talk,' Silas said. 'You're friends with some unusual people.'

'Do you mean Gabriel and the people from beyond our skies?' I asked.

'Whatever you wish to call them. I saw them take your grandfather away. I wasn't in the cell at that point. I was in the courtyard, as I had just been released. I'll never get over seeing that. It also shook my father up. But they've visited us throughout history.'

'Have they?'

'I found documents in the library,' Silas said. 'Quite a number of people have seen them down the years.'

'Your— the mayor, said he'd seen one of them when he was a child, too.'

Envy interrupted our conversation by growling.

I followed her gaze back to the flickering candles, but I couldn't see anything.

Then she barked.

It reverberated through the sparse cavern.

A tapping and shuffling sound came from the shadows, and a man stepped into the candlelight by the crypt entrance.

It was the man with half a face.

Silas slid forward and stood between me and the disfigured man.

Envy snarled as the man with half a face approached us. He morphed into a dark silhouette framed by candlelight.

'What do you want?' Silas asked.

'Why do you always want to cause trouble?' the man with half a face asked back, his speech slurred through his disfigurement.

'You were in the prison working as a guard,' I said. 'I'd seen you before that dressed as a soldier in the square. You said you'd been wounded in the war.'

'Did I?' the man said, as he drew ever closer.

Envy leapt forward and barked again.

Her barking appeared more distressed.

I pulled her back to me.

'Our father wanted to use you as a prop,' Silas said, 'and you let him.'

'Your father?' I said.

'Yes, this is my brother, Gideon. Great family,' Silas said, as he rolled his eyes.

'What do you care about family?' Gideon asked.

'I care about honour,' Silas said.

'But not honouring the family?'

'Honouring lies? Not my thing.'

'You dishonoured our father,' Gideon said.

'He dishonoured himself,' Silas said. 'As did you.'

'What happened to your face?' I asked, as Gideon now stood before us. 'Since there's no war, how could you be so badly injured?'

'It's not an injury,' Silas said, 'and it's not just his face. You see, Gideon ran away as a boy—'

'I learned my lesson,' Gideon said.

'He ran off through the forest to escape our father,' Silas continued. 'That's right. At the time, he used to hate him too. He was gone for months. When he returned, he had a small rash on his face. The rash disappeared, and all was forgotten. Until the rash returned several years later. Then it got worse. He said he couldn't feel his hands or feet. Parts of his body went numb. I was lucky I never caught it from him.'

'What is it?' I asked.

'Some kind of skin disease, from what we understand in the medical journals and books. Living in an isolated town, we forgot what was out there, and we had no immunity. We are weak and vulnerable to everything now.'

'This thing makes you lose your face?' I said, horrified.

'Not just your face, anywhere,' Silas said. 'This disease eats away at your flesh, it seems.'

I stared at Gideon's gloved hands.

He grinned at me.

'I learned my lesson. This was my punishment,' Gideon said, as he began to remove a glove.

He raised his glove-free hand into the candlelight. Some of his fingers had turned to stumps. His body was broken from decay. If his toes had gone the same way, it explained the limp.

'I had found sanctuary in the forest with others who had fled their towns,' Gideon said. 'Only I realised too late that some of them were outcasts.'

'Now no one will touch him without gloves,' Silas said. 'I wouldn't get too close if I were you. I don't.'

'Is there a cure?' I asked.

'Yes, there was,' Silas said. 'But because our backwards authorities decided to denounce the past and create a new world, we didn't have any medication for it. We had lost the knowledge. We didn't know what the rash was. Until it was too late. Plus now our mother has it. She won't leave the house.'

I hadn't even considered that the mayor had a wife. I hadn't really thought about him having a family. She must have been in the house the night when the mayor wanted to see me in his private residence. I imagined a woman bedridden and ashamed, with parts of her hands and feet missing. Perhaps even her face, too.

'I never meant to give it to her,' Gideon said. 'How could I have known?'

'My brother. Her darling boy came home sick and she smothered him with love, and in return she became infected.'

'I never meant to,' Gideon said, hanging his head.

‘I can’t decide if that’s the main reason why you pander to the whim of our father, guilt. He’s used you for his own gain, and you let him,’ Silas said.

‘I’m already dead. It doesn’t matter.’

‘You have a death sentence alright,’ Silas said. ‘But you could be your own man. You don’t have to follow him.’

‘Why do you assume I wouldn’t agree with him even if this hadn’t happened?’ Gideon said, as he lost grip of his stick in apparent frustration. It landed with a thwack across the stone floor and echoed through the crypt as he stumbled to the ground.

Silas stepped forward as though to help his brother, and then reconsidered.

‘I brought this back to Eden,’ Gideon said, showing us his hands. ‘I condemned our mother. I know what’s out there. Eden is better isolated.’

‘If we’d known what you had, we could have cured you,’ Silas said. ‘The real ancestors who came before us were medically advanced. Anyway, people from elsewhere could bring diseases into Eden. It’s the medical knowledge which would protect us, not the physical isolation.’

‘You want to ruin everything our father achieved?’ Gideon asked.

‘He hasn’t achieved anything,’ Silas said. ‘He’s simply continued on with the lie. Which is wrong. Eden is waking up. You must realise this. It’s over.’

‘Then I’m glad I’m dying,’ Gideon said.

‘Well, you’ve come to the right place,’ Silas said. ‘Since you want to spend the rest of your days in darkness, I’ll leave you down here with the dead.’

Silas turned to me.

‘Come on, let’s go. You shouldn’t have to listen to this.’

Silas strode towards the light from all the candles near the entrance to the crypt.

Envy and I followed. But I peered back over my shoulder and beheld a crumpled and dejected man.

'Are you really going to leave your brother down here?' I asked, as we reached the mass of candles. 'He looks like he can barely walk, and I don't think he can get up now, even if he could walk.'

'He'll get up. Eventually,' Silas said. 'Wallowing in self-pity is a terrible waste of life. The self-pity is where most of his anger comes from. That and the anger from guilt, for passing it onto our mother. It's a self-inflicted misery really.'

'But he *is* sick,' I said.

'I know. But he could do something good with his final years. Although it appears he won't.'

We climbed the stone steps which led to the cathedral nave. I was glad for some air. The crypt had become stale and oppressive.

I glanced back down the steps. I could no longer register any candlelight.

'Don't worry about him,' Silas said.

'But he's all alone down there.'

'Gives him time to reflect. Anyway, he's not alone,' Silas said, with a wink.

A cool breeze travelled through the cathedral, and all my hairs stood on end.

'How do we get everyone out of prison?' I asked.

'I'm working on it. I told you. I have friends on the inside.'

'Inside of what?'

'You are funny,' Silas said with a laugh.

'I don't think I am,' I said, wondering why both Gabriel and Silas found me hilarious.

'Please, trust me,' Silas said, 'and try not to get yourself into any more trouble. Leave that to me.'

I peeked down the steps once more.

'Obviously I'm not going to leave him down there forever,'

Silas said. 'But there's something I want to do first. Something I've been wanting to do for a while.'

Silas grinned at me. Now I think back on that grin, I realise it was full of mischief.

'Go home and look after your grandfather,' he said. 'Be proud of yourself too. You've told enough of the townsfolk the truth, and they will pass this truth on. Let me deal with the prison.'

'But you said I shouldn't go back to the square yet. They'll be looking for me, remember. I don't know how long I've been in here.'

'You've been in here a while. But I'll distract them anyway.'

'From inside the temple … I mean cathedral?' I asked.

'Absolutely,' Silas said. 'Now go.'

As I headed for the cathedral door, I heard footsteps upon a stone staircase. I turned back to find that Silas had disappeared, and assumed he had gone back down to the crypt.

Envy and I were departing through the gardens, when a great chime rang out from the heavens.

The chime caused the birds to fly from the cathedral rafters.

Another chime shook the sky. Followed by another, and another. A great bell rang from the top of the central tower. It reminded me of the day when the cathedral had come to life during one of the storms.

As I stood in awe of the chimes, more and more townsfolk arrived in the temple gardens.

Some soldiers appeared, and a couple of them darted into the cathedral. I thought that was it for Silas. I envisioned him being dragged through the door, thrown into a carriage, and whisked back to prison, never to be seen again. Even if he was the mayor's son.

But instead the bell continued. Then a second bell joined in. Then a third. The cathedral came alive once more. The chimes vibrated across the old citadel. Waking Eden from its ignorant slumber.

I burst through the cottage door, which startled my grandfather, and he jolted awake in his armchair.

Envy leapt upon my grandfather's lap.

'The temple – I mean cathedral – bells were ringing. It was beautiful,' I said.

'Thought I heard something,' my grandfather said. 'At first I thought someone was banging dustbin lids together. Then I thought something was clanging about inside my brain.'

'Why haven't you moved out of the armchair, Grandad?'

'I'm a little tired, poppet.'

'I saw Silas,' I said. 'He's not one of the liars. He says he has a plan.'

'You thought he was a liar? A plan about what?' my grandfather asked.

'A plan to get the men out of prison.'

'Why did you think he was a liar?'

'It's a long story,' I said. 'It doesn't matter now.'

'He's a good man,' my grandfather said. 'He'll make something of himself one day. I hope I get to see it.'

'Are you really poorly?' I asked.

'I think the prison finished me off. The cold. The damp. The food. How's an old man to continue? The damn cold is in my bones now.'

'Why don't you move the armchair closer to the log burner. Here, I'll do it,' I said, as I manoeuvred behind the chair, readying myself to give it a big shove.

'No, no, poppet. I'm close enough. Even if I was sitting on top of the log burner, I don't think it would do any good now.'

'But, Grandad, don't give up.'

'I'm tired, poppet.'

'But things will change,' I said. 'If Silas is going to help, things will improve. Don't you want to see what will happen to Eden when everyone knows the truth?'

My grandfather nodded.

'Perhaps you should go up to bed,' I said. 'You can't be comfortable in the chair all day and night. Or should I get you an extra blanket? Will that help?'

'I have two already, but maybe another one will help,' my grandfather said, with another nod before he closed his eyes.

I retrieved another blanket and wrapped it around him as best I could. He woke a little as I moved his arms. I had to also move Envy. She leapt straight back into his lap once I had positioned the blanket, as though I had arranged the blanket for her.

While upstairs, I had also collected some books from my room. I sat in the armchair opposite and read while keeping an eye on my grandfather's faint breathing, although if he were to stop breathing, I had the feeling Envy would sense it first.

As Silas had mentioned the disappearance of many past civilisations, I decided to investigate this further. I had the perfect book, *Civilisations From Around the World: Ancient to Medieval*, which I had taken during one of my first visits to the House of Books.

I was shocked to discover how many had reached great achievement and then fallen. It was true, no civilisation stayed for too long. They all met their end.

The Sumerians declined when their lands got swallowed up within the Akkadian Empire. Then the Akkadian Empire later fell. Other near-eastern empires rose and collapsed: the Babylonians, the Hittites, the Phoenicians, the Assyrians, the Achaemenids, the Parthians, and the Sassanids. In North Africa, the pharaohs of the ancient Egyptian kingdoms reigned for a few thousand years, until foreign rulers from neighbouring lands took over. In Asia they had the Indus Valley civilisations, the Shang dynasty, the Mauryan Empire, the Qin dynasty, and the Han dynasty. The Americas had the Chavin, the Olmecs, the Zapotecs, the Maya, the Paracas, the Nazca, and the Moche. In Europe it was the Minoans, the Mycenaeans, the ancient

Greeks, and the Romans. The Celts were tribes who occupied Central and Western Europe until the Romans pushed them into the far west margins. There were also nomadic tribes across grasslands, known as the steppes, between Eastern Europe and China. The people of the steppes were the Scythians, the Huns, and the Kushans.

These were the people of the ancient and classical worlds. I knew I pronounced every name incorrectly inside my head. But I also knew that no one in Eden would know how to pronounce any of these civilisations either.

I ceased reading due to struggling with all the names. Plus, the list of fallen empires, dynasties, and civilisations went on and on into the medieval period. I knew I wouldn't be able to take it all in, or as Gabriel would say, *digest* it, in one sitting.

Mostly it transpired these civilisations had been attacked by outsiders who took their lands. It seemed everybody wanted to take something from someone else and claim it for their own. These invaders formed new civilisations, until they too were destroyed by another invading force. Then the cycle began once more. What also struck me is that the civilisations appeared to simply give up and die. People came into their worlds, and some of them didn't fight back, they were so complacent they enabled the invading force to win. I considered my ancestors, how they must have given up and died when the people with bad ideas told them to lie. They transformed what was my history. They never considered their descendants. I had told the mayor I thought the ancestors who went along with the lie had been cowards, but perhaps they were frightened? I don't know if that made it better. I don't think it did. They gave in without a fight either way. It was suicide really.

I had had enough of reading about defeated civilisations and thought I would learn something about volcanoes instead from the *General Knowledge Encyclopaedia*. Mars wasn't the only place where volcanoes existed. We had plenty here on Earth, which meant more destruction. But at least it was nature this time, and there is nothing you can do about nature.

Volcanic eruptions can cause volcanic winters, as the gas and smoke fill the sky forming a humongous dust cloud, which blocks out the sun and spreads across the globe. Some volcanic winters can last years, meaning crops don't grow and people starve. The year 1816 is known as the year without summer. When Mount Tambora erupted in Indonesia in 1815, the explosion was so huge it sent a giant ash cloud high into the atmosphere, which caused temperatures to drop globally as the heat from the sun couldn't get through the cloud. This caused a prolonged winter in the northern hemisphere. Neither spring nor summer appeared in 1816. Frosts destroyed crops. Snow fell. Flooding occurred. An ice dam even formed in the mountains of Switzerland.

One volcanic eruption, in one part of the world, caused a global catastrophe. It made me realise how lucky we were to be alive. How lucky we were to have evolved at all. Life is so precious. All the destruction reminded me of something the mayor had said: *The forebears of Eden didn't want you to know that humanity can easily disappear from the face of the Earth*. They hadn't wanted us to know that our home planet could destroy us. Aside from the beauty and the wonder, Earth had a darker side. And humans cannot control this dark side.

Earth even has gargantuan volcanoes, which have been dubbed supervolcanoes. Although supervolcano is a non-scientific term. A supervolcano resides under Yellowstone National Park in the United States. The magma chamber is so enormous, when it goes, it has the potential to wipe out all life. But this is not the only supervolcano. Earth harbours at least twenty others. I read with some relief that these types of major volcanic eruptions occur every one hundred thousand years. But my relief turned to concern when I realised I had no idea when the last one had been.

People had gone before, and people would come after. If this all happened in the past, it could happen in the future. My grandfather, Gabriel, and Silas had all said that people may have gone before us a long, long time ago. But I also considered that despite all this natural destruction, our authorities were possibly our biggest threat. Between malice, greed, and ineptitude – and sometimes a combination of all three – our authorities would kill us all. Governments didn't own the people. They were supposed to work *for* the people, not against them. As Silas had pointed out to me, the duty of any government should be to carry out the wishes of that nation's people. Therefore, consecutive governments, prior to my time, had failed in the one job they had. They appeared to believe they were more beholden to themselves, or someone else, or something else. The authorities were not influenced by the people; they were influenced by this nefarious other. And this nefarious other had condemned humanity. Somewhere out there, way beyond Eden, there was a larger authority in a giant version of the Guildhall, running everything, or more importantly, running everyone.

The volcanoes got me thinking I had overlooked something. Something about the future fate of Earth. But I suppose no one wishes to dwell upon the most terrifying of realities.

Sometimes destruction comes from within the dark internal soul.

Chapter 18

My mother's sewing machine thudded and whirled away in the little backroom off the kitchen as I stared into the flames from the log burner. Such a mesmerising sight. Flickers of orange, red, and yellow danced and spat upon the blackened logs behind the glass. The vibrant colours and warmth beckoned me to draw closer. But no one should get too close to the flames. Within the beauty lay the path to death.

I thought about Gabriel. About how his people were living on that barren and dusty planet with the red sky. I contemplated why his people were here.

Gabriel knows too much about everything. It's as though he's existed forever. How could Gabriel know all about Earth's history? He knows the past, he understands the present, he appears to know the future.

Gabriel and his people all know Earth's future.

Because Earth is their home.

I hadn't been on an expedition to another realm or planet with Gabriel. I had stood upon the Earth of the future.

The realisation of where Gabriel came from filled me with sadness. No one should have to exist like that. Gabriel's people were future humans, and they lived a dark existence. Gabriel had shown me what was to come. I could understand why they were here in their past. I would want to escape the furnace. What I couldn't understand was how they were able to travel into their past. Nor why Gabriel was insistent on leaving when they were safer on Earth in my present.

'*My people can't stay here if we want to live*,' I said to myself.

'What?' my grandfather asked, as he jolted awake.

'That's what Gabriel said to me the last time I saw him.'

'Said what?'

'My people can't stay here if we want to live.'

'Yes, that place where they live is awful. If that's what I saw,' my grandfather said.

'That place is Earth. In the future.'

'Is it?'

'We were shown a planet in turmoil,' I said. 'I saw them underwater. They appeared in tunnels. I don't know if they live in those tunnels. They possibly live underground. I assume it's the only way they can survive the hostile environment. Gabriel and his people are no longer as they were before. Because after centuries of living underground, or under the water, they have evolved.'

'They're future humans?' my grandfather asked.

'When Gabriel showed me the ruined planet, something felt familiar. Plus, I felt glass and metal under the water. How could I feel glass and metal on another planet? They come from inside the Earth of the future. They have adapted to living in darkness. Well, no natural light and no fresh oxygen. Gabriel must have gotten sick because he's not equipped to live here in this time. I've been reading about space exploration, and I've learned about hostile planets. I have learned that one day our own planet will become hostile to us, and that's what has happened in Gabriel's time. I understand where Gabriel's from. But I don't understand how he's here. I also don't understand the specific reason Earth is in peril. I thought Gabriel might come from the time when the sun has begun to expand. But there are so many threats to Earth, it could be something else. It could be a combination of catastrophes. Anything could happen to Earth before our sun finally swallows us.'

'What a horrible way to go,' my grandfather said.

'But no life will have survived even before the Earth gets swallowed,' I said. 'The environment will have already killed us all.'

'Good to know,' he said. 'Not so good to know that a myriad of catastrophes awaits us.'

I thought about earthquakes, tsunamis, volcanoes, asteroids, and land masses disappearing under a new sea.

'Gabriel never told you how he's able to be here? In this time, I mean?' my grandfather asked.

'No,' I said. 'But when they come here, we see past, present, and future. The people of our past come to life as shadow figures. All the buildings return to how they had functioned in their time. When I was with Gabriel and his people on the Earth of the future, I think I saw their ships underwater. Because this area must be under a huge deep river, or rather our river, but it's swallowed the town and even the citadel. They have travelled back and forth throughout time. People from the past have seen them.'

'I've seen them too,' my mother said, as she emerged from the kitchen.

I hadn't realised the sewing machine had stopped, and she'd been listening behind the kitchen door.

'When I was a girl I saw them,' she said. 'The first time, I was playing in the field with a friend. Heavy clouds rolled across what had been a clear sky. Lightning tore through the sudden darkness and thunder shook our world. The clouds opened and a river rained down. Spirits appeared above us. Or rather, beings who resembled spirits. I believe one of the beings watched me as it approached where we stood. My friend and I ran home screaming. The second time, I recall I was a few years older and in my bedroom. My room darkened as the storm arrived. I saw the spirits again. I believe the same being as before floated towards my window. It smiled softly. I knew it was no danger to me. When the storms returned recently, and I heard they were back in the citadel, I couldn't tell you I'd seen them before. I had to keep up the charade. Like everyone in Eden. We've all had to maintain various charades.'

This was true, I thought. Even the lies had been maintained behind closed doors. Had the townsfolk thought the walls could hear them? That the walls would pass on information to the mayor and his cronies?

I was about to collect the *General Knowledge Encyclopaedia* and *Civilisations From Around the World: Ancient to Medieval* from the little table next to the armchair, when I realised both heavy tomes had disappeared.

'My books have gone,' I said.

'How can they just vanish?' my grandfather asked.

'I put them on the table. I'm sure I did. I was just reading from them.'

'Did they fall on the floor?' he asked.

'I would have heard them drop. They're large books,' I said, as I searched under the armchair.

'I don't recall seeing any books on the table just now,' my mother said.

I couldn't fathom it. I wondered if I had forgotten that I'd taken them back upstairs. But I was sure I hadn't moved from the armchair. I hadn't wanted to leave my grandfather alone.

I considered going upstairs to my bedroom to check, but a commotion arose outside, and I stood paralysed by the log burner.

Envy barked as a myriad of footsteps pummelled along the lane.

Beyond our cottage, some of the neighbours screamed, while others cried. In that instance I thought they sounded terrified. But as I was soon to discover, they were screams of joy.

The front door flew open and in burst my father.

He had a full beard, and he wore his uniform. I recalled all those uniforms my mother and I had sewn six years earlier. It looked as though my father had worn his uniform for six years. It was tattered and torn.

My mother rushed to him. As did Envy.

My grandfather beamed through tears, but he couldn't rise from his armchair.

My mother and father cried together.

At first, I thought I must be dreaming. How could my father suddenly be home? If I was dreaming, then I was fully aware that I was dreaming, and that meant I would wake shortly. But I didn't wake. Instead, I could still detect our neighbours crying. Everyone appeared to be crying except me. It was real. I was pleased to see him. I was glad he had come home. But the passing of time had meant that I didn't know him anymore. Six years had passed, and I felt awkward.

'How you've grown,' my father said as he stared at me. 'You're a young woman. And I've missed it all.'

He grimaced through tears at those final words, and while he held my mother in one arm, he opened out his free arm for me to join the embrace.

I did so.

My father smelt of damp walls and straw.

Envy leapt at our legs, and I stroked her.

'Glad to see you home, son,' my grandfather said, as he struggled to his feet.

My father let go of my mother and me, and hugged my grandfather.

They weren't father and son. They were father and son-in-law, but through marriage their bond had been like that of father and son.

'Did those other menfolk get you out?' my grandfather asked.

'What other menfolk? Do you mean soldiers?'

'It was the soldiers?' I asked.

'Some of them, yes,' my father said. 'I think they must've had enough rebels to take charge of the prison.'

'Silas stayed true to his word,' my grandfather said.

'Who's this Silas?' my father asked.

'Andromeda and I spoke to him through our cell doors. When we were imprisoned.'

'You were both in the prison? When? How did you get out?'

'It's a long story,' I said.

'I've got all night,' my father said. 'What's been going on?'

'We'll tell you later,' my grandfather said. 'Why did they lock you all away for so long?'

'They said we were a danger to Eden,' my father said.

'Balderdash. I know who I believe the real danger to be.'

We stepped outside for some air.

The joyful cries continued.

All the men of Eden had returned. They stood outside their homes, wrapped in the arms of their families. The men all wore their ragged uniforms. The true soldiers. They had fought to stay alive in the face of real adversity. Imprisoned for being men. Men who might question. Men who had questioned.

The townsfolk lit their bonfires, but in celebration this time. They laughed, and they danced and sang.

In that moment, the entire town knew everything about Eden was a lie.

I pondered on how the lie had started. I wondered what year it had been exactly when the lie began. The mayor didn't appear to know the exact details, or that was part of the story he had been keeping from me. In a way it didn't matter. All the previous years had been wiped from history, and everyone started over again. There were townsfolk who had to change their family name in order to begin the lie. They had lied to their children. Their children grew up and had children of their own. Some of the townsfolk may have lived long enough to see great grandchildren. The children and adults all lived in ignorance. The elderly never spoke. Then they passed away, and the truth died with them. Their secret left this Earth within the flames which consumed their bodies. I thought about the last one of their kind. The final elderly resident with the knowledge, about two hundred years ago. I wondered if they knew they were the last of their kind with a secret. It was them … and the authorities. Then they too passed, and all knowledge was lost amongst the remaining townsfolk. It was easy to lie, I concluded. And far too easy to live a lie.

I glanced across at my father and found him smiling at me.

'They asked me why we'd named you Andromeda,' he said. 'I didn't know what they meant. I didn't know what they were driving at.'

'What did you tell them?' I asked.

'At first, I told them it was none of their damn business. But I received a beating for that. So I told them the truth. The word is on a building in the citadel. I'd liked it since I was a small child. My father had first pointed the word out to me when I was atop his shoulders. My father had asked me if I could read it. The soldiers didn't believe me. They thought I knew something. I don't know what they thought I knew. No matter how much they beat me, I couldn't know any more than I did. I couldn't give them anything else.'

'Did they beat you a lot?' I asked.

'Yes, in the beginning. All the men were. If it wasn't you, it was someone else receiving a beating. We could all hear it.'

I couldn't stand to think that my father had been punched and kicked. All because of my name. I hung my head.

My father stroked my hair.

'It's not your fault. I was the one who named you after a plaque on a building. That was my undoing. Clearly the authorities had never noticed the name.'

'It's not just a building,' I said. 'Andromeda is a Greek princess, and our neighbouring galaxy was named after her.'

'What's a neighbouring galaxy? And what's a Greek princess? How do you know these things?'

'Because she's been investigating,' my mother said.

'Is that why you ended up in prison?' my father asked.

'Only for one night,' I said. 'The mayor did it to frighten me. I have so much to tell you, Dad.'

'Sounds like you do.'

We embraced again, and I felt more comfortable in his arms this time.

Shouting and jeering came from somewhere beyond the cottages.

Most of my neighbouring townsfolk vacated the lanes and headed for the main road, apart from some of the elderly, including my grandfather, who struggled to walk any further than the top of our lane.

Once we reached the road, we came across a bewildering sight. Former prisoners in shabby uniforms, along with soldiers in their neater attire, stampeded through the streets. They held burning torches. All except four men, who instead held aloft an elaborate chair. And in that chair sat the mayor.

But from the way he sat, it was clear this was no celebration. This was his crucifixion. He clung to the arms of the chair as he lolled about in the seat, and he glared in terror. Some of the townsfolk threw dirt and gravel at him, which they had scooped up from the road. The mayor bellowed at the men to let him go. He berated the townsfolk for their retribution. Some gravel landed in his eyes and he yelled. He couldn't wipe his eyes clean. Had he attempted to, he would have tumbled from the chair, which wobbled above the men of Eden.

Silas appeared within the throng. Our eyes met and he

winked at me. He held his flaming torch aloft and cheered along with the townsfolk.

The men carrying him charged in the direction of the wall. All the townsfolk followed.

The men overpowered the guard at the gatehouse in the wall. Then the gate swung open and the men barged through, with the mayor still clutching the arms of the chair and demanding to be released. He may have even been crying by this point. Some of the townsfolk continued on into the forest with the men. But most of us stayed behind.

I felt a pang of guilt for a brief moment. I had suggested this. Now, Silas and the men of Eden were carrying out my wish. The guilt disappeared when I thought of how the mayor had referred to our history as from a long-dead era. It reminded me of how repugnant I considered him. How he was riddled with malice. I couldn't understand how he could utter such a thing. I may have referred to the ancients as long-dead ancestors, but I said those words out of reverence. Otherwise I wouldn't have used the word ancestor. His reference to long-dead era implied contempt. This had also been apparent from the tone of his voice. To me there was something charming about the distant past. To him, it could be rewritten and destroyed simply because it was old.

The hubris of the man. What a pathetic specimen of a mayor. Mayors should not destroy. Mayors should view their role as one of protector of their respective town or citadel's history. As I told him, he should have been a custodian.

We watched as the torch lights grew dim and the forest consumed the group.

I wondered if the men had considered taking the pathetic specimen all the way to the prison, or whether they would dispose of him somewhere else in the forest. Either way, he knew he was no longer required, but more importantly, no longer respected. If indeed he ever had earnt any respect from the townsfolk. We as a town had simply put up with what we were given. We hadn't known any different. Now we had knowledge. All our lives would change for the better. Eden had a future.

My family and I headed back for the cottage, and my grandfather.

He remained standing at the top of the lane.

'Why didn't you go back inside, Dad?' my mother asked.

'What was going on?' my grandfather asked.

'The mayor's gone,' I said. 'They've taken him into the forest.'

'The prison?' he asked.

'Maybe,' I said. 'Or they might just leave him all alone amongst the trees.'

'Good riddance,' my grandfather said. 'The mayor's always been full of horse manure. A bloody ton of it.'

My father laughed and kissed my grandfather upon his forehead.

The sky ignited in a flash of white.

Clouds billowed and clashed, as huge dark shapes floated within.

A polyphony of choral voices descended, as did the rain and tiny orbs of light. Plus, the bitter acrid scent spliced with sulphur rose in the saturated air. A scent which came from the Earth of the future.

The townsfolk huddled together, not sure whether to run back inside their houses or watch with awe, it seemed. No one screamed this time. Perhaps by now they had realised no harm would befall them. The harm had already been done. By the mayor, and all the previous mayors. We had all been deceived. Manipulated. Silenced.

I searched for Gabriel amongst his kind, as the angels danced above me.

Another shock of lightning blazed across the valley. I realised the large dark shapes were ships hovering above the angels. The ships fanned out in formation within the clouds.

Gabriel floated towards me.

He stood on something, like steps extending from the cloud above. He didn't float of his own accord at all. He held something in his arms. And he radiated once more.

I wanted to run to him. I realised how much I had missed him. But my awkwardness once again prevented me from doing so.

I waited for him to reach me. But instead of acknowledging me, he acknowledged my mother.

'Hello again,' he said.

'You're Gabriel?' my mother asked.

'Yes, I am. I suppose to you it feels like years since you first saw me. But for me it's only been a matter of days.'

'You were who my mum saw as a child?' I asked.

'The only two women with red hair I know of,' Gabriel said.

He held out the items he carried. They were a small pile of neatly folded clothes. I realised they were the clothes I had provided Gabriel with when we ventured into the forest to locate the prison but located all the man-made monsters instead, and the deceased future human.

'I believe these are yours, sir,' Gabriel said to my father.

My father's eyes darted between my mother, Gabriel, and me.

'Is there something I should know?' he asked, as he retrieved his old clothes and examined them.

'This is Andromeda's friend, Gabriel,' my mother said. 'I don't know how he came to have your clothes though?'

My father regarded me, as a smirk spread across his face.

An intense heat rose within me. I wondered if I would ever grow out of blushing. I was glad for the evening darkness. My humiliation was softened by a subdued amber glow from the gas lamps. The gas lamps could never outshine the sun.

I may have had no problem giving the dejected mayor a piece of my mind in the past few days, but I still couldn't hold eye contact if I became embarrassed. I stared at the ground until Gabriel stood closer. His large eyes softened as he smiled upon me. He reached out a hand and I accepted it.

Ours had become a friendship between two humans millennia apart.

Chapter 19

The storm abated but the rain continued to fall. Although this, too, eased.

Gabriel tucked a section of my hair behind an ear.

'That's better. I can see your face,' he said.

I scowled at him and ruffled my hair back to how it had originally fallen.

He chuckled.

'You'll always be a funny one,' he said.

'I think you might be the funny one actually,' I said.

'If you say so,' he said, shrugging.

'Why are you here?' I asked. 'I know where you come from, I understand that now. But why and how are you here, in my time?'

'Because Earth in the future is moaning and shaking, and it's causing some kind of fracture in time. We accidently travel through time whenever we try to depart Earth. We believe it will be easier to leave Earth from your time instead.'

'You're leaving Earth? For good?' I asked.

'We must. I showed you Earth in my time.'

'That really was Earth in the future?' my grandfather asked. 'That dying planet is our fate?'

'Yes,' Gabriel confirmed.

'I think I need to sit down,' my grandfather said.

'Come inside, Dad,' my mother said, as she gently grabbed my grandfather's arm.

'You can also explain to me what's going on,' my father said.

Both my mother and father helped my grandfather back inside the house. But they proceeded to spy on Gabriel and me from one of the windows. Even the rest of the townsfolk had retreated closer to their cottages, but they continued to observe us, clearly curious.

'So you live underground in the future?' I asked.

'We have to,' Gabriel said. 'We have created a vast tunnel network all leading to underground cities, which are really cavernous spaces with small homes, if you could call them that. The dwellings are built into the rockface.'

'The tunnels I saw underwater, what are they for?'

'They lead to the ships,' Gabriel said. 'We needed more space to build the ships. But the water has acted like a portal, which, incidentally, is how the really ancient ancestors perceived a body of water.'

'They thought water was a portal?'

'Yes, to another realm or spirit place,' Gabriel said.

'It feels like you come from another realm. I would say they had it right,' I said.

'We humans of the future are in decay,' Gabriel said. 'But only the ones who remained on Earth. Humans aren't supposed to live underground. Some had already left to begin the colonisation of space and save themselves. We call them the first pioneers, as they were the first to leave Earth with no intention of returning. Although who's to say how they're living on one of the moons. But I expect they live on the surface, with a view of the sky. They went on an ark, of sorts. Those who left knew we had no future if we all remained. But those who didn't believe in the plan, or weren't financially capable, or weren't required or considered valuable, they stayed. They are my ancestors, and your descendants. They were the majority of the population. They had no choice. Plus, the ones who remained in charge of those who stayed behind were ignorant to what would happen. They told the people it would be okay, and they didn't need to leave. But then the planet changed, becoming inhospitable for humans and animals. Of course, then most of the people decided they did want to leave. But they were too late. They didn't know how to build the ships. All that knowledge had gone with the first pioneers. The planet became chaotic. The planet *shifted.* My ancestors went to war with the natural world. Nature began to reclaim everything they had created. Nature was not under their control. They were fools to think the natural world ever had been. They couldn't win against her destructive side. The heat became intense. Everything they needed to survive began to disappear. They had a planetary war over resources, which resulted in famine. Most of my ancestors died. The selfish ones had ruined it for everyone. The smart ones tried to change things, but the ignorant humans won. My ancestors hid underground and evolved in the darkness. Humans transformed.'

'I'm sorry, Gabriel,' I said, as sat on the little stone wall which ran along the perimeter of our front garden, and Envy leapt into my lap. 'I can't even begin to imagine what that must have been like. Even though I've been learning all about natural disasters, and how the authorities thoroughly enjoy lying to the citizens. I had only been thinking recently how our authorities would be the ones to kill us all. Between malice, greed, and ineptitude, they will be the death of everyone.'

'It certainly was a combination of those, but mostly malice,' Gabriel said, as he joined me on the wall. 'But no one had anticipated what would happen. Even those who had planned for disaster and left the Earth behind. I don't think they could've imagined where the disaster would come from. The ignorant ones in charge forgot about life and death in nature. Everything dies in the end. *Everything*. Some didn't want to go because leaving Earth went against their beliefs. The thought of being alone in the darkness of space terrified them. Ironically, they stayed behind to live in darkness within the Earth instead. Now those of us who remain are all leaving. The Earth gave birth to us. She's been our nursery, plus our school, college, and university. Now it's time to explore. If we want to survive until the entire universe becomes hostile to life, we have to leave.'

'You mentioned the planet shifted? What do you mean exactly?' I asked, thinking how I hadn't come across shifting planets in my recent studies.

'An incredible, once in a million years phenomenon. Or so it seemed,' Gabriel said. 'Matter had seeped from Earth's inner core into the outer core. The Earth spilled her insides out. Molten liquid burst forth from every single volcano, all at once. But even that wasn't enough to ease all the exploding pressure. What had happened was like the equivalent of a bomb going off within the Earth's core.'

'A bomb?'

'A bomb struck your beloved House of Books and destroyed it,' Gabriel said. 'Imagine a bomb, but a million times worse, going off inside the Earth.'

I couldn't imagine it. I had never heard the word *bomb*, for one. But I recalled the gaping wound in the citadel skyline, and the rubble strewn across the square the day the black dragon – sent on the mayor's order – fell from the sky. I also recalled reading something in the *Space Encyclopaedia* about how Mars' molten core had changed. Although in Mars' case it became cooler. Then Mars lost its magnetic field and became a frozen wasteland as the planet lost its atmosphere and the temperature dropped. What had once been our solar system's first water world became inhospitable to life. Despite all the natural disasters that could befall us, I hadn't even entertained the idea that the Earth's core could change, too. I think I hadn't wanted to consider for even a moment that it could.

'The tectonic plates all began to grind,' Gabriel continued, 'which created a worldwide earthquake. This sent the continents on the move. Countries which had resided in the cooler northern hemisphere found themselves repositioned in the tropics. Desert countries ended up at the South Pole. It became chaos. The weather turned violent. Every coastal town and city was destroyed by a tsunami. And this all happened within hours. Across the whole planet. No safe place existed, which is why most of the population died. But this was part of a pattern. This had happened before. Although rarely spoken about, that type of cataclysmic event happens every six to ten thousand years or thereabouts. Not every one million years. My ancestors – your descendants – should have expected it, but they didn't, because they thought we were invincible. Because we forgot that we live upon a moving rock, with a molten core and a shifting crust.'

'So now you're all leaving from my time?' I asked.

'We've tried to leave many times before,' Gabriel said. 'But it appears that some we thought had gone got trapped instead.'

'You mean the dead one in the forest?' I said. 'There must be more of them inside that part of the ship underground. How did the ship get trapped?'

'I can't say for sure what happened, my guess is they were just unlucky,' he said. 'Perhaps the portal literally transported them to the exact spot where the ship was stationed in my time, and that meant underground in the past. Or perhaps they even crashed when they arrived hundreds, if not thousands of years ago, and were consumed by the surrounding earth as the landscape changed over the centuries. Accidental time travel means ... well, accidents, and unfortunate accidents at that. But we're all ready to leave now. Would you like to leave with us? It's a good time; Jupiter and Saturn are almost aligned at present and will be on the same side of the sun, which will make it easier for us to stay together until we get to the first moon. My family are part of the group going to Jupiter's Ganymede. Others are going to Saturn's Enceladus. Both have water ice. The moons of the gas giants are our saviours, although an asteroid could hit us on Ganymede. But we could also get hit on another moon, or another planet. We're not entirely safe anywhere.'

'You want me to leave with you?' I asked.

'Well … you don't have to. But I have to leave.'

'You don't have to leave,' I said.

'I've already evolved differently from you.'

'Not that much,' I said, annoyed that he thought he was so different he couldn't stay.

'Humans will venture out into space and have a rebirth, and evolve again,' Gabriel said. 'We must keep moving on, further out into the universe. We cannot allow ourselves to disappear in the dark. A speck of dust. A grain of sand that once was. We owe it to ourselves and the stars to continue. Although I think there will be more hostile planets than safe ones. By hostile, I mean the environment. I hope the moons across the universe will be safer for us humans to build our bases as we keep exploring. Our planet could be one of many planets which harbour life. Intelligence may not be unique to Earth. Intelligence is not even unique to humans. A myriad of magnificent creatures who have evolved and survived alongside us are testament to this. Plus, the conditions which have enabled life here could enable life anywhere. Every chemical here exists out there. Why assume life could only thrive here? But also, why assume all life requires the same conditions we require?'

'Do you think maybe Earth is not our true home?' I asked.

'You think maybe humans originally came from somewhere else?' Gabriel asked, sounding puzzled.

'You've got me thinking, with all your going off to find new moons and planets. Perhaps this has all happened before,' I said. 'But after the previous first pioneers arrived here, their descendants were never informed of the journey across the stars to find a hospitable home.'

'Do you really believe that?'

'Don't know,' I said. 'You've just got me pondering. Who is to say what other lies we've been told throughout our history. I suppose in my heart I feel we are from Earth. But now I wonder, when we do find a suitable planet to settle on in another solar system, the first pioneers who arrive may not tell their descendants what really happened.'

'That could be the case. They may not want to terrify them,' Gabriel confirmed.

'Then the lies will begin all over again,' I said, feeling more than a little frustrated with how easy it was to eradicate history.

'They may not lie. Humans really should have learned from that mistake by the time we find Earth version two.'

'Or version three, if it happened before,' I said.

Gabriel chuckled.

'So, would you like to go to Ganymede?' he asked.

'No, thank you. I love the stars,' I said, turning my face to the sky, 'but I love to look at the stars from Earth. Earth isn't in trouble in my time. I'm staying put. Plus it frightens me. I understand why some of my descendants didn't want to leave.'

'Why be afraid? Think of it this way: the pagan ancestors considered that their gods lived all around them, gods of the sky, the rivers, the forest, etcetera. Their gods created everything. Why not the universe? But even if you believe in one god, could that god not be present in the sky, the river, the forest? If you believe God created Earth, God could have also created the universe. Leaving Earth is nothing to be terrified of. The entire universe is our home. It doesn't matter if we're alone. It doesn't matter if we discover other beings out there on other habitable planets. We all come from the same place. We are all made from stardust.'

'I know what you're saying. But I'm happy to stay here and appreciate Earth in a time when she's considered safe. I haven't explored my own land because I didn't know what existed out there. Now I know, I want to see it all. I want to see as much as I can of my home before I die. My descendants may need to leave in order to save themselves, but I don't need to. I want to die on Earth. That is my wish.'

'You really don't want to go?' Gabriel asked, a little disappointed it seemed. 'You'll be one of the true first pioneers. Because we've time travelled, the first pioneers will no longer be the first pioneers to colonise space. We will. We'll be the first to set up a base on Ganymede. You don't want to be part of history?'

'I'm ready for an adventure,' I said, thinking how I had been confined to Eden for far too long. 'But not amongst the stars. And you don't have to go. You could all live here now, in this land, since you've time travelled. You haven't evolved that much from me.'

'I don't believe we could all stay. The population would increase in the thousands, in an instant. That places a lot of pressure on your resources. Where would we all live? We would have to live in all the prisons in the forest.'

'Don't be ridiculous,' I said.

'Anyway, we've planned to leave for years,' Gabriel stated, matter-of-factly.

'But *you* could stay,' I pleaded. 'One more person won't put pressure on resources. You could live with us.'

'I don't know if I have a reason to stay.'

I think I baulked at his comment.

All I ever wanted was to be understood. I had that and so much more, thanks to Gabriel. I even understood myself better. I accepted myself.

I leaned forward and kissed Gabriel on the lips.

The rain ceased and the sky cleared. The air rang with beautiful angelic song. The sky pulsated as large obsidian ships drew away from each other and fanned outwards. The enormity and number of ships became apparent when they blocked out the stars.

The first pioneers were on the way to their new homes.

Chapter 20

The ships set fire to the sky. They ascended in a vortex of red, orange and gold. Gabriel wrapped an arm around me and explained how his family and the rest of the future humans were travelling through the troposphere, stratosphere, mesosphere, thermosphere, and into the exosphere all within a minute. The streams of colour dissipated once they were through Earth's protective atmosphere. The townsfolk watched until the flaming light became tiny flecks. Then the first pioneers vanished.

I thought about how the real First Ancestors appeared to have had a deeper connection to our world and the cosmos, even though they could not venture beyond our planet. Their eyes were open. The night sky shone through the darkness, and they beheld the galaxy. They realised the significance of the stars. They built statues and temples to the gods who they imagined had created all the heavens and the rock upon which they stood. Aside from the gods on Earth, a god resided within the sun. Another in the moon. Each star became a god. How else could they explain their reason for being? Nature consisted of gods. They gave the gods physical bodies in order to pay humble respect, give thanks, and to offer devotion for the life bestowed upon them. Respecting nature will hold humanity in better stead as we leave the Earth. Especially accepting we are part of nature, not separate from it. Life is an opportunity.

The descendants of the first pioneers will go through a metamorphosis in order to live and survive in the universe. Humans will become unrecognisable to the humans of today. Caterpillars to butterflies.

The first pioneers have set this in motion. They have begun to light the way.

We do belong out there. If it is said that a god created Earth, who is to say this divine being hasn't created the universe? *Something* is continually creating everything in the universe. The universe grows every day. There is a presence. There is *something*. We living creatures are not nothing. The universe is not nothing. We and the universe are everything.

Gabriel and I remained outside with Envy, despite the chill which had hung in the air since the clouds and ships departed.

'I'm glad I didn't leave,' Gabriel said. 'You're right. We should explore this land while we can. I want to see Earth in the light.'

He gazed at the stars.

'My people are out there in the darkness now,' he said.

'Do you think, because we see Jupiter as a star, Earth would be a star in the sky of Ganymede?' I asked.

'I like that idea. When they turn back to look at where they came from, they will see a small but brilliant star glowing a bluish hue.'

'A blue star is beautiful,' I said, trying to picture this wonder against a dark sky. 'But I suppose if an intergalactic race should discover our solar system through their telescopes, they wouldn't imagine all the wonder on that blue star. All the beauty. And all the life which treads upon the land, flies through the skies, and swims within the seas. Earth is the humble gem of our solar system. I value her, and I want to see as much of her as I can. I appreciate what the ancestors began. It's a miracle we're here at all, what with all the possible natural disasters on Earth and from space which can cause our demise. It helps me to appreciate life and all the abundance of life here. I know it won't last forever, but in a way that's what makes everything here even more precious. To experience life is actually amazing.'

'I have a surprise for you,' Gabriel said.

'I hate— what surprise do you have?' I asked.

Gabriel chuckled.

'I did what I believe you would have wished I could do,' he said, cryptically.

'Pardon?'

'Think about it. I've been able to time travel. Albeit by mistake. What would you have wished for?'

'I can't think of anything,' I said, perplexed. How could his accidental time travelling help me?

'You wouldn't have wished for anything? Not even since your favourite place was destroyed?' he said.

'You can be very tiresome sometimes. Do you know that?'

'I believe you would've wished we could have saved the books,' he said. 'And I have, with the help of my family and some others. On our most recent accidental jaunt back in time, we collected all the books and rehomed them.'

'You did?' I asked, leaping to my feet, which caused poor Envy to fall from my lap in the process.

'But you may find all the books you had taken previously have disappeared from your home. As we went back long before I introduced you to the House of Books and your authorities had begun removing volumes.'

'Ah, that explains how those books vanished from the sitting room,' I said.

'I don't know at what specific point in time we arrived,' Gabriel said. 'Could have been decades ago. But at least it was before the bomb fell. By the way, that was an unmanned flying bomb which destroyed the House of Books. Doodlebugs they called them in the second world war.'

'I don't care about doodlebugs,' I said. 'You went back in time and saved all the books?'

'Yes. Aren't you going to throw your arms around me and give me another kiss?' he said, grinning like an idiot.

'There's no need to be smug, Gabriel. If you've saved the books, where are they?'

'In a real house of books,' he stated.

'Am I supposed to guess where my books are?'

'*Your* books?' he said, raising an eyebrow.

'Yes, mine,' I said. 'Have you really saved them all?'

'Yes, and they're very close to you.'

I glanced back at my cottage. All those magnificent tomes would never fit in my humble home.

Gabriel grabbed my hand.

'Let's go for a short walk,' he said. 'Come on, Envy.'

Envy rose at Gabriel's command and waited for us to advance.

'See, she's keen,' he said.

We strolled along the lane until we reached the gate of the abandoned manor house.

'In there?' I asked.

'In every room, stacked up high, you'll find every book.'

I flung my arms around Gabriel and kissed him on his cheek. He would be lucky if he got another kiss on the lips anytime soon, I thought. Not with his smugness. But I forgave him since it appeared he had saved the contents of the House of Books.

'Can we go in now?' I asked.

‘But it’s dark.’

‘I don’t care,’ I said.

I ran up the overgrown path and threw open the door. It creaked in indignation at the disturbance. I danced through the hallway of towering books and explored every room in the moonlight. I tripped up the staircase in excitement. I decided in an instant it was my new favourite place.

‘Are the books still in order?’ I asked.

‘Yes, I believe so,’ Gabriel said. ‘Although I’m sure you’ll have fun logging which books are in which room.’

I would, I thought.

My life was about to change again. But if I could prepare for changes, I could deal with them. I embraced this change because I considered this change a positive. I possessed all the knowledge in the world. I had even more knowledge than I should have for my time of 1273. Or 2273, or whatever it was. Because I had Gabriel. A man from the future.

The manor house looked even better in daylight, now it heaved with dusty tomes. It was a real House of Books.

With the help of some professionals, my family, Gabriel, and I, spent several weeks cleaning and fixing up the house in preparation for a grand opening of the House of Books to the townsfolk.

Doctor Hartnell popped in to see what was happening in the old manor house. I thanked her for the book about autism. She thought it was great that I had taken on the responsibility as guardian to the beautiful building, and that I would be loaning out all the unknown books.

Silas also popped by. He informed us there would be an election campaign and he would be running for mayor. We would have Eden’s first ever democratic vote. The townsfolk would have their say. Their opinions mattered. Therefore it would be a real democratic vote. We all thought it was a wonderful idea that Silas would run for mayor. He had none of his father's characteristics, which was his selling point. He said he only put himself forward as a candidate as he had so many ideas, and he wanted to get things going.

He wanted to open all the abandoned buildings to the public. He envisioned Eden becoming a tourist hotspot, due to most of the surrounding towns and citadels beyond the forest all having had their history removed. The buildings were ugly, he said, they had no charm or character. Every building had been made to the specification of the mundane and generic, built by people who wanted their populace to live in the dark, in so many ways. Silas also explained how the towns and citadels had no gardens or surrounding fields, confirming what the previous mayor had told me. The towns were concrete monstrosities. Eden, however, did have green space. Silas said tourists would come from miles around to marvel at the fields and gardens and honey stone buildings which the true ancestors created. This would bring in revenue and help the town. I realised I still had Stonburh Museum and Stonburh Art Gallery to explore. I wondered what hidden gems lay behind their façades.

Silas wanted my opinion on the bomb-damaged House of Books. If his tourism idea worked out, there should be money to spend on restoration. He would have the House of Books and the Theatre Royal rebuilt. But I said to leave the House of Books and the Theatre Royal as they stood. It would serve as a reminder of mankind's stupidity and how easy it was to destroy what someone else in the past had lovingly created.

Within the month, Silas was elected as mayor. He had no real competition. It helped that he knew the history of the town and the old citadel, and understood the lives of the ancestors. He, like me, wanted everyone to understand where and who they had come from, and we would never have our ancestors lives and achievements taken from us again. The townsfolk were free to roam the forest and encounter the stone circle of the truly ancient ancestors.

Silas said he didn't know if Eden should remain as Eden or revert back to Stonburh. I liked the name Eden, I told him. Stonburh was another word I couldn't get used to. My grandfather agreed. But of course, Silas had to ask all the townsfolk for their opinion.

We were permitted to listen to music. It came over the wireless daily. I couldn't really understand the concept of music at first. I had only ever heard voices over the wireless. The only *music* I had previously known was the jangling chimes from the clock on the Guildhall, so listening to music for enjoyment was a bit of an adjustment. But I grew to love music. Plus Gabriel and I discovered a gramophone in the attic of the manor house. The following day we came across several boxes of records. I jumped out of my skin when Gabriel placed the gramophone's needle on a record. I recalled the music from the gramophone in the mayor's house, but the music Gabriel played had a much faster tempo. Once I got used to the rhythm, we played the joyous music all day, and danced around the piles of books while Envy leapt at our legs.

We also found an upright piano in a small backroom. Gabriel showed me how the piano worked. He ran his fingers over the keys. If the piano was in tune, then Gabriel wasn't.

We opened the manor house as the House of Books. To me, the word *library* continued to have little meaning. A house of books still made more sense, and it was literal in this case.

We placed the gramophone in the entrance hall and played some of the classical music we had found.

The townsfolk would come and go all day long to soak up the knowledge of the ages, and more importantly, to learn the truth about our existence. It felt good to know I had a part to play in enabling their awakening. I had wanted the lie of Eden revealed, and it had been. I had wanted all the knowledge in the world. Now the townsfolk had access to all the knowledge, too.

We shuffled things around in the manor house, and even managed to turn one of the large rooms on the ground floor into a café, which my mother and father ran. My mother baked all the cakes and my father made all the sandwiches. We had proper tea and coffee, so Eden no longer suffered the indignity of beverages made from watered-down shoe polish, much to my grandfather's delight.

I loved my new life. Once the House of Books closed for the day, Gabriel and I would sit and read on the sofa. We lived within some of the bedrooms on the upper floor. The rooms became our sanctuary in the evenings and weekends.

Prendergast Books expanded. Now the whole world had opened up again, a plethora of new and updated books appeared. The townsfolk wished to purchase these books, not just loan older volumes from the House of Books. The townsfolk also tried to get to grips with fiction. However, I still struggled with the idea of made-up stories in print.

After much discussion, Eden became known as Eden-Stonburh. This way it wasn't too confusing for the townsfolk, and it also honoured the previous residents. New signage was made for the square. It carried an explanation as to why Stonburh had been renamed Eden. People of the past had done so to eradicate history. Now we righted the wrong and paid our respects.

It had transpired that when Stonburh became Eden, the authorities had adjusted the year to 1000 CE. They had considered amending the year to zero, but they felt that the idea of the First Ancestors needed to go farther back, to make it more realistic. Silas and the other incoming authorities of the land stuck with the year 1273 when they took charge of running the towns and citadels. Amending the year to over a thousand years in the future was deemed too confusing. But instead of keeping Common Era, the year became known as

1273 RE. Which stood for Renaissance Era. No one in Eden had any concept of Common Era anyway. Our new era of rebirth honoured the past, whereas the new era conjured up by the previous mayors did not.

Posters and banners decorated the square and the omnibuses. The war posters were gone and replaced with advertisements for the opening of the Assembly Rooms, the museum, and the art gallery. Plus the openings of new shops and restaurants.

Once the Assembly Rooms opened in the citadel, I took my grandfather along to witness the beautiful frescos on the ceilings. Since music was permitted, some musicians came to play in the Assembly Rooms for the opening. A pianist played in one of the rooms, while two celloists played in another. I was in awe. My grandfather and I flitted between both rooms as we didn't want to miss out on either. We couldn't get enough of the music, which swam around the high ceilings and enhanced the enjoyment of both frescos. We had a little dance around the room with the celloists playing, until my grandfather needed a sit down. He loved it, and wished my grandmother could have seen the stunning frescos and heard the beautiful music.

Silas said he would use the Assembly Rooms not just for entertainment but as a meeting place. Everybody would be welcome to come along once a month and have their say about the future of Eden-Stonburh.

Eden-Stonburh Museum housed a permanent exhibition on the history of the town. It transpired that the stone circle had been erected by the ancient Britons during the Neolithic Age. This meant that the stones had stood strong for at least six thousand years. The word *lithic* meant stone.

Parts of the old citadel had existed since Anglo-Saxon times, with the first-known structures being built between the real eighth and ninth centuries, including the citadel wall, which was built to defend the citadel from a Viking invasion. Although you could say this failed eventually, since the Norman invaders – who arrived during the late eleventh century – were descendants of the Vikings. The Normans took the citadel for a period and built their giant cathedral. I was upset to learn that when the Normans began building the cathedral the construction destroyed a pre-existing eighth century Anglo-Saxon church. The Norman invasion had been a brutal period in English history, particularly in the north of England. The Normans rampaged through the northern counties, burning crops and slaughtering people and animals. Those who survived either fled England or starved to death. This became known as the Harrying of the North. Some historians believed that the Harrying of the North caused the death or migration of seventy-five per cent of the population. Despite this initial and probable genocide, over time, the remaining Anglo-Saxons and invading Normans intermarried and became known as the Anglo-Normans.

It appeared the later people of Stonburh honoured their heritage when they named the square after an Anglo-Saxon king and erected a statue. Aethelwulf, King of Wessex, had fought in a great battle only a few miles from Stonburh. A battle in which he was victorious over the Vikings. This meant all the surrounding towns and citadels were saved from attack. The statue of Aethelwulf, King of Wessex was discovered in the storeroom of the museum. Silas had the statue reinstated in the square upon a newly sculpted stone plinth. The king rose again, in the exact spot he had once stood proud for centuries, before he was ignominiously removed by the people who wanted us kept ignorant.

The museum had a huge chart on display depicting all the different ages and time periods down the centuries. I could finally see where I fit in with the history of my town. Numerous photographs of Stonburh had been uncovered. Some were of the House of Books in its prime. Plus we had moving pictures, which freaked me out a little. Some were in black and white, while others were in colour. Some of the images were of Stonburh during the Great War, which became the First World War. Some even showed the men on the real front line. It wasn't a town. It was an horrendous place. There were photographs of when the war memorial was first erected in honour of the men of Stonburh who had died. It was surrounded by wreaths made from poppies. From the black-and-white photographs, you wouldn't have realised the poppy flower was a vivid red. But the museum had a poppy wreath on display, and wreaths were regularly laid upon the war memorial once more. The poppy became a symbol of honour to the war dead after the Napoleonic wars, which had taken place before the Great War. Barren fields in Northern France and Flanders had become battlefields during these wars. However, deep within the soil, poppy seeds which had lain dormant began to rise to the surface as the soldiers churned the rain-soaked fields over with their boots. When the Napoleonic wars ended, the bodies remained strewn across the mud. Poppy flowers burst into full bloom around the corpses, creating a carpet of blood red. These fields became battlegrounds again during the Great War. And when that war was over, the poppies bloomed once more to honour the fallen.

Other photographs and moving pictures taught us about World War Two. Stonburh even had something called motorcars at this time. They looked terrifying. People had been allowed to drive into the old citadel at one point. The horses had been made redundant.

Eden-Stonburh Art Gallery housed some beautiful paintings. My favourite painting was of a spirited-looking woman with red hair. I was a rarity in Eden-Stonburh after all. I found myself drawn to the woman with dark eyes and red hair. The artwork was one of three known versions of a painting known as the *Armada Portrait*. Eden-Stonburh was lucky to have one of the artworks. The woman was a queen. Queen Elizabeth

I. I knew she was important by the size of her dress. I never realised a woman with red hair had ever been so notable. I stood mesmerised before her portrait for some time. Gabriel said I got lost in the painting. I even stroked the ends of my hair while I gazed upon her. I don't recall doing that, but he swears I did.

My grandfather passed away only a few months after the House of Books opened, but not before exploring all the previous abandoned buildings.

He died in his favourite armchair in front of the log burner. He must have known he was going to leave us that night, as my mother said he had his wedding photograph in his lap.

Gabriel and I rang the local church bells in his memory. I wondered if the bells could be heard all across Eden-Stonburh.

Envy passed the following year; she got to sixteen, which was a good age for a dog. We scattered her ashes in the forest, which had become her favourite place for snooping. Of course, I remained devastated for weeks. I had lost my best friend of sixteen years. But I did have Gabriel; he was my new friend. He was more than a friend.

The forest had also become my favourite place, the stone circle especially. I had many new favourite places, but I realised the forest topped the list. I still loved the beauty of the cathedral, because I could see the cathedral had been forged by masters of their craft, and for a higher purpose, even if they were Norman invaders. But something stronger drew me towards the stones and the trees and the land. Everything had been stolen from me, including the forest. And now the forest was mine. A place the long-dead ancestors had trodden. They left their remnants in the soil and I walked in their footsteps. I felt a connection to something greater. A connection to the very thing they had also revered.

I forgot about my autism most days. I no longer cared I had a *thing*. I accepted it and moved on. Gabriel said he didn't mind that I sometimes had trouble comprehending his sarcasm, stupid jokes, and weird facial expressions. I couldn't comprehend how my family regularly noted that I misunderstood their sarcasm, while at the same time they pulled me up on the apparent sarcastic comments I made. How, on the one hand, could I not understand sarcasm, and yet according to them, on the other hand, be sarcastic myself? Gabriel would just chuckle if I misunderstood a joke, then I would throw a small book at him, which I always later regretted, because if it landed well the pages would crumple.

We explored the land together. We discovered sandy beaches and craggy cliffs. Plus the island was home to more rivers, and even man-made canals. The island had lakes and mountains, although apparently modest compared to others around the world. The beauty of nature surrounded us. We encountered crumbling castles and more gothic cathedrals. I was also heartened to find that other stone circles made their mark upon the landscape. We occasionally even took boat trips to nearby lands. One time we got to witness the northern lights on one of those trips.

As we got older, I said I wanted to live in a house with a sea view. We found the perfect cottage overlooking a natural cove. We would spend the day upon the sand, under a giant parasol, reading, writing, discussing Eastern and Western philosophy further, the differences, the similarities, how much positivity we could take from both. I believe Gabriel enjoyed the sea breeze. It would refresh our senses and renew our energy, which we required for the climb back up the rock face. Winding wooden steps returned us to the cliff top, and we would linger to soak in the complete vista until the sun sank into the sea.

Sometimes on the way home Gabriel would tell me a ghost story. He knew I hated them, but equally found them fascinating.

He would recount these stories after dark, but I found them too scary. I told him straight, if he wanted to regale me with frightening stories, he could narrate them before the sunlight died. Although I would still spend the evening peering over my shoulder if I thought I heard a noise. The Japanese ghost stories were the most terrifying. The Japanese, it seemed, loved to be frightened out of their wits in the name of entertainment, and from that I deduced the Japanese were a crazy kind of people.

Some days, Gabriel didn't like to be outside for too long. For one thing he required an awful lot of sunblock. As he had lived underground his entire childhood and young adult life, he had a weak immune system. Plus he had allergies. The poor man appeared to be allergic to most things. He often got sick in the early years of our relationship, but he always recovered. His immune system got a little stronger until latter middle age, when it began to decline again, and his fair hair turned completely white.

I came to love my red hair just as it began to lighten and sprout strands of brilliant white. I scolded myself for my own idiocy and wasted years of dissatisfaction with my fiery crown.

Old age took Gabriel from me eleven years ago in 1332.

I smile at the memory of him. My funny future man who introduced me to the House of Books, opened the world up to me, and showed me what it truly meant to be alive.

I'm on my own now, as I sit here at my writing bureau, composing my story for you, whoever you are. I want you to know I'm grateful for my life, even if it began with lies. My life bloomed once I learned the truth. Now I'm ready for my next adventure.

Gabriel had said to me numerous times down the years that we could travel to the stars one day. I could even visit Andromeda. I had always said that was impossible as it was too far away, but he would reply: nothing is impossible. It cannot be impossible when one is made from stars.

Gabriel and I were blessed with two children and five grandchildren. My children and grandchildren are preparing to leave Earth. As am I. But I won't be going on the ship.

I'm ready to be with Gabriel, my family elders, Envy, and all her successors again. I'm ready to leave and join the first pioneers. I'm ready to witness the vastness amongst all the space dust and planets, while my atoms float free on the way to Andromeda.

Acknowledgements

Firstly, I would like to thank my editors, Russel D McLean (through Jericho Writers) and Richard Sheehan. Their professional guidance, enthusiasm, and encouragement gave me the confidence to push forward.

I would also like to thank Sarah Houldcroft and the team at Goldcrest Books. It's thanks to Sarah's expertise and passion for books that the manuscript turned from a simple word doc into the fabulous book you hold in your hands.

Finally, I would like to thank Ellen Brock, a freelance editor on YouTube. I have found her video content to be exceptionally informative and useful. Ellen's writing advice really helped me understand scene and story structure. The woman is worth her weight in gold.

About the Author

Tanya Savage discovered she was on the autistic spectrum in February 2021, during Britain's third lockdown for the Covid pandemic. The discovery came about while she was researching autism and Asperger syndrome for another manuscript, which was later abandoned for a whole new idea: *The House of Enlightenment*.

Printed in Great Britain
by Amazon

55071256R00196